ENLIGHTE

Bahá'ís revere the *Bhagavad-Gita*, the *Bible*, the *Qu'rán,* as well as the teachings of Buddha and Zoroaster. Rather than seeking to abrogate the Divine revelations of the past, Bahá'ís view their faith as the latest in a long line of revelations linking humanity to the Creator. Moreover, in the teachings of their faith, Bahá'ís see the most effective solution for overcoming the ethnic and religious strife, as well as the economic and environmental injustice which afflict our world. In *Enlightened Views* you will encounter a revelation, which, like its predecessors, is dazzling in style, extraordinary in its claims and stirring in its prophetic implications. Within the pages of *Enlightened Views*, a uniquely spiritual yet thoroughly workable model for a global society unfolds, which respects cultural identity, rejects excessive centralization and sees, as its goal, the unification of the entire human race. In a like manner, you will readily understand why the Bahá'í Faith, in just over a 100 years, has grown to become the second most widespread religion on the planet, with millions of adherents in more than 100,000 localities scattered in over 230 countries and territories around the globe.

Alan Bryson holds a Bachelor of Arts degree from the University of Nevada and a Master's degree from the University of South Carolina.

Published by
Sterling Publishers Private Limited

ENLIGHTENED VIEWS

ALAN BRYSON

A Sterling Paperback

STERLING PAPERBACKS
An imprint of
Sterling Publishers (P) Ltd.
L-10, Green Park Extension, New Delhi-110016
Ph.: 6191784, 6191785, 6191023 Fax: 91-11-6190028
E-mail: sterlin.gpvb@axcess.net.in

Enlightened Views
©1998, Alan Bryson
ISBN 81 207 2082 2
First Edition 1996
Second Revised & Enlarged Edition 1998

All rights are reserved. No part of this publication may be reproduced, stored in a retrieval system or transmitted, in any form or by any means, mechanical, photocopying, recording or otherwise, without prior written permission of the publisher.

Published by Sterling Publishers Pvt. Ltd., New Delhi-110016.
Lasertypeset by Vikas Compographics, New Delhi.
Printed at Ram Printograph (India), Delhi-110051.

CONTENTS

	A Note from the Compiler	vii
1.	An introduction to the Bahá'í Faith	1
2.	Why Persia?	7
3.	Excerpts from the Spoken Narrative of Bahiyyih Khanum	10
4.	Why Now?	16
5.	Becoming A True Baha'i	19
6.	On the Bahá'í Faith	40
7.	Search After Truth	59
8.	The Oneness of Religion	62
9.	Relation to Other Faiths	68
10.	Promulgation of the Faith	74
11.	God	84
12.	Creation	91
13.	Nature	95
14.	Love	98
15.	The Prophets	102
16.	Prayer, Reflection & Worship	110
17.	Selection of Baha'i Prayers	117
18.	Places of Worship	120
19.	The Station of Man	123
20.	The Soul	130
21.	Life After Death	133
22.	Self	140
23.	Deeds & Actions	143
24.	Trials & Difficulties	146
25.	Materialism	148
26.	Family	154

27.	Child Development	156
28.	Education	159
29.	Science	165
30.	Prejudice	170
31.	The Equality of Women	174
32.	Work and Occupation	179
33.	Economics	181
34.	Dealing with Crime	187
35.	Health and Nutrition	191
36.	Music	195
37.	Unity and Justice	198
38.	Peace	206
39.	Political Questions	211
40.	Baha'i Consultation	215
41.	Government	218
42.	International Auxiliary Language	225
43.	World Government	227
44.	Civilization	232
45.	The Báb	240
46.	Bahá'u'lláh	251
47.	Miracles	264
48.	The Station of Bahá'u'lláh	267
49.	'Abdu'l-Bahá The Most Great Branch	272
50.	Shoghi Effendi The Guardian	277
51.	The Covenant	280
52.	Laws and Commandments	289
53.	The Current Age	305
54.	Religion	311
55.	Superstition	315
56.	Free-Will & Predestination	317
57.	Non-Existence of Evil	319
58.	Confession	320
59.	Leaders of Religion	322
60.	Calumny and Opposition	327
	Bibliography	330
	Index	333

A NOTE FROM THE COMPILER

As the independent investigation of truth is one of the fundamental principles of the Bahá'í Faith, a conscious effort was made to limit the contents of this volume to direct quotations from the *Bahá'í Sacred Writings,* as well as the tablets, letters and talks of those persons who were empowered to act as its authorized interpreters. The only exceptions are documented first-hand accounts of persons who were actually in the presence of the central figures of the Bahá'í Faith, in addition, chapter and section headings were included for the sake of clarity and cohesion.

Those familiar with the copiousness of the sources available can attest to the sheer impossibility of presenting a comprehensive yet concise volume of the tenets and history of a religion whose Founder alone penned over one hundred volumes. By the same token, the vastness of the Bahá'í Revelation justifies the attempt to assist those, especially non-Bahá'ís, who are interested in its study. It should be noted, however, that several volumes, each of equal length and covering these same subjects, could be compiled from the *Bahá'í Sacred Writings* without repeating any passage contained in this volume.

Cognizant of the limitations of this endeavour I am nevertheless confident that the reader will gain a thorough understanding of what the Bahá'í Faith claims to be, of what an individual Bahá'í should strive to be, and many of the beliefs shared by Bahá'ís throughout the world.

During a few magical days in the summer of 1969 mankind's collective view of itself was forever altered. As we gazed at the Moon, aware that humans were at that moment exploring its surface, the age-old dream of travelling to another celestial sphere was finally realized, moreover, the pictures of our own planet taken from space enabled many to recognize for the first time that all people share a common destiny. Apart from the technological implications, it truly was a giant leap for mankind. Interestingly, the vision of one world, inhabited by one people and worshipping one God has been the cornerstone of the Bahá'í Faith for 150 years.

To truly appreciate the stupendous vision with which the Bahá'í Revelation is endowed, one must consider the Age in which it was revealed. The mid-nineteenth century was a time of unbridled nationalism and militarism, institutionalized racism, sexism and colonialism, and virtually unrestrained worker exploitation. In addition, the cleft between religion and science was growing ever wider. When we continue to narrow our focus with respect to place, we encounter in nineteenth century Iran, the birthplace of the Bahá'í Faith, a religious climate of unrivalled bigotry, intolerance and fanaticism. One can hardly conceive of a more fitting place to demonstrate the transforming power of a fresh revelation. What greater proof of the prophetic power of the Bahá'í Revelation could be imagined than the fact that an individual reared in nineteenth century Persia could proclaim that Faith in God should be expressed through service to humanity, aided by scientific knowledge, built upon a foundation of love, tempered with wisdom, justice and reason and dedicated to the unification of humanity? Moreover, Bahá'u'lláh, the Prophet Founder of the Bahá'í Faith, proclaimed the equality of women, forbade slavery, annulled differences of race and nationality, advocated universal compulsory education for boys and girls, declared the unity of science and religion, called for the establishment of a world federation of nations, the adoption of a universal auxiliary language, and the establishment of the Most Great Peace.

Bahá'ís recognize the validity of all the great religions of the past and see their faith as the latest in a long line of divine revelations connecting mankind to God the creator. Revelation in the Bahá'í view is continuous and progressive, tailored to the needs of the age in which it is revealed. For example:

Krishna stated, "When goodness grows weak, when evil increases, I make myself a body. In every age I come back to deliver the holy, to destroy the sin of the sinner, to establish righteousness."

According to Buddha, "I am not the first Buddha who came upon earth, nor shall I be the last. In due time another Buddha will arise in the world, a Holy One, a supremely enlightened One, endowed with wisdom in conduct, auspicious, knowing the universe, an incomparable leader of men, a master of angels and mortals. He will reveal to you the same eternal truths which I have taught you. He will preach his religion, glorious in its origin, glorious at the climax, and glorious at the goal, in

A Note from the Compiler

the spirit and in the letter. He will proclaim a religious life, wholly perfect and pure; such as I now proclaim."

Jesus said, "I have yet many things to say unto you, but ye cannot bear them now. Howbeit when he, the Spirit of truth, is come, he will guide you unto all truth."

Although "a new great teacher" is expected by all faiths, the appearance of such an individual is generally met with animosity by those awaiting His arrival. Both Jesus and Muhammad attest this fact:

"Elijah has already come, and they did not know him, but did to him whatever they pleased. So also the Son of man will suffer at their hands."

(Jesus)

"And verily We gave unto Moses the Scripture and We caused a train of messengers to follow after him, and We gave unto Jesus, son of Mary, clear proofs of God's sovereignty, and We supported him with the holy Spirit. It is ever so, that, when there cometh unto you a messenger from God with that which ye yourselves desire not, ye grow arrogant, and some ye disbelieve and some ye slay?"

(Muhammad)

We need not expect that our "modern" world would react differently. The noted Christian theologian, Father Raymond Brown, has stated that were Jesus to now appear He would in all probability be arrested and found guilty by those calling themselves Christians.

"Know thou, that they who are truly wise have likened the world unto the human temple. As the body of man needeth a garment to clothe it, so the body of mankind must needs be adorned with the mantle of justice and wisdom. Its robe is the Revelation vouchsafed unto it by God. Whenever this robe hath fulfilled its purpose, the Almighty will assuredly renew it. For every age requireth a fresh measure of the light of God. Every Divine Revelation hath been sent down in a manner that befitted the circumstances of the age in which it hath appeared."

(Bahá'u'lláh)

Bahá'u'lláh summoned mankind to immerse itself in the ocean of His words and objectively investigate the validity of His claims. He expressly forbade His followers to recount events associated with Him which they held to be miracles, as He considered them unworthy of mention and an unsound basis for belief. Spreading His message by recounting such events would only serve to degrade the sanctity of the divine revelation which He was entrusted to impart to mankind. His message, revealed under circumstances of severe persecution and harsh imprisonment, was clothed in a powerful style incorporating the transcendental spirituality of Krishna, the wisdom of Moses, the prophetic insight of Isaiah, the tenderness of Christ, the compassion of the Buddha and the authority of Muhammad. Indeed, Shoghi Effendi, to whom we are indebted for many of the English translations of Bahá'u'lláh's works, has testified that His words "...are impregnated with such power and reveal such beauty as only those who are versed in the languages in which they were originally revealed can claim to have sufficiently appreciated." The majesty of Bahá'u'lláh's literary style is mirrored in a penetrating vision of unparalleled profundity.

Bahá'u'lláh instructed His followers to turn to His eldest son, 'Abdu'l-Bahá, for guidance after His passing. At the age of nine, 'Abdu'l-Bahá, in the company of his father, began a life of exile and imprisonment which was to last until the age of sixty-four. After over fifty years as an exile and a prisoner 'Abdu'l-Bahá was released from captivity by a general amnesty granted after the fall of the Ottoman Empire. Shortly thereafter, at the age of sixty-seven, he travelled to Europe and North America to proclaim the message of Bahá'u'lláh to the peoples of the west. Although deprived of a formal education, 'Abdu'l-Bahá exhibited an almost supernatural knowledge and wisdom which, coupled with a saintly character and a demeanour described as majestic yet exceedingly humble, seldom failed to win the respect of those with whom he came in contact—from the mission poor to the university president.

Equally impressive was his energy and stamina. Many of the passages contained in this volume are taken from unprepared talks recorded during his travels in North America. Although travelling from coast to coast he managed to deliver 139 talks within the span of 244 days, from April until early December 1912. His words are not divine Revelation and thus are not considered equal in rank to those of Bahá'u'lláh, however, according to Bahá'u'lláh, they do possess equal validity.

After returning to the Holy Lands shortly before World War I 'Abdu'l-Bahá took steps to set aside grain before the onslaught of the impending chaos. This grain was later distributed free of charge to the inhabitants of Haifa and thus averted mass starvation. For this and many other humanitarian deeds he was Knighted by the British Government. Many of the officers and officials who made his acquaintance recorded their impressions. Here is a brief sample:

"There was never a more striking instance of one who desired that mankind should live in peace and goodwill and have love for others by the recognition of their inherent divine qualities. At Haifa, in 1919, I well

remember seeing a white figure seated by the roadside; when he arose and walked the vision of a truly and holy saintly man impressed itself on me."
(Lord Lamington)

"It was a wonderful experience in the midst of the chaos of war conditions to visit the Master at His Mount Carmel home, which even at that time was a haven of peace and refreshment.

"I can remember Him, majestic yet gentle, pacing up and down His garden whilst He spoke to me about eternal realities, at a time when the whole material world was rocking on its foundations. The divine power of the spirit shone through His presence, giving one the feeling that a great prophet from Old Testament days had risen up in a war-stricken world, as an inspirer and spiritual guide for the human race."
(Major Tudor-Pole)

"I was impressed, as was every visitor, by 'Abdu'l-Bahá's dignity, grace, and charm...his strong features and lofty expression lent to his personality an appearance of majesty."
(Sir Herbert Samuel, G.C.B., C.B.E.)

"...I never failed to visit him whenever I went to Haifa. His conversation was indeed a remarkable planing, like that of an ancient prophet, far above the perplexities and pettinesses of Palestine politics, and elevating all problems into first principles."
(Sir Ronald Storrs, K.C.M.G., C.B.E.)

In his will and testament 'Abdu'l-Bahá appointed his grandson, Shoghi Effendi, as the Guardian of the Bahá'í Faith. From 1921 until 1957 he guided the affairs of the steadily growing Bahá'í World Community and helped solidify the administrative institutions outlined in the writings of Bahá'u'lláh and 'Abdu'l-Bahá. Shoghi Effendi's contributions to the Bahá'í Faith stagger the imagination. His translations of the *Sacred Writings* from Persian and Arabic into English (plus the account of the early history of the faith written by the historian Nabil) would by themselves be deemed a remarkable achievement. Yet in addition he established the World Centre of the Bahá'í Faith in Haifa, Israel, acting simultaneously as architect, project manager, landscaper, diplomat and the administrative head of the Bahá'í World Community. His writings are not held in the same rank as those of Bahá'u'lláh or 'Abdu'l-Bahá, but their validity is explicitly attested by 'Abdu'l-Bahá.

In the year 1963 the Universal House of Justice was established, that institution envisioned by Bahá'u'lláh to rule upon matters not specifically addressed in the *Sacred Writings* and to guide the affairs of the Bahá'í Community. It is currently composed of nine members who are democratically elected by the members of the Bahá'í Spiritual Assemblies of the nations of the world, who gather every five years in Haifa, Israel, for this purpose. The seat of the Universal House of Justice and the World Centre of Bahá'í Faith are situated on Mount Carmel in Israel in fulfilment of the Prophet Isaiah's vision:

> Now it shall come to pass in the later days
> That the mountain of the Lord's house
> Shall be established on the top of the mountains,
> And shall be exalted above the hills,
> And all nations shall flow to it...
> For out of Zion shall go forth the Law.
>
> **Isaiah**

In order to stifle Bahá'u'lláh's ever growing influence, He was tortured, imprisoned and finally exiled to the Holy Lands in 1868. Once there He pitched His tent on the slopes of Mount Carmel, under the gaze of German Christians who had gathered to await the return of Jesus Christ, and revealed these words:

> Render thanks unto Thy Lord, O Carmel...
> Rejoice, for God hath in this Day established upon thee His throne,
> hath made thee the dawning-place of the signs
> and the dayspring of the evidences of His Revelation...
> He, verily, loveth the spot which hath been made
> the seat of His throne, which His footsteps have trodden,
> which hath been honoured by His presence,
> from which He raised His call...
> Call out to Zion, O Carmel,
> and announce the joyful tidings:
> He that was hidden from mortal eyes is come!
>
> **Bahá'u'lláh**

1
AN INTRODUCTION TO THE BAHÁ'Í FAITH

From the writings of Shoghi Effendi (1897-1957)
The Guardian of the Bahá'í Faith

This Cause is too evident to be obscured, and too conspicuous to be concealed. It shineth as the sun in its meridian glory.

Bahá'u'lláh

AN INDEPENDENT WORLD RELIGION

The Faith established by Bahá'u'lláh was born in Persia about the middle of the nineteenth century and has, as a result of the successive banishments of its Founder, culminating in His exile to the Turkish penal colony of 'Akká, and His subsequent death and burial in its vicinity, fixed its permanent spiritual centre in the Holy Land, and is now in the process of laying the foundations of its world administrative centre in the city of Haifa.

Alike in the claims unequivocally asserted by its Author and the general character of the growth of the Bahá'í community in every continent of the globe, it can be regarded in no other light than a world religion.

...this Faith is now increasingly demonstrating its right to be recognized, not as one more religious system superimposed on the conflicting creeds which for so many generations have divided mankind and darkened its fortunes, but rather as a restatement of the eternal verities underlying all the religions of the past, as a unifying force instilling into the adherents of these religions a new spiritual vigour, infusing them with a new hope and love for mankind, firing them with a new vision of the fundamental unity of their religious doctrines, and unfolding to their eyes the glorious destiny that awaits the human race.

THE BASIC TENETS OF THE BAHÁ'Í FAITH

The fundamental principle enunciated by Bahá'u'lláh, the followers of His Faith firmly believe, is that religious truth is not absolute but relative, that Divine Revelation is a continuous and progressive process, that all the great religions of the world are divine in origin, that their basic principles are in complete harmony, that their aims and purposes are one and the same, that their teachings are but facets of one truth, that their functions are complementary, that they differ only in the non-essential aspects of their doctrines, and that their missions represent successive stages in the spiritual evolution of human society.

The aim of Bahá'u'lláh, the Prophet of this new and great age which humanity has entered upon...is not to destroy but to fulfil the Revelations of the past, to reconcile rather than accentuate the divergencies of the conflicting creeds which disrupt present-day society.

This purpose, far from belittling the station of the Prophets gone before Him or of whittling down their teachings, is to restate the basic truths which these teachings enshrine in a manner that would conform to the needs, and be in consonance with the capacity, and be applicable to the problems, the ills, the perplexities, of the ages in which we live. His mission is to proclaim that the ages of the infancy and of the childhood of the human race are past, that the convulsions associated with the present stage of its adolescence are slowly and painfully preparing it to attain the stage of manhood, and are heralding the approach of that Age of Ages when swords will be beaten into plowshares, when the Kingdom promised by Jesus Christ will have been established, and the peace of the planet definitely and permanently ensured. Nor does Bahá'u'lláh claim finality for His own Revelation, but rather stipulates that a fuller measure of the truth He has been commissioned by the Almighty to vouchsafe to humanity, at so critical a juncture in its fortunes, must needs be disclosed at future stages in the constant and limitless evolution of mankind.

The Bahá'í Faith upholds the unity of God, recognizes the unity of His Prophets, and inculcates the principle of the oneness and wholeness of the entire human race. It proclaims the necessity and inevitability of the unification of mankind, asserts that it is gradually approaching, and claims that nothing short of the transmuting spirit of God, working through His chosen Mouthpiece in this day, can ultimately succeed in bringing it about. It, moreover, enjoins upon its followers the primary duty of an unfettered search after truth, condemns all manner of prejudice and superstition, declares the purpose of religion to be the

An Introduction to the Bahá'í Faith

promotion of amity and concord, proclaims its essential harmony with science, and recognizes it as a foremost agency for the pacification and the orderly progress of human society. It unequivocally maintains the principle of equal rights, opportunities, and privileges for men and women, insists on compulsory education, eliminates extremes of poverty and wealth, abolishes the institution of priesthood, prohibits slavery, asceticism, mendicancy, and monasticism, prescribes monogamy, discourages divorce, emphasizes the necessity of strict obedience to one's government, exalts any work performed in the spirit of service to the level of worship, urges either the creation or the selection of an auxiliary international language, and delineates the outlines of those institutions that must establish and perpetuate the general peace of mankind.

THE BAB

The Bahá'í Faith revolves around three central Figures, the first of whom was a youth, a native of Shiráz, named Mírzá 'Alí-Muhammad, known as the Báb (Gate), who in May 1844, at the age of twenty-five, advanced the claim of being the Herald Who, according to the sacred Scriptures of previous Dispensations, must needs announce and prepare the way for the advent of One greater that Himself, Whose mission would be, according to those same Scriptures, to inaugurate an era of righteousness and peace, an era that would be hailed as the consummation of all previous Dispensations, and initiate a new cycle in the religious history of mankind. Swift and severe persecution, launched by the organized forces of Church and State in His native land, precipitated successively His arrest, His exile to the mountains of Adhirbáyján, His imprisonment in the fortresses of Máh-Kú and Chihríq, and His execution, in July 1850, by a firing squad in the public square of Tabriz. No less than twenty thousand of his followers were put to death with such barbarous cruelty as to evoke the warm sympathy and the unqualified admiration of a number of Western writers, diplomats, travellers, and scholars, some of whom were witnesses of these abominable outrages, and were moved to record them in their books and diaries.

BAHÁ'U'LLÁH

Mírzá Husayn-'Alí, surnamed Bahá'u'lláh (the Glory of God), a native of Mázindarán, Whose advent the Báb had foretold, was assailed by those same forces of ignorance and fanaticism, was imprisoned in

Tihrán, was banished, in 1852, from His native land to Baghdád, thence to Constantinople and Adrianople, and finally to the prison city of 'Akká, where He remained incarcerated for no less than twenty-four years, and in whose neighbourhood He passed away in 1892. In the course of His banishment, and particularly in Adrianople and 'Akká, He formulated the laws and ordinances of His Dispensation, expounded, in over a hundred volumes, the principles of His Faith, proclaimed His Message to the kings and rulers of both the East and the West, both Christian and Muslim, addressed the Pope, the Caliph of Islám, the Chief Magistrates of the Republics of the American continent, the entire Christian sacerdotal order, the leaders of Shi'ih and Sunní Islam, and the high priests of the Zoroastrian religion. In these writings He proclaimed His Revelation, summoned those whom He addressed to heed His call and espouse His Faith, warned them of the consequences of their refusal, and denounced, in some cases, their arrogance and tyranny.

'ABDU'L-BAHÁ

His eldest son, 'Abbás Effendi, known as 'Abdu'l-Bahá (the Servant of Bahá), appointed by Him as His lawful successor and the authorized interpreter of His teachings, Who since early childhood had been closely associated with His Father, and shared His exile and tribulations, remained a prisoner until 1908, when, as a result of the Young Turk Revolution, He was released from His confinement. Establishing His residence in Haifa, He embarked soon after on His three-year journey to Egypt, Europe, and North America, in the course of which He expounded before vast audiences, the teachings of His Father and predicted the approach of that catastrophe that was soon to befall mankind. He returned to His home on the eve of the first World War, in the course of which He was exposed to constant danger, until the liberation of Palestine by the forces under the command of General Allenby, who extended the utmost consideration to Him and to the small band of His fellow-exiles in 'Akká and Haifa. In 1921 He passed away, and was buried in a vault in the mausoleum erected on Mount Carmel, at the express instruction of Bahá'u'lláh, for the remains of the Báb, which had previously been transferred from Tabriz to the Holy Land after having been preserved and concealed for no less than sixty years.

THE ADMINISTRATIVE ORDER

The passing of 'Abdu'l-Bahá marked the termination of the first and Heroic Age of the Bahá'í Faith and signalized the opening of the

Formative Age destined to witness the gradual emergence of its Administrative Order, whose establishment had been foretold by the Báb, whose laws were revealed by Bahá'u'lláh, whose outlines were delineated by 'Abdu'l-Bahá in His Will and Testament, and whose foundations are now being laid by the national and local councils which are elected by the professed adherents of the Faith, and which are paving the way for the constitution of the World Council, to be designated as the Universal House of Justice [established in 1963], which, in conjunction with me, as its appointed Head and the authorized interpreter of the Bahá'í teachings, must co-ordinate and direct the affairs of the Bahá'í community, and whose seat will be permanently established in the Holy Land, in close proximity to its world spiritual centre, the resting-places of its Founders.

The Administrative Order of the Faith of Bahá'u'lláh, which is destined to evolve into the Bahá'í World Commonwealth, and has already survived the assaults launched against its institutions by such formidable foes as the kings of the Qájár dynasty, the Caliphs of Islam, the ecclesiastical leaders of Egypt, and the Nazi regime in Germany, has already extended its ramifications to every continent of the globe, stretching from Iceland to the extremity of Chile, has been established in no less than eighty-eight countries of the world [187 countries and 45 territories as of this writing], has gathered within its pale representatives of no less than thirty-one races [over 2100 ethnic and tribal groups], numbers among its supporters Christians of various denominations, Muslims of both Sunní and Shí'ih sects, Jews, Hindus, Sikhs, Zoroastrians, and Buddhists. It has published and disseminated, through its appointed agencies, Bahá'í literature in forty-eight languages [over 800]; has already consolidated its structure through the incorporation of five National Assemblies and seventy-seven local Assemblies [currently 165 national & 18,232 local Assemblies], in lands as far apart as South America, India, and the Antipodes-incorporations that legally empower its elected representatives to hold property as trustees of the Bahá'í community. ...It [the Administrative Order]...enjoys in several countries the privilege of official recognition by the civil authorities, enabling it to secure exemption from taxation for its endowments and to solemnize Bahá'í marriage...

This Administrative Order, unlike the systems evolved after the death of the Founders of the various religions, is divine in origin, rests securely on the laws, the precepts, the ordinances and institutions which the Founder of the Faith has Himself specifically laid down and unequivocally established, and functions in strict accordance with the interpretations of the authorized Interpreters of its holy scriptures. Though fiercely assailed, ever since its inception, it has, by virtue of its character, unique in the annals of the world's religious history, succeeded in maintaining the unity of the diversified and far-flung body of its supporters, and enabled them to launch, unitedly and systematically, enterprises in both Hemispheres, designed to extend its limits and consolidate its administrative institutions.

The Faith which this order serves, safeguards, and promotes is, it should be noted in this connection, essentially **supernatural, supranational, entirely non-political, non-partisan,** and diametrically opposed to any policy or school of thought that seeks to exalt any particular race, class or nation. It is free from any form of ecclesiasticism, has neither priesthood nor rituals, and is supported exclusively by voluntary contributions made by its avowed adherents. Though loyal to their respective governments, though imbued with the love of their own country, and anxious to promote, at all times, its best interests, the followers of the Bahá'í Faith, nevertheless, viewing mankind as one entity, and profoundly attached to its vital interests, will not hesitate to subordinate every particular interest, be it personal, regional or national, to the over-riding interest of the generality of mankind, knowing full well than in a world of interdependent peoples and nations the advantage of the part is best to be reached by the advantage of the whole, and that no lasting result can be achieved by any of the component parts if the general interests of the entity itself are neglected.[1]

Shoghi Effendi

---

1. Guidance for Today and Tomorrow, A selection from the Writings of Shoghi Effendi, Bahá'í Publishing Trust, London, 1973 edition. pages 1-10.

2
WHY PERSIA?

...it should always be borne in mind, nor can it be sufficiently emphasized, that the primary reason why the Báb and Bahá'u'lláh chose to appear in Persia, and to make it the first repository of their Revelation, was because, of all the peoples and nations of the civilized world, that race and nation had, as so often depicted by 'Abdu'l-Bahá, sunk to such ignominious depths, and manifested so great a perversity, as to find no parallel among its contemporaries. For no more convincing proof could be adduced demonstrating the regenerating spirit animating the Revelations proclaimed by the Báb and Bahá'u'lláh than their power to transform what can be truly regarded as one of the most backward, the most cowardly, and perverse of peoples into a race of heroes, fit to effect in turn a similar revolution in the life of mankind.

Shoghi Effendi

INDEPENDENT CONFIRMATIONS

Now it appears to me that the history of the Bábi movement must be interesting in different ways to others besides those who are directly engaged in the study of Persian. To the student of religious thought it will afford no little matter for reflection; for here he may contemplate such personalities as by lapse of time pass into heroes and demi-gods still unobscured by myth and fable; he may examine by the light of concurrent and independent testimony one of those strange outbursts of enthusiasm, faith, fervent devotion, and indomitable heroism...which we are accustomed to associate with the earlier history of the human race; he may witness, in a word, the birth of a faith which may not impossibly win a place amidst the great religions of the world. To the ethnologist also it may yield food for thought as to the character of a people who, stigmatised as they often have been as selfish, mercenary, avaricious, egotistical, sordid, and cowardly, are yet capable of exhibiting under the influence of a strong religious impulse a degree of devotion, disinterestedness, generosity, unselfishness, nobility, and courage which may be paralleled in history, but can scarcely be surpassed.

Professor Edward G. Browne, Cambridge (1862-1926)

AN EYEWITNESS ACCOUNT

But follow me, my friend, you who lay claim to a heart and European ethics, follow me to the unhappy ones who, with gouged-out eyes must eat, on the scene of the deed, without any sauce, their own amputated ears; or whose teeth are torn out with inhuman violence by the hand of the executioner; or whose bare skulls are simply crushed by blows from a hammer; or where the bázár is illuminated with unhappy victims, because on right and left the people dig deep holes in their breasts and shoulders and insert burning wicks in the wounds. I saw some dragged in chains through the bázár, preceded by a military band, in whom these wicks had burned so deep that now the fat flickered convulsively in the wounds like a newly-extinguished lamp. Not seldom it happens that the unwearying ingenuity of the Orientals leads to fresh tortures. They will skin the soles of the Bábí's feet, soak the wound in boiling oil, shoe the foot like the hoof of a horse, and compel the victim to run. No cry escapes from the victim's breast; the torment is endured in dark silence by the numbed sensation of the fanatic; now he must run; the body cannot endure what the soul has endured; he falls. Give him the coup de grâce! Put him out of his pain! No! The executioner swings the whip, and-I myself have had to witness it-the unhappy victim of hundred-fold tortures runs! This is the beginning of the end. As for the end itself, they hang the scorched and perforated bodies by their hands and feet to a tree head downwards, and now every Persian may try his marksmanship to his heart's content from a fixed but not too proximate distance on the noble quarry placed at his disposal. I saw corpses torn by nearly 150 bullets...When I read over again what I have written I am overcome by the thought that those who are with you in our dearly beloved Austria may doubt the full truth of the picture, and accuse me of exaggeration. Would to God that I had not lived to see it! But by the duties of my profession I was unhappily often, only to often, a witness of these abominations. At present I never leave my house, in order not to meet with fresh scenes of horror. After their death the Bábis are hacked in two and either nailed to the city gate, or cast out into the plain as food for the dogs and jackals. Thus the punishment extends even beyond the limits which bound this bitter world, for Musulmáns who are not buried have no right to enter the Prophet's Paradise. Since my whole soul revolts against such infamy, against such abominations as recent times, according to the judgement of all, present, I will no longer maintain my connection with the scene of such crimes.

*from the Austrian officer, Captain von Goumoens
in a letter to friends dated October 17, 1852*

A REFLECTION ON CERTITUDE

Reflect : Who in this world is able to manifest such transcendent power, such pervading influence? All these stainless hearts and sanctified souls have, with absolute resignation, responded to the summons of His decree. Instead of complaining, they rendered thanks unto God, and amidst the darkness of their anguish they revealed naught but radiant acquiescence to His will. It is evident how relentless was the hate, and how bitter the malice and enmity entertained by all the peoples. The persecution and pain they inflicted on these holy and spiritual beings were regarded by them as means unto salvation, prosperity, and everlasting success. Hath the world, since the days of Adam, witnessed such tumult, such violent commotion? Notwithstanding all the torture they suffered, and manifold the afflictions they endured, they became the object of universal opprobrium and execration. Methinks, patience was revealed only by virtue of their fortitude, and faithfulness itself was begotten only by their deed.

Do thou ponder these momentous happenings in thy heart, so that thou mayest apprehend the greatness of this Revelation, and perceive its stupendous glory. Then shall the spirit of faith, through the grace of the Merciful, be breathed into thy being, and thou shalt be established and abide upon the seat of certitude. The one God is My witness! Wert thou to ponder a while, thou wilt recognize that, apart from all these established truths and above-mentioned evidences, the repudiation, cursing, and execration, pronounced by the people of the earth, are in themselves the mightiest proof and the surest testimony of the truth of these heroes of the field of resignation and detachment. Whenever thou dost meditate upon the cavils uttered by all the people, be they divines, learned or ignorant, the firmer and the more steadfast wilt thou grow in the Faith. For whatsoever hath come to pass, hath been prophesied by them who are the Mines of divine knowledge, and Recipients of God's eternal law.

Bahá'u'lláh

3
EXCERPTS FROM THE SPOKEN NARRATIVE OF BAHIYYIH KHANUM

(THE DAUGHTER OF BAHÁ'U'LLÁH)

I remember dimly very happy days with my beloved father and mother, and my brother 'Abbás, who was two years my senior.

My father was Mírzá Husayn-'Alí [Bahá'u'lláh] of Núr, who married my beautiful mother, Asíyíh Khánum, when she was very young. She was the only daughter of a Persian Vizier, of high degree, Mírzá Ismá'íl. He, as well as Mirzá Abbás Burzug, my paternal grandfather, possessed great wealth.

When the brother of my mother married my father's sister, the double alliance of the two noble families roused much interest throughout the land. "It is adding wealth to wealth," the people said. Asíyíh Khánum's wedding treasures were extensive, in accordance with the usual custom in families of their standing; forty mules were loaded with her possessions when she came to her husband's home...

I wish you could have seen her as I first remember her, tall, slender, graceful, eyes of dark blue-a pearl, a flower amongst women.

I have been told that even when very young, her wisdom and intelligence were remarkable. I always think of her in those earliest days of my memory as queenly in her dignity and loveliness, full of consideration for everybody, gentle, of a marvellous unselfishness, no action of hers ever failed to show the loving-kindness of her pure heart; her very presence seemed to make an atmosphere of love and happiness wherever she came, enfolding all comers in the fragrance of gentle courtesy.

Even in the early years of their married life, they, my father and mother, took part as little as possible in State functions, social ceremonies, and the luxurious habits of ordinary highly-placed and

Excerpts from the Spoken Narrative of Bahíyyih Khánum

wealthy families in the land of Persia; she, and her noble-hearted husband, counted these worldly pleasures meaningless, and preferred rather to occupy themselves in caring for the poor, and for all who were unhappy, or in trouble.

From our doors nobody was ever turned away; the hospitable board was spread for all comers. Constantly the poor women came to my mother, to whom they poured out their various stories of woe, to be comforted and consoled by her loving helpfulness. Whilst the people called my father, "The Father of the Poor," they spoke of my mother as "The Mother of Consolation," though, naturally, only the women and little children ever looked upon her face unveiled.

So our peaceful days flowed on.

We used to go to our house in the country sometimes; my brother 'Abbás and I loved to play in the beautiful gardens, where grew many kinds of wonderful fruits and flowers and flowering trees; but this part of my early life is a very dim memory.

One day I remember very well, though I was only six years old at the time. It seemed that an attempt had been made on the life of the Sháh by a half-crazy young Bábí.

My father was away at his country house in the village of Níavirán, which was his property, the villagers of which were all and individually cared for by him.

Suddenly and hurriedly a servant came rushing in great distress to my mother.

"The master, the master, he is arrested- I have seen him! He has walked many miles! Oh, they have beaten him! They say he has suffered the torture of the bastinado! His feet are bleeding! He has no shoes on! His turban has gone! His clothes are torn! There are chains upon his neck!"

My poor mothers face grew whiter and whiter. We children were terribly frightened and could only weep bitterly.

Immediately everybody, all our relations, and friends, and servants fled from our house in terror, only one man-servant, Isfadíyár, remained, and one woman. Our palace, and the smaller houses belonging to it were very soon stripped of everything; furniture, treasures, all were stolen by the people.

Mirzá Músá, my father's brother, who was always very kind to us, helped my mother and her three children to escape into hiding. She succeeded in saving some few of the marriage treasures, which were all of our vast possessions left to us. These things were sold; with the money my mother was able to pay the gaolers to take food to my father in the prison, and to meet other expenses incurred later on.

We were now in a little house, not far from the prison...Oh, the terrible anxiety my beloved mother suffered at that time! Surely greater than any woman, about to become a mother (as I afterwards knew), could possible have strength to bear.

The prison into which my father had been cast was a terrible place, seven steps below the ground; it was ankle-deep in filth, infested with horrible vermin, and of an indescribable loathsomeness. Added to this, there was no glimmer of light in that noisome place. Within its walls forty Bábís were crowded; murderers and highway robbers were also imprisoned there.

My noble father was hurled into this black hole, loaded with heavy chains; five other Bábís were chained to him night and day, and here he remained for four months. Picture to yourself the horror of these conditions. Any movement caused the chains to cut deeper and deeper not only into the flesh of one, but of all who were chained together; whilst sleep or rest of any kind was not possible. No food was provided, and it was with the utmost difficulty that my mother was able to arrange to get any food or drink taken into that ghastly prison.

Meanwhile, the spirit which upheld the Bábís never quailed for a moment, even under these conditions...They chanted prayers night and day. Every morning one or more of these brave and devoted friends would be taken out to be tortured and killed in various way of horror.

When religious fanaticism was aroused against a person or persons, who were accused of being infidels, as was now the case with the Bábís, it was customary not simply to condemn them to death and have them executed by the State executioner, but to hand the victims over to various classes of the populace.

The butchers had their methods of torture; the bakers theirs; the shoemakers and blacksmiths yet others of their own. They were all given opportunities of carrying out their pitiless inventions on the Bábís.

The fanatics became more and more infuriated when they failed to quench the amazing spirit of these fearless, devoted ones, who remained unflinching, chanting prayers, asking God to pardon and bless their murderers, and praising Him, as long as they were able to breathe. The mob crowed to these fearful scenes, and yelled their execrations, whilst all through the fiendish work, a drum was loudly beaten.

These horrible sounds I well remember, as we three children clung to our mother, she not knowing whether the victim was her own adored husband. She could not find out whether he was still alive or not until late at night, or very early in the morning, when she determined to venture out, in defiance of the danger to herself and to us, for neither women or children were spared.

How well I remember cowering in the dark, with my little brother, Mírzá Midhí, the Purest Branch, at that time two years old, in my arms, which were not very strong, as I was only six. I was shivering with terror, for I knew of some of the horrible things that were happening, and was aware that they might have seized even my mother.

So I waited and waited until she should come back. The Mírzá Músá, my uncle, who was in hiding, would venture in to hear what tidings my mother had been able to gather.

My brother ʻAbbás usually went with her on these sorrowful errands.

We listened eagerly to the accounts she gave to my uncle.

This information came through the kindness of a sister of my grandfather, who was married to Mírzá Yúsif, a Russian subject, and a friend of the Russian Consul in Tihrán. This gentleman, my great uncle by marriage, used to attend the courts to find out some particulars as to the victims chosen for execution day by day, and thus was able to relieve to some extent my mother's overwhelming anxiety as these appalling days passed over us.

It was Mírzá Yúsif who was able to help my mother about getting food taken to my father, and who brought us to the two little rooms near the prison, where we stayed in close hiding. He had to be very careful in thus defying the authorities, although the danger in this case was mitigated by the fact of his being under the protection of the Russian Consulate, as a Russian subject.

Nobody at all, of all our friends and relations, dared to come to see my mother during these days of death, but the wife of Mírzá Yúsif, the aunt of my father.

One day the discovery was made by Mírzá Yúsif that our untiring enemies, the most fanatical of the mullás, were plotting the death of Mírzá Husayn ʻAlí Núri [Baháʼuʼlláh], my father.

Mírzá Yúsif consulted the Russian Consul; that powerful friend determined that this plan should be at once frustrated.

An amazing scene took place in the Court, where the sentences of death were passed. The Russian Consul rose and fearlessly addressed those in court:

"Hearken to me! I have words of importance to say to you" (his voice rang out, the president and officials were too amazed to reply).

"Have you not taken enough cruel revenge? Have you not already murdered a large enough number of harmless people, because of this accusation, of the absurd falseness of which you are quite aware? Has there not been sufficient of this orgy of brutal torture to satisfy you? How is it possible that you can even pretend to think that this august prisoner planned that silly attempt to shoot the Sháh?

"It is not unknown to you that the stupid gun, used by that poor youth, could not have killed a bird. Moreover, the boy was obviously insane. You know very well that this charge is not only untrue, but palpably ridiculous.

"There must be an end to all this.

"I have determined to extend the protection of Russia to this innocent nobleman; therefore beware! For if one hair of his head be hurt from this moment, rivers of blood shall flow in your town as punishment.

"You will do well to heed my warning, my country is behind me in this matter."

An account of this scene was given to my mother by Mírzá Yúsif that night, and told by her to my uncle, Mírzá Músá, when he came for tidings.

Needless to say how eagerly my brother and I listened, and how we all wept for joy.

Very soon afterwards we heard that, fearing to disregard the stern warning of the Russian Consul, the Governor gave orders that my father should be permitted to come forth from that prison with his life. It was also decreed that he and his family were banished.

They were to leave Tihrán for Baghdád. Ten days were allowed for preparation, as the beloved prisoner was very ill indeed.

And so he came to our two little rooms.

Oh, the joy of his presence!

Oh, the horror of that dungeon, where he had passed those four terrible months.

[He] spoke very little of the terrible sufferings of that time! We, who saw the marks of what he had endured, where the chains had cut into the delicate skin, especially that of his neck, his wounded feet so long untended, evidence of the torture of the bastinado, how we wept with my dear mother.

He, on his part, told of the steadfast faith of the friends, who had gone forth to meet their death at the hands of their torturers, with joy and gladness...

Excerpts from the Spoken Narrative of Bahíyyih Khánum

[Bahá'u'lláh] had a marvellous divine experience whilst in that prison. We saw a new radiance seeming to enfold him like a shining vesture, its significance we were to learn years later. [There He received the intimation of His Mission]. At that time we were only aware of the wonder of it, without understanding, or even being told the details of the sacred event.

My mother did her best to nurse our beloved, that he might have some strength to set out upon that journey on which we were to start in ten days time.

Now was a time of great difficulty. How could she prepare?

The poor, dear lady sold almost all that remained of her marriage treasures, jewels, embroidered garments, and other belongings...With this money she was able to make some provision for the terrible journey. (The Government provided nothing for those whom they exiled.)

This journey was filled with indescribable difficulties. My mother had no experience, no servants, no provisions, and very little money left. My father was extremely ill, not having recovered from the ordeals of the torture and the prison. No one of all our friends and relations dared to come to our help, or even to say good-bye, but one old lady, the grandmother of Asíyíh Khánum.

At length we started on that fearful journey, which lasted about four weeks; the weather was bitterly cold, snow was upon the ground...My poor mother! How she suffered on this journey, riding in a takht-raván, borne on a jolting mule! And this took place only six weeks before her youngest son was born![1]

---

1. For the full account of this and many other fascinating first hand chronicles refer to "The Chosen Highway", by Lady Blomfield, Bahá'í Publishing Trust, Wilmette, Illinois, 1970. pp. 39-46

4
WHY NOW?

THE NECESSITY OF A NEW REVELATION

The recrudescence of religious intolerance, of racial animosity, and of patriotic arrogance; the increasing evidences of selfishness, of suspicion, of fear and of fraud; the spread of terrorism, of lawlessness, of drunkenness and of crime; the unquestionable thirst for, and the feverish pursuit after, earthly vanities, riches and pleasures; the weakening of family solidarity; the laxity in parental control; the lapse into luxurious indulgence; the irresponsible attitude towards marriage and the consequent rising tide of divorce; the degeneracy of art and music, the infection of literature, and the corruption of the press...these appear as the outstanding characteristics of a decadent society, a society that must either be reborn or perish.

Shoghi Effendi

So marked a decline in the strength and cohesion of the elements constituting Christian society has led, in its turn, as we might well anticipate, to the emergence of an increasing number of obscure cults, of strange and new worships, of ineffective philosophies, whose sophisticated doctrines have intensified the confusion of a troubled age. In their tenets and pursuits they may be said to reflect and bear witness to the revolt, the discontent, and the confused aspirations of the disillusioned masses that have deserted the cause of the Christian churches and seceded from their membership.

Shoghi Effendi

Who, contemplating the helplessness and fears and miseries of humanity in this day, can any longer question the necessity for a fresh revelation of the quickening power of God's redemptive love and guidance? Who, witnessing on one hand the stupendous advance achieved in the realm of human knowledge, of power, of skill and inventiveness, and viewing on the other the unprecedented character of the sufferings that afflict, and the dangers that beset, present-day society, can be so blind as to doubt that the hour has at last struck for the advent of a new Revelation, for a re-statement of the Divine Purpose, and for the consequent revival of those forces that have, at fixed intervals, rehabilitated the fortunes of human society? Does not the very operation of the world-unifying forces that are at work in this age necessitate that He Who is the Bearer of the Message of God in this day should not only reaffirm that self-same exalted standard of individual conduct inculcated by the Prophets gone before Him, but embody in His appeal, to all governments and peoples, the essentials of that social code, that Divine Economy, which must guide humanity's concerted efforts in establishing that all-embracing federation which is to signalize the advent of the Kingdom of God on this earth?

Shoghi Effendi

HUMANITY IN A STAGE OF TRANSITION

What we witness at the present time...is the adolescent stage in the slow and painful evolution of humanity, preparatory to the attainment of the stage of manhood, the stage of maturity, the promise of which is embedded in the teachings, and enshrined in the prophecies, of Bahá'u'lláh. The tumult of this age of transition is characteristic of the impetuosity and irrational instincts of youth, its follies, its prodigality, its pride, its self-assurance, its rebelliousness, and contempt of discipline.

The ages of its infancy and childhood are past, never again to return, while the Great Age, the consummation of all ages, which must signalize the coming of age of the entire human race, is yet to come. The convulsions of this transitional and most turbulent period in the annals of humanity are the essential prerequisites, and herald the inevitable approach, of that Age of Ages, "the time of the end," in which the folly and tumult of strife that has, since the dawn of history, blackened the annals of mankind, will have been finally transmuted into the wisdom and the tranquillity of an undisturbed, a universal, and lasting peace, in which the discord and separation of the children of men will have given way to the world-wide reconciliation, and the complete unification of the divers elements that constitute human society.

This will indeed be the fitting climax of that process of integration which, starting with the family, the smallest unit in the scale of human organization, must, after having called successively into being the tribe, the city-state and the nation, continue to operate until it culminates in the unification of the whole world, the final object and the crowing glory of human evolution on this planet. It is this stage which humanity, willingly or unwillingly, is resistlessly approaching.

Shoghi Effendi

THE FOLLOWERS OF BAHÁ'U'LLÁH

Conscious of their high calling, confident in the society-building power which their Faith possesses, they press forward, undeterred and undismayed, in their efforts to fashion and perfect the necessary instruments wherein the embryonic World Order of Bahá'u'lláh can mature and develop. It is this building process, slow and unobtrusive, to which the life of the world-wide Bahá'í Community is wholly consecrated, that constitutes the one hope of a stricken society...

In a world the structure of whose political and social institutions is impaired, whose vision is befogged, whose conscience is bewildered, whose religious systems have become anemic and lost their virtue, this healing Agency, this leavening Power, this cementing force, intensely alive and all-pervasive, has been taking shape, is crystallizing into institutions, is mobilizing its forces, and is preparing for the spiritual conquest and the complete redemption of mankind. Though the society which incarnates its ideals be small, and its direct and tangible benefits as yet inconsiderable, yet the potentialities with which it has been endowed, and through which it is destined to regenerate the individual and rebuild a broken world, are incalculable.

Shoghi Effendi

5
BECOMING A TRUE BAHA'I

Their concern hath ever been and now is for the betterment of the world. Their purpose is to obliterate differences, and quench the flame of hatred and enmity, so that the whole earth may come to be viewed as one country.

Bahá'u'lláh

My first counsel is this: Possess a pure, kindly and radiant heart, that thine may be a sovereignty ancient, imperishable and everlasting.

Bahá'u'lláh

LOVE THE FIRST SIGN OF FAITH

A man may be a Bahá'í in name only. If he is a Bahá'í in reality, his deeds and actions will be decisive proof of it. What are the requirements? Love for mankind, sincerity toward all, reflecting the oneness of the world of humanity, philanthropy, becoming enkindled with the fire of the love of God, attainment of the knowledge of God and that which is conducive to human welfare.

...Associate most kindly with all; be as one family; pursue this same pathway. Let your intentions be one that your love may permeate and affect the hearts of others so that they may grow to love each other and all attain to this condition of oneness.

The world of humanity is filled with darkness; you are its radiant candles...It is exceedingly debased; you must be the cause of its exaltation...According to the teachings of Bahá'u'lláh you must love and cherish each individual member of humanity.

The first sign of faith is love. The message of the holy, divine Manifestations is love; the phenomena of creation are based upon love; the radiance of the world is due to love; the well-being and happiness of the world depend upon it. Therefore, I admonish you that you must strive throughout the human world to diffuse the light of love. The people of this world are thinking of warfare; you must be peacemakers. The nations are self-centered; you must be thoughtful of others rather than yourselves. They are neglectful; you must be mindful. They are asleep; you should be awake and alert. May each one of you be as a shining star in the horizon of eternal glory. This is my wish for you and my highest hope.

'Abdu'l-Bahá

DISTINCTION

From the standpoint of color there are white, black, yellow and red people. From the standpoint of physiognomy there is a wide difference and distinction among races. The Asian, African and American have different physiognomies; the men of the North and men of the South are very different in type and features. From an economic standpoint in the law of living there is a great deal of difference. Some are poor, others wealthy; some are wise, others ignorant; some are patient and serene, some impatient and excitable; some are prone to justice, others practice injustice and oppression; some are meek, others arrogant. In brief, there are many points of distinction among humankind.

I desire distinction for you. The Bahá'ís must be distinguished from others of humanity. But this distinction must not depend upon wealth-that they should become more affluent than other people. I do not desire for you financial distinction. It is not an ordinary distinction I desire; not scientific, commercial, industrial distinction. For you I desire spiritual distinction-that is, you must become distinguished for loving humanity, for unity and accord, for love and justice. In brief, you must become distinguished in all the virtues of the human world-for faithfulness and sincerity, for justice and fidelity, for firmness and steadfastness, for philanthropic deeds and service to the human world, for love toward every human being, for unity and accord with all people, for removing prejudices and promoting international peace. Finally, you must become distinguished for heavenly illumination and for acquiring the bestowals of God. I desire this distinction for you. This must be the point of distinction among you.

'Abdu'l-Bahá

BE ACTIVE AND PROGRESSIVE

Be ye in that land vanguards of the perfections of humankind; carry forward the various branches of knowledge, be active and progressive in the field of inventions and the arts. Endeavour to rectify the conduct of men, and seek to excel the whole world in moral character.

'Abdu'l-Bahá

The All-loving God created man to radiate the Divine light and to illumine the world by his words, action and life. If he is without virtue he becomes no better than a mere animal...

If ye will follow earnestly the teachings of Bahá'u'lláh, ye shall indeed become the light of the world, the soul for the body of the world, the comfort and help for humanity, and the source of salvation for the whole universe.

'Abdu'l-Bahá

BECOME A POINT OF ATTRACTION

Should any one of you enter a city, he should become a centre of attraction by reason of his sincerity, his faithfulness and love, his honesty and fidelity, his truthfulness and loving-kindness towards all the peoples of the world, so that the people of that city may cry out and say: "This man is unquestionably a Bahá'í, for his manners, his behaviour, his conduct, his morals, his nature, and disposition reflect the attributes of the Bahá'ís." Not until ye attain this station can ye be said to have been faithful to the Covenant and Testament of God. For He hath, through irrefutable Texts, entered into a binding Covenant with us all, requiring us to act in accordance with His sacred instructions and counsels.

'Abdu'l-Bahá

FOR TRUE BAHÁ'ÍS SPEECH IS NOT NEEDED

All over the world one hears beautiful sayings extolled and noble precepts admired...

But all these sayings are but words and we see very few of them carried into the world of action...

But Bahá'ís must not be thus; they must rise above this condition. Actions must be more to them than words. By their actions they must be merciful and not merely by their words. They must on all occasions confirm by their actions what they proclaim in words. Their deeds must prove their fidelity, and their actions must show forth Divine light.

Let your actions cry aloud to the world that you are indeed Bahá'ís, for it is actions that speak to the world and are the cause of the progress of humanity.

If we are true Bahá'ís speech is not needed. Our actions will help on the world, will spread civilization, will help the progress of science, and cause the arts to develop. Without action nothing in the material world can be accomplished, neither can words unaided advance a man in the spiritual Kingdom. It is not through lip-service that the elect of God have attained to holiness, but by patient lives of active service they have brought light into the world.

Therefore strive that your actions day by day may be beautiful prayers. Turn towards God, and seek always to do that which is right and noble. Enrich the poor, raise the fallen, comfort the sorrowful, bring healing to the sick, reassure the fearful, rescue the oppressed, bring hope to the hopeless, shelter the destitute!

This is the work of a true Bahá'í, and this is what is expected of him. If we strive to do all this, then are we true Bahá'ís, but if we neglect it, we are not followers of the Light, and we have no right to the name.

God, who sees all hearts, knows how far our lives are the fulfilment of our words.

'Abdu'l-Bahá

HUMILITY

You must manifest complete love and affection toward all mankind. Do not exalt yourselves above others, but consider all as your equals, recognizing them as the servants of one God. Know that God is compassionate toward all; therefore, love all from the depths of your hearts, prefer all religionists before yourselves, be filled with love for every race, and be kind toward the people of all nationalities. Never speak disparagingly of others, but praise without distinction. Pollute not your tongues by speaking evil of another. Recognize your enemies as friends, and consider those who wish you evil as the wishers of good. You must not see evil as evil and then compromise with your opinion, for to treat in a smooth, kindly way one whom you consider evil or an enemy is hypocrisy, and this is not worthy or allowable. You must consider your enemies as your friends, look upon your evil-wishers as your well-wishers and treat them accordingly. Act in such a way that your heart may be free from hatred. Let not your heart be offended with anyone. If some one commits an error and wrong toward you, you must instantly forgive him. Do not complain of others. Refrain from reprimanding them, and if you wish to give admonition or advice, let it be offered in such a way that it will not burden the bearer. Turn all your thoughts toward bringing joy to hearts. Beware! Beware! lest ye offend any heart. Assist the world of humanity as much as possible. Be the source of consolation to every sad one, assist every weak one, be helpful to every indigent one, care for every sick one, be the cause of glorification to every lowly one, and shelter those who are overshadowed by fear.

In brief, let each one of you be as a lamp shining forth with the light of the virtues of the world of humanity. Be trustworthy, sincere, affectionate and replete with chastity. Be illumined, be spiritual, be divine, be glorious, be quickened of God, be a Bahá'í.

'Abdu'l-Bahá

MAGNANIMITY

Never become angry with one another. Let your eyes be directed toward the kingdom of truth and not toward the world of creation. Love the creatures for the sake of God and not for themselves. You will never become angry or impatient if you love them for the sake of God. Humanity is not perfect. There are imperfections in every human being, and you will always become unhappy if you look toward the people themselves. But if you look toward God, you will love them and be kind to them, for the world of God is the world of perfection and complete mercy. Therefore, do not look at the shortcomings of anybody; see with the sight of forgiveness. The imperfect eye beholds imperfections. The eye that covers faults looks toward the Creator of souls. He created them, trains and provides for them, endows them with capacity and life, sight and hearing; therefore, they are the signs of His grandeur. You must love and be kind to everybody, care for the poor, protect the weak, heal the sick, teach and educate the ignorant.

'Abdu'l-Bahá

The noblest of men is he who serves humankind, and he is nearest the threshold of God who is the least of His servants.

'Abdu'l-Bahá

PURITY

God loveth those who are pure. Naught ...in the sight of God is more loved than purity and immaculate cleanliness...

God desireth not to see...any soul deprived of joy and radiance. He indeed desireth that under all conditions, all may be adorned with such purity, both inwardly and outwardly, that no repugnance may be caused even to themselves, how much less unto others.

The Báb

DETACHMENT

I sorrow not for the burden of My imprisonment. Neither do I grieve over My abasement, or the tribulation I suffer at the hands of Mine enemies. By My life! They are My glory, a glory wherewith God hath adorned His own Self. Would that ye know it!

The shame I was made to bear hath uncovered the glory with which the whole creation had been invested, and through the cruelties I have endured, the Day Star of Justice hath manifested itself, and shed its splendor upon men.

My sorrows are for those who have involved themselves in their corrupt passions, and claim to be associated with the Faith of God, the Gracious, the All-Praised.

It behoveth the people of Bahá to die to the world and all that is therein, to be so detached from all earthly things that the inmates of Paradise may inhale from their garment the sweet smelling savor of sanctity, that all the peoples of the earth may recognize in their faces the brightness of the All-Merciful, and that through them may be spread abroad the signs and tokens of God, the Almighty, the All-Wise. They that have tarnished the fair name of the Cause of God, by following the things of the flesh-these are in palpable error!

Bahá'u'lláh

The days of your life are far spent, O people, and your end is fast approaching...Delight not yourselves in things of the world and its vain ornaments, neither set your hopes on them. Let your reliance be on the remembrance of God, the Most Exalted, the Most Great...

Lay not on any soul a load which ye would not wish to be laid upon you, and desire not for any one the things ye would not desire for yourselves. This is My best counsel unto you, did ye but observe it.

Bahá'u'lláh

OBLIGATION TO THE POOR

If ye meet the abased or the down-trodden, turn not away disdainfully from them, for the King of Glory ever watcheth over them and surroundeth them with such tenderness as none can fathom except them that have suffered their wishes and desires to be merged in the Will of your Lord, the Gracious, the All-Wise. O ye rich ones of the earth! Flee not from the face of the poor that lieth in the dust, nay rather befriend him and suffer him to recount the tale of the woes with which God's inscrutable Decree hath caused him to be afflicted...Blessed are the learned that pride not themselves on their attainments; and well is it with the righteous that mock not the sinful, but rather conceal their misdeeds, so that their own shortcomings may remain veiled to men's eyes.

Bahá'u'lláh

OVERCOMING XENOPHOBIA

When a man turns his face to God he finds sunshine everywhere. All men are his brothers. Let no conventionality cause you to seem cold and unsympathetic when you meet strange people from other countries. Do not look at them as though you suspected them of being evil-doers, thieves and boors. You think it necessary to be very careful, not to expose yourselves to the risk of making acquaintance with such possibly, undesirable people.

I ask you not to think only of yourselves. Be kind to the strangers, whether come they from Turkey, Japan, Persia, Russia, China or any other country in the world...

Let those who meet you know, without your proclaiming the fact, that you are indeed a Bahá'í. Put into practice the Teaching of Bahá'u'lláh, that of kindness to all nations. Do not be content with showing friendship in words alone, let your heart burn with loving kindness for all who may cross your path...

What profit is there in agreeing that universal friendship is good, and talking of the solidarity of the human race as a grand ideal? Unless these thoughts are translated into the world of action, they are useless...

People make much profession of goodness, multiplying fine words because they wish to be thought greater and better than their fellows, seeking fame in the eyes of the world. Those who do most good use fewest words concerning their actions.

The children of God do the works without boasting, obeying His laws.

My hope for you is that you will ever avoid tyranny and oppression; that you will work without ceasing till justice reigns in every land, that you will keep your hearts pure and your hands free from unrighteousness.

This is what the near approach to God requires from you, and this is what I expect of you.

'Abdu'l-Bahá

KINDNESS TO ALL

Beware lest ye harm any soul, or make any heart to sorrow; lest ye wound any man with your words, be he known to you or a stranger, be he friend or foe. Pray ye for all; ask ye that all be blessed, all be forgiven. Beware, beware, lest any of you seek vengeance, even against one who is thirsting for your blood. Beware, beware, lest ye offend the feelings of another, even though he be an evil-doer, and he wish you ill. Look ye not upon the creatures, turn ye to their Creator. See ye not the never-yielding people, see but the Lord of Hosts. Gaze ye not down upon the dust, gaze upward at the shining sun, which hath caused every patch of darksome earth to glow with light.

'Abdu'l-Bahá

It is your duty to be exceedingly kind to every human being, and to wish him well; to work for the upliftment of society; to blow the breath of life into the dead; to act in accordance with the instructions of Bahá'u'lláh and walk His path-until ye change the world of man into the world of God.

'Abdu'l-Bahá

OVERLOOKING FAULTS IN OTHERS

If ye become aware of a sin committed by another, conceal it, that God may conceal your own sin.

Bahá'u'lláh

One must see in every human being only that which is worthy of praise. When this is done, one can be a friend to the whole human race. If, however, we look at people form the standpoint of their faults, then being a friend to them is a formidable task.

It happened one day in the time of Christ-may the life of the world be a sacrifice unto Him-that He passed by the dead body of a dog, a carcass reeking, hideous, the limbs rotting away. One of those present said: 'How foul its stench!' And another said: 'How sickening! How loathsome!' To be brief, each one of them had something to add to the list.

But then Christ Himself spoke, and He told them: 'Look at that dog's teeth! How gleaming white!'

The Messiah's sin-covering gaze did not for a moment dwell upon the repulsiveness of that carrion. The one element of that dead dog's carcass which was not abomination was the teeth: and Jesus looked upon their brightness.

Thus is it incumbent upon us, when we direct our gaze toward other people, to see where they excel, not where they fail.

'Abdu'l-Bahá

Let your thoughts dwell on your own spiritual development, and close your eyes to the deficiencies of other souls. Act ye in such wise, showing forth pure and goodly deeds, and modesty and humility, that ye will cause others to be awakened.

Never is it the wish of 'Abdu'l-Bahá to see any being hurt, nor will He make anyone to grieve; for man can receive no greater gift than this, that he rejoice another's heart.

'Abdu'l-Bahá

SPIRITUAL PHYSICIANS

It is incumbent upon thee to summon the people, under all conditions, to whatever will cause them to show forth spiritual characteristics and goodly deeds, so that all may become aware of that which is the cause of human upliftment, and may, with the utmost endeavor, direct themselves towards the most sublime Station and the Pinnacle of Glory.

Bahá'u'lláh

The world is even as a human being who is diseased and impotent, whose eyes can see no longer, whose ears have gone deaf, all of whose powers are corroded and used up. Wherefore must the friends of God be competent physicians who, following the holy Teachings, will nurse this patient back to health. Perhaps, God willing, the world will mend, and become permanently whole, and its exhausted faculties will be restored, and its person will take on such vigour, freshness and verdancy that it will shine out with comeliness and grace...

They must cleanse their hearts from even the slightest trace of hatred and spite, and they must set about being truthful and honest, conciliatory and loving to all humankind-so that East and West will, even as two lovers, hold each other close; that hatred and hostility will perish from the earth, and universal peace be firmly rooted in their place.

O ye lovers of God! Be kind to all peoples; care for every person; do all ye can to purify the hearts and minds of men; strive ye to gladden every soul. To every meadow be a shower of grace, to every tree the water of life; be as sweet musk to the sense of humankind, and to the ailing be a fresh, restoring breeze. Be pleasing waters to all those who thirst, a careful guide to all who have lost their way; be father and mother to the orphan, be loving sons and daughters to the old, be an abundant treasure to the poor. Think ye of love and good fellowship as the delights of heaven, think ye of hostility and hatred as the torments of hell.

'Abdu'l-Bahá

THE ATTITUDE OF THE TRUE SEEKER

He must never seek to exalt himself above any one, must wash away from the tablet of his heart every trace of pride and vainglory, must cling unto patience and resignation, observe silence, and refrain from idle talk. For the tongue is a smouldering fire, and excess of speech a deadly poison. Material fire consumeth the body, whereas the fire of the tongue devoureth both heart and soul. The force of the former lasteth but a time, whilst the effects of the latter endure a century.

That seeker should also regard backbiting as grievous error, and keep himself aloof from its dominion, inasmuch as backbiting quencheth the light of the heart, and extinguisheth the life of the soul. He should be content with little, and be freed from all inordinate desire. He should treasure the companionship of those that have renounced the world, and regard avoidance of boastful and worldly people a precious benefit. At the dawn of every day he should commune with God, and with all his soul persevere in the quest of his Beloved. He should consume every wayward thought with the flame of His loving mention, and, with the swiftness of lighting, pass by all else save Him. He should succour the dispossessed, and never withhold his favour from the destitute. He should show kindness to animals, how much more unto his fellow-man, to him who is endowed with the power of utterance. He should not hesitate to offer up his life for his Beloved, nor allow the censure of the people to turn him away from the Truth. He should not wish for others that which he doth not wish for himself, nor promise that which he doth not fulfil. With all his heart should the seeker avoid fellowship with evil doers, and pray for the remission of their sins. He should forgive the sinful, and never despise his low estate, for none knoweth what his own end shall be...Our purpose in revealing these convincing and weighty utterances is to impress upon the seeker that he should regard all else beside God as transient, and count all things save Him, Who is the Object of all adoration, as utter nothingness.

Bahá'u'lláh

VIRTUES EXPECTED OF THE PEOPLE OF BAHÁ

The sword of a virtuous character and upright conduct is sharper than blades of steel.

Bahá'u'lláh

O people of Bahá! Ye are the dawning-places of the love of God and the daysprings of His loving-kindness. Defile not your tongues with the cursing and reviling of any soul, and guard your eyes against that which is not seemly. Set forth that which ye possess. If it be favourably received, your end is attained; if not, to protest is in vain. Leave that soul to himself and turn unto the Lord, the Protector, the Self-Subsisting. Be not the cause of grief, much less of discord and strife. The hope is cherished that ye may obtain true education in the shelter of the tree of His tender mercies and act in accordance with that which God desireth. Ye are all the leaves of one tree and the drops of one ocean.

Bahá'u'lláh

Fix your gaze upon wisdom in all things, for it is an unfailing antidote.

Bahá'u'lláh

The people of Bahá must under all circumstances observe that which is meet and seemly and exhort the people accordingly.
...They that are endued with sincerity and faithfulness should associate with all the peoples and kindreds of the earth with joy and radiance, inasmuch as consorting with people hath promoted and will continue to promote unity and concord, which in turn are conducive to the maintenance of order in the world and to the regeneration of nations. Blessed are such as hold fast to the cord of kindliness and tender mercy and are free from animosity and hatred.

This Wronged One exhorteth the peoples of the world to observe tolerance and righteousness, which are two lights amidst the darkness of the world and two educators for the edification of mankind. Happy are they who have attained thereto and woe betide the heedless.

...The light of a good character surpasseth the light of the sun and the radiance thereof. Whoso attaineth unto it is accounted as a jewel among men. The glory and the upliftment of the world must needs depend upon it.

...O people of Bahá! Trustworthiness is in truth the best of vestures for your temples and the most glorious crown for your heads. Take ye fast hold of it at the behest of Him Who is the Ordainer, the All-Informed.

Bahá'u'lláh

O ye friends of God in His cities and His loved ones in His lands! This Wronged One enjoineth on you honesty and piety. Blessed the city that shineth by their light. Through them man is exalted, and the door of security is unlocked before the face of all creation. Happy the man that cleaveth fast unto them, and recognizeth their virtue, and woe betide him that denieth their station.

Bahá'u'lláh

Beautify your tongues, O people, with truthfulness, and adorn your souls with the ornament of honesty. Beware, O people, that ye deal not treacherously with any one. Be ye the trustees of God amongst His creatures, and the emblem of His generosity amidst His People.

Bahá'u'lláh

Dispute not with any one concerning the things of this world and its affairs, for God hath abandoned them to such as have set their affection upon them. Out of the whole world He hath chosen for Himself the hearts of men-hearts which the hosts of revelation and of utterance can subdue.

Bahá'u'lláh

O people of Bahá! The source of crafts, sciences and arts is the power of reflection. Make ye every effort that out of this ideal mine there may gleam forth such pearls of wisdom and utterance as will promote the well-being and harmony of all the kindreds of the earth.

Bahá'u'lláh

If thine eyes be turned towards mercy, forsake the things that profit thee and cleave unto that which will profit mankind. And if thine eyes be turned towards justice, choose thou for thy neighbour that which thou choosest for thyself. Humility exalteth man to the heaven of glory and power, whilst pride abaseth him to the depths of wretchedness and degradation.

Bahá'u'lláh

O people of God! Do not buy yourselves in your own concerns; let your thoughts be fixed upon that which will rehabilitate the fortunes of mankind and sanctify the hearts and souls of men. This can best be achieved through pure and holy deeds, through a virtuous life and a goodly behaviour. Valiant acts will ensure the triumph of this Cause, and a saintly character will reinforce its power. Cleave unto righteousness, O people of Bahá! This, verily, is the commandment which this Wronged One hath given unto you, and the first choice of His unrestrained Will for every one of you.

Bahá'u'lláh

Be of them whom the tumult of the world, however much it may agitate them in the path of their Creator, can never sadden, whose purpose the blame of the blamer will never defeat.

Bahá'u'lláh

O ye loved ones! Do not forsake prudence. Incline your hearts to the counsels given by the Most Exalted Pen and beware lest your hands or tongues cause harm unto anyone among mankind.

Bahá'u'lláh

O people of God! I admonish you to observe courtesy, for above all else it is the prince of virtues. Well is it with him who is illumined with the light of courtesy and is attired with the vesture of uprightness.

Bahá'u'lláh

It is Our wish and desire that every one of you may become a source of all goodness unto men, and an example of uprightness to mankind...If any differences arise amongst you, behold Me standing before your face, and overlook the faults of one another for My name's sake and as a token of your love for My manifest and resplendent Cause. We love to see you at all times consorting in amity and concord within the paradise of My good-pleasure, and to inhale from your acts the fragrance of friendliness and unity, of loving-kindness and fellowship.

Bahá'u'lláh

The more grievous their woes, the greater waxed the love of the people of Bahá.

Bahá'u'lláh

In all matters moderation is desirable. If a thing is carried to excess, it will prove a source of evil.

Bahá'u'lláh

He is not to be numbered with the people of Bahá who followeth his mundane desires, or fixeth his heart on things of the earth. He is My true follower who, if he come to a valley of pure gold, will pass straight through it aloof as a cloud, and will neither turn back, nor pause. Such a man is, assuredly, of Me...And if he met the fairest and most comely of women, he would not feel his heart seduced by the least shadow of desire for her beauty. Such a one, indeed, is the creation of spotless chastity. Thus instructeth you the Pen of the Ancient of Day, as bidden by your Lord, the Almighty, the All-Bountiful.

Bahá'u'lláh

It behoveth, likewise, the loved ones of God to be forbearing towards their fellow-men, and to be so sanctified and detached from all things, and to evince such sincerity and fairness, that all the peoples of the earth may recognize them as the trustees of God amongst men.

Bahá'u'lláh

Be generous in prosperity, and thankful in adversity. Be worthy of the trust of thy neighbor, and look upon him with a bright and friendly face. Be a treasure to the poor, an admonisher to the rich, an answerer to the cry of the needy, a preserver of the sanctity of thy pledge. Be fair in thy judgement, and guarded in thy speech. Be unjust to no man, and show meekness to all men. Be as a lamp unto them that walk in darkness, a joy to the sorrowful, a sea for the thirsty, a haven for the distressed, an upholder and defender of the victim of oppression. Let integrity and uprightness distinguish all thine acts. Be a home for the stranger, a balm to the suffering, a tower of strength for the fugitive. Be eyes to the blind, and a guiding light unto the feet of the erring. Be an ornament to the countenance of truth, a crown to the brow of fidelity, a pillar of the temple of righteousness, a breath of life to the body of mankind, an ensign of the hosts of justice, a luminary above the horizon of virtue, a dew to the soil of the human heart, an ark on the ocean of knowledge, a sun in the heaven of bounty, a gem on the diadem of wisdom, a shining light in the firmament of thy generation, a fruit upon the tree of humility.

Bahá'u'lláh

THE CAUSE

The supreme cause for creating the world and all that is therein is for man to know God...Having reached this lofty station a twofold obligation resteth upon every soul. One is to be steadfast in the Cause with such steadfastness that were all the peoples of the world to attempt to prevent him from turning to the Source of Revelation, they would be powerless to do so. The other is observance of the divine ordinances which have streamed forth from the wellspring of His heavenly-propelled Pen. For man's knowledge of God cannot develop fully and adequately save by observing whatsoever hath been ordained by Him and is set forth in His heavenly Book.

Bahá'u'lláh

Arise for the triumph of My Cause, and, through the power of thine utterance, subdue the hearts of men. Thou must show forth that which will ensure the peace and well-being of the miserable and the downtrodden. Gird up the loins of thine endeavor, that perchance thou mayest release the captive from his chains, and enable him to attain unto true liberty.

Bahá'u'lláh

They who are the beloved of God, in whatever place they gather and whomsoever they may meet, must evince, in their attitude towards God, and in the manner of their celebration of His praise and glory, such humility and submissiveness that every atom of dust beneath their feet may attest the depth of their devotion. The conversation carried by these holy souls should be informed with such power that these same atoms of dust will be thrilled by its influence...

Show forbearance and benevolence and love to one another. Should any one among you be incapable of grasping a certain truth, or be striving to comprehend it, show forth, when conversing with him, a spirit of extreme kindliness and good-will. Help him to see and recognize the truth, without esteeming yourself to be, in the least, superior to him, or to be possessed of greater endowments...

Nothing whatever can, in this Day, inflict a greater harm upon this Cause than dissension and strife, contention, estrangement and apathy, among the loved ones of God. Flee them, through the power of God and His sovereign aid, and strive ye to knit together the hearts of men, in His Name, the Unifier, the All-Knowing, the All-Wise.

Beseech ye the one true God to grant that ye may taste the savor of such deeds as are performed in His path, and partake of the sweetness of such humility and submissiveness as are shown for His sake...

We dare not, in this Day, lift the veil that concealeth the exalted station which every true believer can attain, for the joy which such a revelation must provoke might well cause a few to faint away and die...

Whoso hath searched the depths of the oceans that lie hid within these exalted words, and fathomed their import, can be said to have discovered a glimmer of the unspeakable glory with which this mighty, this sublime, and most holy Revelation hath been endowed. From the excellence of so great a Revelation the honor with which its faithful followers must needs be invested can be well imagined. By the righteousness of the one true God! The very breath of these souls is in itself richer than all the treasures of the earth. Happy is the man that hath attained thereunto, and woe betide the heedless.

Bahá'u'lláh

He is truly wise whom the world and all that is therein have not deterred from recognizing the light of this Day, who will not allow men's idle talk to cause him to swerve from the way of righteousness. He is indeed as one dead who, at the wondrous dawn of this Revelation, hath failed to be quickened by its soul-stirring breeze.

Bahá'u'lláh

THE BETTERMENT OF THE WORLD AND THE PROMOTION OF THE CAUSE

This is a Revelation that infuseth strength into the feeble, and crowneth with wealth the destitute.

With the utmost friendliness and in a spirit of perfect fellowship take ye counsel together, and dedicate the precious days of your lives to the betterment of the world and the promotion of the Cause...He, verily, enjoineth upon all men what is right, and forbiddeth whatsoever degradeth their station.

Bahá'u'lláh

Whoso ariseth, in this Day, to aid Our Cause, and summoneth to his assistance the hosts of a praiseworthy character and upright conduct, the influence flowing from such an action will, most certainly, be diffused throughout the whole world.

Bahá'u'lláh

How sad if any man were, in this Day, to rest his heart on the transitory things of this world! Arise, and cling firmly to the Cause of God. Be most loving one to another. Burn away, wholly for the sake of the Well-Beloved, the veil of self with the flame of the undying Fire, and with faces joyous and beaming with light, associate with your neighbor.

...Please God, ye will regard this blessed night as the night of unity, will knit your souls together, and resolve to adorn yourselves with the ornament of a goodly and praiseworthy character. Let your principal concern be to rescue the fallen from the slough of impending extinction, and to help him embrace the ancient Faith of God. Your behavior towards your neighbor should be such as to manifest clearly the signs of the one true God...

Bahá'u'lláh

DEALING WITH OPPOSITION

If they oppose you be gentle with them, if they contradict be firm in your faith, if they desert you and flee from before you, seek them out and treat them kindly. Do harm to nobody; pray for all; try to make your light shine in the world and let your banner fly high in the Heavens. The beautiful perfume of your noble lives will permeate everywhere. The light of truth kindled in your hearts will shine out of the distant horizon!

The indifference and scorn of the world matters not at all, whereas your lives will be of the greatest importance.

All those who seek truth in the Heavenly Kingdom shine like the stars; they are like fruit trees laden with choice fruit, like seas full of precious pearls.

Only have faith in the Mercy of God, and spread the Divine Truth.

'Abdu'l-Bahá

PEACE BEGINS WITH INDIVIDUALS

...peace must first be established among individuals until it leadeth in the end to peace among nations. Wherefore, O ye Bahá'ís, strive ye with all your might to create, through the power of the Word of God, genuine love, spiritual communion and durable bonds among individuals. This is your task.

'Abdu'l-Bahá

This people need no weapons of destruction, inasmuch as they have girded themselves to reconstruct the world. Their hosts are the hosts of goodly deeds, and their arms the arms of upright conduct...

Bahá'u'lláh

SHINING EXAMPLES UNTO MANKIND

O people of the world! Forsake all evil, hold fast that which is good. Strive to be shining examples unto all mankind, and true reminders of the virtues of God amidst men. He that riseth to serve My Cause should manifest My wisdom, and bend every effort to banish ignorance from the earth. Be united in counsel, be one in thought. Let each morn be better than its eve and each morrow richer than its yesterday. Man's merit lieth in service and virtue and not in the pageantry of wealth and riches. Take heed that your words be purged from idle fancies and worldly desires and your deeds be cleansed from craftiness and suspicion. Dissipate not the wealth of your precious lives in the pursuit of evil and corrupt affection, nor let your endeavours be spent in promoting your personal interest. Be generous in your days of plenty, and be patient in the hour of loss. Adversity is followed by success and rejoicings follow woe. Guard against idleness and sloth, and cling unto that which profiteth mankind, whether young or old, whether high or low. Beware lest ye sow tares of dissension among men or plant thorns of doubt in pure and radiant hearts.

O ye beloved of the Lord! Commit not that which defileth the limpid stream of love or destroyeth the sweet fragrance of friendship. By the righteousness of the Lord! Ye were created to show love one to another and not perversity and rancour. Take pride not in love for yourselves but in love for all mankind. Let your eye be chaste, your hand faithful, your tongue truthful and your heart enlightened.

Bahá'u'lláh

A SWIFTLY-PASSING WORLD

These few brief days shall pass away, this present life shall vanish from our sight; the roses of this world shall be fresh and fair no more, the garden of this earth's triumphs and delights shall droop and fade. The spring season of life shall turn into the autumn of death, the bright joy of palace halls give way to moonless dark within the tomb. And therefore is none of this worth loving at all, and to this the wise will not anchor his heart.

He who hath knowledge and power will rather seek out the glory of heaven, and spiritual distinction, and the life that dieth not. And such a one longeth to approach the sacred Threshold of God; for in the tavern of this swiftly-passing world the man of God will not lie drunken, nor will he even for a moment take his ease, nor stain himself with any fondness for this earthly life.

'Abdu'l-Bahá

GRATITUDE FOR THE BOUNTY OF BECOMING A BAHÁ'Í

O ye peoples of the Kingdom! How many a soul expended all its span of life in worship, endured the mortification of the flesh, longed to gain an entry into the Kingdom, and yet failed, while ye, with neither toil nor pain nor self-denial, have won the prize and entered in.

It is even as in the time of the Messiah, when the Pharisees and the pious were left without a portion, while Peter, John and Andrew, given neither to pious worship nor ascetic practice, won the day. Wherefore, thank ye God for setting upon your heads the crown of glory everlasting, for granting unto you this immeasurable grace.

The time hath come when, as a thank-offering for this bestowal, ye should grow in faith and constancy as day followeth day, and should draw ever nearer to the Lord, your God, becoming magnetized to such a degree, and so aflame, that your holy melodies in praise of the Beloved will reach upward to the Company on high; and that each one of you, even as a nightingale in this rose garden of God, will glorify the Lord of Hosts, and become the teacher of all who dwell on earth.

'Abdu'l-Bahá

Be thankful to God for having enabled you to recognise His Cause. Whoever has received this blessing must, prior to his acceptance, have performed some deed which, though he himself was unaware of its character, was ordained by God as a means whereby he has been guided to find and embrace the Truth...We cherish the hope that you, who have attained to this light, will exert your utmost to banish the darkness of superstition and unbelief from the midst of the people. May your deeds proclaim your faith and enable you to lead the erring into the paths of eternal salvation.

Bahá'u'lláh

A FINAL WORD

These are my final words of exhortation. I have repeatedly summoned you to the cause of the unity of the world of humanity, announcing that all mankind are the servants of the same God, that God is the creator of all; He is the Provider and Life-giver; all are equally beloved by Him...Therefore, you must manifest the greatest kindness and love toward the nations of the world, setting aside fanaticism, abandoning religious, national and racial prejudice.

This earth is one native land, one home; and all mankind are the children of one Father. God has created them, and they are the recipients of His compassion. Therefore, if anyone offends another he offends God. It is the wish of our heavenly Father that every heart should rejoice and be filled with happiness, that we should live together in felicity and joy. The obstacle to human happiness is racial or religious prejudice, the competitive struggle for existence and inhumanity toward each other.

Your eyes have been illumined, your ears are attentive, your hearts knowing. You must be free from prejudice and fanaticism, beholding no difference between the races and religions...

...Direct your whole effort toward the happiness of those who are despondent, bestow food upon the hungry, clothe the needy, and glorify the humble. Be a helper to every helpless one, and manifest kindness to your fellow creatures in order that ye may attain the good pleasure of God. This is conducive to the illumination of the world of humanity and eternal felicity for yourselves. I seek from God everlasting glory in your behalf; therefore, this is my prayer and exhortation.

Consider what is happening in the Balkans. Human blood is being shed, properties are destroyed, possessions pillaged, cities and villages devastated. A world-enkindling fire is astir in the Balkans. God has created men to love each other; but instead, they kill each other with cruelty and bloodshed. God has created them that they may cooperate and mingle in accord; but instead, they ravage, plunder and destroy in the carnage of battle. God has created them to be the cause of mutual felicity and peace; but instead, discord lamentation and anguish rise from the hearts of the innocent and afflicted.

As to you: Your efforts must be lofty. Exert yourselves with heart and soul so that, perchance, through your efforts the light of universal peace may shine and this darkness of estrangement and enmity may be dispelled from amongst men, that all men may become as one family and consort together in love and kindness...for all are the inhabitants of one planet...

...It is my hope that you may become successful in this high calling so that like brilliant lamps you may cast light upon the world of humanity and quicken and stir the body of existence like unto a spirit of life. This is eternal glory. This is everlasting felicity. This is immortal life. This is heavenly attainment. This is being created in the image and likeness of God...

'Abdu'l-Bahá

We remember every one of you, men and women, and from this spot -the Scene of incomparable glory- regard you all as one soul and send you the joyous tidings of divine blessings which have preceded all created things, and of My remembrance that pervadeth everyone, whether young or old. The glory of God rest upon you, O people of Bahá. Rejoice with exceeding gladness through My remembrance, for He is indeed with you at all times.

Bahá'u'lláh

6
ON THE BAHÁ'Í FAITH

THE SPIRIT OF A NEW ERA

...every era hath a spirit; the spirit of this illumined era lieth in the teachings of Bahá'u'lláh. For these lay the foundation of the oneness of the world of humanity and promulgate universal brotherhood. They are founded upon the unity of science and religion and upon investigation of truth. They uphold the principle that religion must be the cause of amity, union and harmony among men. They establish the equality of both sexes and propound economic principles which are for the happiness of individuals. They diffuse universal education, that every soul may as much as possible have a share of knowledge. They abrogate and nullify religious, racial, political, patriotic and economic prejudices and the like. These teachings that are scattered throughout the Epistles and Tablets are the cause of the illumination and the life of the world of humanity.

'Abdu'l-Bahá

ITS FUNDAMENTAL PURPOSE

O ye that dwell on earth! The distinguishing feature that marketh the preeminent character of this Supreme Revelation consisteth in that We have, on the one hand, blotted out from the pages of God's holy Book whatsoever hath been the cause of strife, of malice and mischief amongst the children of men, and have, on the other, laid down the essential prerequisites of concord, of understanding, of complete and enduring unity. Well is it with them that keep My statutes.

...Unveiled and unconcealed, this Wronged One hath, at all times, proclaimed before the face of all the peoples of the world that which will serve as the key for unlocking the doors of sciences, of arts, of knowledge, of well-being, of prosperity and wealth...I earnestly beseech

God that He may protect and purge the people of Bahá from the idle fancies and corrupt imaginings of the followers of the former Faith.

Bahá'u'lláh

It is incumbent upon every man of insight and understanding to strive to translate that which hath been written into reality and action...That one indeed is a man who, today, dedicateth himself to the service of the entire human race...Blessed and happy is he that ariseth to promote the best interests of the peoples and kindreds of the earth...It is not for him to pride himself who loveth his own country, but rather for him who loveth the whole world. The earth is but one country, and mankind its citizens.

Bahá'u'lláh

The purpose of God in creating man hath been, and will ever be, to enable him to know his Creator and to attain His Presence. To this most excellent aim, this supreme of objective, all the heavenly Books and the divinely-revealed and weighty Scriptures unequivocally bear witness.

Bahá'u'lláh

O ye children of men! The fundamental purpose animating the Faith of God and His Religion is to safeguard the interests and promote the unity of the human race, and to foster the spirit of love and fellowship amongst men. Suffer it not to become a source of dissension and discord, of hate and enmity. This is the straight Path, the fixed and immovable foundation. Whatsoever is raised on this foundation, the changes and chances of the world can never impair its strength, nor will the revolution of countless centuries undermine its structure.

Bahá'u'lláh

Is not the object of every Revelation to effect a transformation in the whole character of mankind, a transformation that shall manifest itself, both outwardly and inwardly, that shall affect both its inner life and external conditions? For if the character of mankind be not changed, the futility of God's universal Manifestations would be apparent.

Bahá'u'lláh

O contending peoples and kindreds of the earth! Set your faces towards unity, and let the radiance of its light shine upon you. Gather ye together, and for the sake of God resolve to root out whatever is the source of contention amongst you. Then will the effulgence of the world's great

Luminary envelop the whole earth, and its inhabitants become the citizens of one city, and the occupants of one and the same throne. This wronged One hath, ever since the early days of His life, cherished none other desire but this, and will continue to entertain no other wish except this.

Bahá'u'lláh

The basis of the teaching of Bahá'u'lláh is the Unity of Mankind, and his greatest desire was that love and goodwill should live in the heart of men.

'Abdu'l-Bahá

The harmony of religious belief with reason is a new vista which Bahá'u'lláh has opened for the soul of man.

'Abdu'l-Bahá

UNBIASED INVESTIGATION

So great is the glory of the Cause of God that even the blind can perceive it, how much more they whose sight is sharp, whose vision is pure. The blind, though unable to perceive the light of the sun, are, nevertheless, capable of experiencing its continual heat. The blind in heart, however...are impotent, no matter how long the Sun may shine upon them, either to perceive the radiance of its glory, or appreciate the warmth of its rays...

Purge your sight, that ye may perceive its glory with your own eyes, and depend not on the sight of any one except your self, for God hath never burdened any soul beyond its power. Thus hath it been sent down unto the Prophets and Messengers of old, and been recorded in all the Scriptures.

Bahá'u'lláh

It behoveth every man to blot out the trace of every idle word from the tablet of his heart, and to gaze, with an open and unbiased mind, on the signs of His Revelation, the proofs of His Mission, and the tokens of His glory.

Bahá'u'lláh

Immerse yourselves in the ocean of My words, that ye may unravel its secrets, and discover all the pearls of wisdom that lie hid in its depths...This is the changeless Faith of God, eternal in the past, eternal in the future. Let him that seeketh, attain it; and as to him that hath refused to seek it-verily, God is Self-Sufficient, above any need of His creatures.

Bahá'u'lláh

Do not allow difference of opinion, or diversity of thought to separate you from your fellow-men, or to be the cause of dispute, hatred and strife in your hearts.

Rather, search diligently for the truth and make all men your friends.

'Abdu'l-Bahá

Sanctify your souls from whatsoever is not of God, and taste ye the sweetness of rest within the pale of His vast and mighty Revelation... every man hath been, and will continue to be, able of himself to appreciate the Beauty of God, the Glorified. Had he not been endowed with such a capacity, how could he be called to account for his failure? If...any man should, whilst standing in the presence of God, be asked: "Wherefore hast thou disbelieved in My Beauty and turned away from My Self," and if such a man should reply and say: "Inasmuch as all men have erred, and none hath been found willing to turn his face to the Truth, I, too, following their example, have grievously failed to recognize the Beauty of the Eternal," such a plea will, assuredly, be rejected. For the faith of no man can be conditioned by any one except himself.

Bahá'u'lláh

BASIC HISTORY AND TENETS

Bahá'u'lláh was a Persian personage descended from prominent lineage. During His early years a Youth Whose name was 'Alí-Muhammad appeared in Persia. He was entitled the Báb, which means door or gate. The bearer of this title was a great Soul from Whom spiritual signs and evidences became manifest. He withstood the test of time and lived contrary to the custom and usages of Persia. He revealed a new system of faith opposed to the beliefs in His country and promulgated certain principles contrary to the thoughts of people. For this, that remarkable Personality was imprisoned by the Persian government. Eventually, by order of the government He was martyred. The account of this martyrdom, briefly stated, is as follows: He was suspended in a square as a target and shot to death. This revered Personality foreshadowed the advent of another Soul of Whom He said, "When He cometh He shall reveal greater things unto you."

Thus, after the martyrdom of the Báb, Bahá'u'lláh appeared. The government arose against Him. The priesthood in Persia opposed Him, subjecting Him to severe persecution. His possessions were confiscated, His relatives and friends were killed, and He was placed in a dungeon. For a long period He was imprisoned, chained and subjected to severest suffering. Afterward, He was exiled to Iráq, or Mesopotamia, from thence to Constantinople, then transferred to Adrianople and finally to 'Akká, where He underwent the severest ordeals and privations without a day or night of relaxation and repose. Notwithstanding this imprisonment and suffering, He manifested utmost spiritual power and majesty. Although imprisoned, He withstood two tyrant kings and eventually overcame both.

Shortly after His imprisonment He addressed Epistles, or Tablets, to all the kings and rulers of the world, summoning them to universal peace, to unity and international brotherhood. Among these sovereigns was the Shah of Persia, through whose instrumentality chiefly He had been imprisoned. In His letter to that ruler He arraigned him severely and prophesied his downfall, saying, "Thou art a tyrant; thy country will be laid waste; and thy family, humiliated and debased." He wrote to the Sultán of Turkey in similar terms, saying, "Thy dominion will pass away from thee." The Epistles to the kings and rulers summoning them to international peace were written by Bahá'u'lláh fifty years ago [mid 19th century]. Everything He wrote has come to pass. These letters were published in Bombay thirty years ago and are now spread broadcast throughout the world. Briefly, Bahá'u'lláh endured forty years of vicissitudes, ordeals and hardships for the purpose of spreading His teachings, which may be mentioned as follows:

The first teaching is that man should investigate reality, for reality is contrary to dogmatic interpretations and imitations of ancestral forms of belief to which all nations and peoples adhere so tenaciously. These blind imitations are contrary to the fundamental basis of the divine religions, for the divine religions in their central and essential teaching are based upon unity, love and peace, whereas these variations and imitations have ever been productive of warfare, sedition and strife...

The second teaching of Bahá'u'lláh is the principle of the oneness of the world of humanity. God is one; His servants are, likewise, one...

The third teaching of Bahá'u'lláh concerns universal peace among the nations, among the religions, among the races and native lands. He has declared that so long as prejudice-whether religious, racial, patriotic, political or sectarian-continues to exist among mankind, universal peace cannot become a reality in the world...

Furthermore, the teachings of Bahá'u'lláh announce that religion must be in conformity with science and reason; otherwise, it is superstition; for science and reason are realities, and religion itself is the Divine Reality unto which true science and reason must conform. God has bestowed the gift of mind upon man in order that he may weigh every fact or truth presented to him and adjudge whether it be reasonable...

The teachings of Bahá'u'lláh also proclaim equality between man and woman...In the estimation of God there is no gender. The one whose deeds are more worthy...is nearest and dearest in the estimation of God, be that one male or female.

...Bahá'u'lláh teaches that material civilization is incomplete, insufficient and that divine civilization must be established. Material civilization concerns the world of matter or bodies, but divine civilization is the realm of ethics and moralities. Until the moral degree of the nations is advanced and human virtues attain a lofty level, happiness for mankind is impossible...

'Abdu'l-Bahá

These teachings are even as the tree that beareth the best fruits of all trees. Philosophers, for instance, find in these heavenly teachings the most perfect solution of their social problems, and similarly a true and noble exposition of matters that pertain to philosophical questions. In like manner men of faith behold the reality of religion manifestly revealed in these heavenly teachings, and clearly and conclusively prove them to be the real and true remedy for the ills and infirmities of all mankind. Should these sublime teachings be diffused, mankind shall be freed from all perils, from all chronic ills and sicknesses. In like manner are the Bahá'í economic principles the embodiment of the highest aspirations of all wage-earning classes and of economists of various schools.

In short, all sections and parties have their aspirations realized in the teachings of Bahá'u'lláh. As these teachings are declared in churches, in mosques and in other places of worship, whether those of the followers of Buddha or of Confucius, in political circles or amongst materialists, all shall bear witness that these teachings bestow a fresh life upon mankind and constitute the immediate remedy for all the ills of social life.

'Abdu'l-Bahá

The Tablets of Bahá'u'lláh are many. The precepts and teachings they contain are universal, covering every subject. He has revealed scientific explanations ranging throughout all the realms of human inquiry and investigation-astronomy, biology, medical science, etc.. In the Kitab-i-Iqán He has given expositions of the meanings of the Gospel and other heavenly Books. He wrote lengthy Tablets upon civilization, sociology and government. Every subject is considered. His Tablets are matchless in beauty and profundity.

'Abdu'l-Bahá

If ye will trust in the Word of God and be strong; if ye will follow the precepts of Bahá'u'lláh to tend to the sick, raise the fallen, care for the poor and needy, give shelter to the destitute, protect the oppressed, comfort the sorrowful and love the world of humanity with all your hearts, then I say unto you that ere long this meeting-place will see a wonderful harvest. Day by day each member will advance and become more and more spiritual. But ye must have a firm foundation and your aims and ambitions must be clearly understood by each member. They shall be as follows:

1. To show compassion and goodwill to all mankind.
2. To render service to humanity.
3. To endeavour to guide and enlighten those in darkness.
4. To be kind to everyone, and show forth affection to every living soul.
5. To be humble in your attitude towards God, to be constant in prayer to Him, so as to grow daily nearer to God.
6. To be so faithful and sincere in all your actions that every member may be known as embodying the qualities of honesty, love, faith, kindness, generosity, and courage. To be detached from all that is not God, attracted by the Heavenly Breath-a divine soul; so that the world may know that a Bahá'í is a perfect being.

'Abdu'l-Bahá

STATION AND CLAIMS OF BAHÁ'U'LLÁH

Who can ever believe that this Servant of God hath at any time cherished in His heart a desire for any earthly honor or benefit? The Cause associated with His Name is far above the transitory things of this world. Behold Him, an exile, a victim of tyranny, in this Most Great Prison. His enemies have assailed Him on every side, and will continue to do so till the end of His life. Whatever, therefore, He saith unto you is wholly for the sake of God, that haply the peoples of the earth may cleanse their hearts from the stain of evil desire, may rend its veil asunder, and attain unto the knowledge of the one true God-the most exalted station to which any man can aspire. Their belief or disbelief in My Cause can neither profit nor harm Me. We summon them wholly for the sake of God. He, verily, can afford to dispense with all creatures.

Bahá'u'lláh

If ye choose to follow Me, I will make you heirs of My Kingdom; and if ye transgress against Me, I will, in My long-suffering, endure it patiently, and I, verily, am the Ever-Forgiving, the All Merciful.

Bahá'u'lláh

That Bahá'u'lláh should, notwithstanding the overwhelming intensity of His Revelation, be regarded as essentially one of these Manifestations of God, never to be identified with that invisible Reality, the Essence of Divinity itself, is one of the major beliefs of our Faith-a belief which should never be obscured and the integrity of which no one of its followers should allow to be compromised.

Shoghi Effendi

The human temple that has been made the vehicle of so overpowering a Revelation must, if we be faithful to the tenets of our Faith, ever remain entirely distinguished from the "innermost Spirit of Spirits" and "eternal Essence of Essences"-that invisible yet rational God Who, however much we extol the divinity of His Manifestations on earth, can in no wise incarnate His infinite, His unknowable, His incorruptible and all-embracing Reality in the concrete and limited frame of a mortal being. Indeed, the God Who could so incarnate His own reality would, in the light of the teachings of Bahá'u'lláh, cease immediately to be God. So crude and fantastic a theory of Divine incarnation is as removed from, and incompatible with, the essentials of Bahá'í belief as are the no less inadmissible pantheistic and anthropomorphic conceptions of God-both of which the utterances of Bahá'u'lláh emphatically repudiate and the fallacy of which they expose.

Shoghi Effendi

RELATION TO OTHER FAITHS

The Revelation, of which Bahá'u'lláh is the source and center, abrogates none of the religions that have preceded it, nor does it attempt, in the slightest degree, to distort their features or to belittle their value. It disclaims any intention of dwarfing any of the Prophets of the past, or of whittling down the eternal verity of their teachings. It can, in no wise, conflict with the spirit that animates their claims, nor does it seek to undermine the basis of any man's allegiance to their cause. Its declared, its primary purpose is to enable every adherent of these Faiths to obtain a fuller understanding of the religion with which he stands identified, and to acquire a clearer apprehension of its purpose. It is neither eclectic in the presentation of its truths nor arrogant in the affirmation of its claims. Its teachings revolve around the fundamental principle that religious truth is not absolute but relative, that Divine Revelation is progressive, not final. Unequivocally and without the least reservation it proclaims all established religions to be divine in origin, identical in their aims, complementary in their functions, continuous in their purpose, indispensable in their value to mankind.

Shoghi Effendi

THE REHABILITATION OF MANKIND

O people of God! Do not busy yourselves in your own concerns; let your thoughts be fixed upon that which will rehabilitate the fortunes of mankind and sanctify the hearts and souls of men. This can best be achieved through pure and holy deeds, through a virtuous life and a goodly behavior. Valiant acts will ensure the triumph of this Cause, and a saintly character will reinforce its power. Cleave unto righteousness, O people of Bahá! This, verily, is the commandment which this wronged One hath given unto you, and the first choice of His unrestrained Will for every one of you...

Let your vision be world embracing, rather than confined to your own self...

Consort with the followers of all religions in a spirit of friendliness and fellowship. Whatsoever hath led the children of men to shun one another, and hath caused dissensions and divisions amongst them, hath, through the revelation of these words, been nullified and abolished...Of old it hath been revealed: "Love of one's country is an element of the Faith of God." The Tongue of Grandeur hath, however, in the day of His manifestation proclaimed: "It is not his to boast who loveth his country, but it is his who loveth the world." Through the power released by these exalted words He hath lent a fresh impulse, and set a new direction, to the birds of men's hearts, and hath obliterated every trace of restriction and limitation from God's holy Book.

O people of Justice! Be as brilliant as the light, and as splendid as the fire that blazed in the Burning Bush. The brightness of the fire of your love will no doubt fuse and unify the contending people and kindreds of the earth, whilst the fierceness of the flame of enmity and hatred cannot but result in strife and ruin...

Every verse which this Pen hath revealed is a bright and shining portal that discloseth the glories of a saintly and pious life, of pure and stainless deeds. The summons and the message which We gave were never intended to reach or to benefit one land or one people only. Mankind in its entirety must firmly adhere to whatsoever hath been revealed and vouchsafed unto it. Then and only then will it attain unto true liberty...

Bahá'u'lláh

The All-Knowing Physician hath His finger on the pulse of mankind. He perceiveth the disease, and prescribeth, in His unerring wisdom, the remedy. Every age hath its own problem, and every soul its particular aspiration. The remedy the world needeth in its present-day afflictions can never be the same as that which a subsequent age may require. Be anxiously concerned with the needs of the age ye live in, and center your deliberations on its exigencies and requirements.

We can well perceive how the whole human race is encompassed with great, with incalculable afflictions. We see it languishing on its bed of sickness, sore-tried and disillusioned. They that are intoxicated by self-conceit have interposed themselves between it and the Divine and infallible Physician. Witness how they have entangled all men, themselves included, in the mesh of their devices. They can neither discover the cause of the disease, nor have they any knowledge of the remedy. They have conceived the straight to be crooked, and have imagined their friend an enemy.

Incline your ears to the sweet melody of this Prisoner. Arise, and lift up your voices, that haply they that are fast asleep may be awakened.

Bahá'u'lláh

They who are the people of God have no ambition except to revive the world, to ennoble its life, and regenerate its peoples. Truthfulness and good-will have, at all times, marked their relations with all men. Their outward conduct is but a reflection of their inward life, and their inward life a mirror of their outward conduct. No veil hideth or obsureth the verities on which their Faith is established. Before the eyes of all men these verities have been laid bare, and can be unmistakably recognized. Their very acts attest the truth of these words.

Bahá'u'lláh

THE ONENESS OF HUMANITY

We have created you from one tree and have caused you to be as the leaves and fruit of the same tree, that haply ye may become a source of comfort to one another. Regard ye not others save as ye regard your own selves, that no feeling of aversion may prevail amongst you...It behooveth you all to be one indivisible people...

The Báb

Issue forth from your cities, O peoples of the West...Become as true brethren in the one and indivisible religion of God, free from distinction, for verily God desireth that your hearts should become mirrors unto your brethren in the Faith, so that ye find yourselves reflected in them, and they in you. This is the true Path of God, the Almighty, and He is indeed watchful over your actions.

The Báb

It is incumbent upon all the peoples of the world to reconcile their differences, and, with perfect unity and peace, abide beneath the shadow of the Tree of His care and loving-kindness. I behoveth them to cleave to whatsoever will, in this Day, be conducive to the exaltation of their stations, and to promotion of their best interests.

Bahá'u'lláh

The purpose underlying the revelation of every heavenly Book, nay, of every divinely-revealed verse, is to endue all men with righteousness and understanding, so that peace and tranquillity may be firmly established amongst them. Whatsoever ever instilleth assurance into the hearts of men, whatsoever exalteth their station or promoteth their contentment, is acceptable in the sight of God.

Bahá'u'lláh

Address yourselves to the promotion of the well-being and tranquillity of the children of men. Bend your minds and wills to the education of the peoples and kindreds of the earth, that haply the dissensions that divide it may, through the power of the Most Great Name, be blotted out from its face, and all mankind become the upholders of one Order, and the inhabitants of one City. Illumine and hallow your hearts; let them not be profaned by the thorns of hate or the thistles of malice. Ye dwell in one world, and have been created through the operation of one Will. Blessed is he who mingleth with all men in a spirit of utmost kindliness and love.

Bahá'u'lláh

The ideal faculties of man, including the capacity for scientific acquisition, are beyond nature's ken...How shall we utilize these gifts and expend these bounties? By directing our efforts toward the unification of the human race...Then will mankind be as one nation, one race and kind-as waves on one ocean. Although these waves may differ in form and shape, they are waves of the same sea.

'Abdu'l-Bahá

I hope you will continue in unity and fellowship. How beautiful to see blacks and whites together! I hope, God willing, the day may come when I shall see the red men, the Indians, with you, also Japanese and others. Then there will be white roses, yellow roses, red roses, and a very wonderful rose garden will appear in the world.

'Abdu'l-Bahá

RACE AND NATIONALITY OF NO IMPORTANCE TO BAHÁ'ÍS

The whole world must be looked upon as one single country, all the nations as one nation, all men as belonging to one race. Religions, races, and nations are all divisions of man's making only, and are necessary only in his thought...God is God for all, and to Him all creation is one. We must obey God, and strive to follow Him by leaving all our prejudices and bringing about peace on earth.

'Abdu'l-Bahá

Variations of colour, of land and of race are of no importance in the Bahá'í Faith; on the contrary, Bahá'í unity overcometh them all and doth away with all the fancies and imaginations...

Let them look not upon a man's colour but upon his heart. If the heart be filled with light, that man is nigh unto the threshold of His Lord; but if not, that man is careless of His Lord, be he while or be he black.

'Abdu'l-Bahá

Character is the true criterion of humanity. Anyone who possesses a good character, who has faith in God and is firm, whose actions are good, whose speech is good-that one is accepted at the threshold of God no matter what color he may be...

'Abdu'l-Bahá

To discriminate against any race, on the ground of its being socially backward, politically immature, and numerically in a minority, is a flagrant violation of the spirit that animates the Faith of Bahá'u'lláh. The consciousness of any division or cleavage in its ranks is alien to its very purpose, principles, and ideals. Once its members have fully recognized the claim of its Author, and, by identifying themselves with its Administrative Order, accepted unreservedly the principles and laws embodied in its teachings, every differentiation of class, creed, or color must automatically be obliterated, and never be allowed, under any pretext, and however great the pressure of events or of public opinion, to reassert itself.

Shoghi Effendi

THE FAMILY OF MAN

Now must the lovers of God arise to carry out these instructions of His: let them be kindly fathers to the children of the human race, and compassionate brothers to the youth, and self-denying offspring to those bent with years. The meaning of this is that ye must show forth tenderness and love to every human being, even to your enemies, and welcome them all with unalloyed friendship, good cheer, and loving-kindness. When ye meet with cruelty and persecution at anther's hands, keep faith with him; when malevolence is directed your way, respond with a friendly heart. To the spears and arrows rained upon you, expose your breasts for a target mirror-bright; and in return for curses, taunts and wounding words, show forth abounding love. Thus will all peoples witness the power of the Most Great Name, and every nation acknowledge the might of the Ancient Beauty, and see how He hath toppled down the walls of discord, and how surely He hath guided all the peoples of the earth to oneness; how He hath lit man's world, and made this earth of dust to send forth streams of light.

The human creatures are even as children, they are brash and unconcerned. These children must be reared with infinite, loving care, and tenderly fostered in the embraces of mercy, so that they may taste the spiritual honey-sweetness of God's love; that they may become like unto candles shedding their beams across this darksome world, and may clearly perceive what blazing crowns of glory the Most Great Name, the Ancient Beauty, hath set on the brows of His beloved, what bounties He hath bestowed on the hearts of those He holdeth dear, what a love He hath cast into the breasts of humankind, and what treasures of friendship He hath made to appear amongst all men.

'Abdu'l-Bahá

GUIDANCE FOR THE INDIVIDUAL

Act in accordance with the counsels of the lord: that is, rise up in such wise, and with such qualities, as to endow the body of this world with a living soul, and to bring this young child, humanity, to the stage of adulthood. So far as ye are able, ignite a candle of love in every meeting, and with tenderness rejoice and cheer ye every heart. Care for the stranger as for one of your own; show to alien souls the same loving kindness ye bestow upon your faithful friends. Should any come to blows with you, seek to be friends with him; should any stab you to the heart, be ye a healing salve unto his sores; should any taunt and mock at you, meet him with love. Should any heap his blame upon you, praise ye him; should he offer you a deadly poison, give him the choicest honey in exchange; and should he threaten your life, grant him a remedy that will heal him evermore. Should he be pain itself, be ye his medicine; should he be thorns, be ye his roses and sweet herbs. Perchance such ways and words from you will make this darksome world turn bright at last; will make this dusty earth turn heavenly, this devilish prison place become a royal palace of the Lord-so that war and strife will pass and be no more, and love and trust will pitch their tents on the summits of the world. Such is the essence of God's admonitions; such in sum are the teachings for the Dispensation of Bahá.

'Abdu'l-Bahá

EXTINGUISHING THE FLAMES OF RELIGIOUS FANATICISM

The Purpose of the one true God, exalted be His Glory, in revealing Himself unto men is to lay bare those gems that lie hidden within the mine of their true and inmost selves. That the divers communions of the earth, and the manifold systems of religious belief, should never be allowed to foster the feelings of animosity among men, is, in this Day, of the essence of the Faith of God and His Religion. These principles and laws, these firmly-established and mighty systems, have proceeded from one Source, and are the rays of one Light. That they differ one from another is to be attributed to the varying requirements of the ages in which they were promulgated.

Gird up the loins of your endeavor, O people of Bahá, that haply the tumult of religious dissension and strife that agitateth the peoples of the earth may be stilled, that every trace of it may be completely obliterated. For the love of God, and them that serve Him, arise to aid this most sublime and momentous Revelation. Religious fanaticism and hatred are world-devouring fire, whose violence none can quench. The Hand of Divine power can, alone, deliver mankind from this desolating affliction...

The utterance of God is a lamp, whose light is these words: Ye are the fruits of one tree, and the leaves of one branch. Deal ye one with another with the utmost love and harmony, with friendliness and fellowship... So powerful is the light of unity that it can illuminate the whole earth...

Exert yourselves that ye may attain this transcendent and most sublime station, the station that can ensure the protection and security of all mankind. This goal excelleth every other goal, and this aspiration is the monarch of all aspirations...

Consort with all men, O people of Bahá, in a spirit of friendliness and fellowship. If ye be aware of a certain truth, if ye possess a jewel, of which others are deprived, share it with them in a language of utmost kindliness and goodwill. If it be accepted, if it fulfil its purpose, your object is attained. If any one should refuse it, leave him unto himself, and beseech God to guide him. Beware lest ye deal unkindly with him. A kindly tongue is the lodestone of the hearts of men. It is the bread of the spirit, it clotheth the words with meaning, it is the fountain of the light of wisdom and understanding.

Bahá'u'lláh

REJECTION OF RITUALS AND ELABORATE CEREMONIALS

All these divisions we see on all sides, all these disputes and opposition, are caused because men cling to ritual and outward observances, and forget the simple, underlying truth. It is the outward practices of religion that are so different, and it is they that cause disputes and enmity-while the reality is always the same, and one. The Reality is the Truth, and truth has no division. Truth is God's guidance, it is the light of the world, it is love, it is mercy. These attributes of truth are also human virtues inspired by the Holy Spirit.

So let us one and all hold fast to truth, and we shall be free indeed!

'Abdu'l-Bahá

We should also bear in mind that the distinguishing character of the Bahá'í Revelation does not solely consists in the completeness and unquestionable validly of the Dispensation which the teachings of Bahá'u'lláh and 'Abdu'l-Bahá have established. Its excellence lies also in the fact that those elements which in the past Dispensations have, without the least authority from their Founders, been a source of corruption and of incalculable harm to the Faith of God, have been strictly excluded by the clear text of Bahá'u'lláh's writings. Those unwarranted practices, in connection with the sacrament of baptism, of communion, of confession of sins, of asceticism, of priestly domination, of elaborate ceremonials, of holy war, and polygamy, have one and all been rigidly suppressed by the Pen of Bahá'u'lláh; whilst the rigidity and rigour of certain observances, such as fasting, which are necessary to the devotional life of the individual, have been considerably abated.

Shoghi Effendi

LIVING A HOLY LIFE

A chaste and holy life must be made the controlling principle in the behavior and conduct of all Bahá'ís, both in their social relations with the members of their own community, and in their contact with the world at large...

It must be remembered, however, that the maintenance of such a high standard of moral conduct is not to be associated or confused with any form of asceticism, or of excessive and bigoted puritanism. The standard inculcated by Bahá'u'lláh, seeks, under no circumstances, to deny any one the legitimate right and privilege to derive the fullest advantage and benefit from the manifold joys, beauties, and pleasures with which the world has been so plentifully enriched by an All-Loving Creator.

Shoghi Effendi

SOLICITATION OF MONEY PROHIBITED

It would be impossible to conceive any act more contemptible than soliciting, in the name of the one true God, the riches which men possess...

They who are possessed of riches, however, must have the utmost regard for the poor...

Bahá'u'lláh

A WORLD RELIGION

Ceasing to designate itself a movement, a fellowship and the like...the Faith of Bahá'u'lláh is now visibly succeeding in demonstrating its claim and title to be regarded as a World Religion, destined to attain, in the fullness of time, the status of a world-embracing Commonwealth, which would be at once the instrument and the guardian of the Most Great Peace announced by its Author. Far from wishing to add to the number of the religious systems, whose conflicting loyalties have for so many generations disturbed the peace of mankind, this Faith is instilling into each of its adherents a new love for, and a genuine appreciation of the unity underlying, the various religions represented within its pale...

The Faith of Bahá'u'lláh has assimilated, by virtue of its creative, its regulative and ennobling energies, the varied races, nationalities, creeds and classes that have sought its shadow, and have pledged unswerving fealty to its cause. It has changed the hearts of its adherents, burned away their prejudices, stilled their passions, exalted their conceptions, ennobled their motives, coordinated their efforts, and transformed their outlook. While preserving their patriotism and safeguarding their lesser loyalties, it has made them lovers of mankind, and the determined upholders of its best and truest interests. While maintaining intact their belief in the Divine origin of their respective religions, it has enabled them to visualize the underlying purpose of these religions, to discover their merits, to recognize their sequence, their interdependence, their wholeness and unity, and to acknowledge the bond that vitally links them to itself. This universal, this transcending love which the followers of the Bahá'í Faith feel for their fellow-men, of whatever race, creed, class or nation, is neither mysterious nor can it be said to have been artificially stimulated. It is both spontaneous and genuine. They whose hearts are warmed by the energizing influence of God's creative love cherish His creatures for His sake, and recognise in every human face a sign of His reflected glory.

Of such men and women it may be truly said that to them "every foreign land is a fatherland, and every fatherland a foreign land." For their citizenship, it must be remembered, is in the Kingdom of Bahá'u'lláh. Though willing to share to the utmost the temporal benefits and the fleeting joys which this earthly life can confer, though eager to participate in whatever activity that conduces to the richness, the happiness and peace of that life, they can, at no time, forget that it constitutes no more than a transient, a very brief stage of their existence, that they who live it are but pilgrims and wayfarers whose goal is the Celestial City, and whose home the Country of never-failing joy and brightness.

Though loyal to their respective governments, though profoundly interested in anything that affects their security and welfare, though anxious to share in whatever promotes their best interests, the Faith with which the followers of Bahá'u'lláh stand identified is one which they firmly believe God has raised high above the storms, the divisions, and controversies of the political arena. Their Faith they conceive to be essentially non-political, supra-national in character, rigidly non-partisan, and entirely dissociated from nationalistic ambitions, pursuits, and purposes. Such a Faith knows no division of class or of party. It subordinates, without hesitation or equivocation, every particularistic interest, be it personal, regional, or national, to the paramount interests of humanity, firmly convinced that in a world of inter-dependent peoples and nations the advantage of the part is best to be reached by the advantage of the whole, and that no abiding benefit can be conferred upon the component parts if the general interests of the entity itself are ignored or neglected.

Small wonder if by the Pen of Bahá'u'lláh these pregnant words, written in anticipation of the present state of mankind, should have been revealed: "It is not for him to pride himself who loveth his own country, but rather for him who loveth the whole world. The earth is but one country, and mankind its citizen." And again, "That one indeed is a man who today dedicateth himself to the service of the entire human race." "Through the power released by these exalted words," He explains, "He hath lent a fresh impulse, and set a new direction, to the birds of men's hearts, and hath obliterated every trace of restriction and limitation from God's Holy Book."

Their Faith, Bahá'ís firmly believe, is moreover undenominational, non-sectarian, and wholly divorced from every ecclesiastical system, whatever its form, origin, or activities. No ecclesiastical organization, with its creeds, its traditions, its limitation, and exclusive outlook, can be said (as is the case with all existing political factions, parties, systems and programs) to conform, in all its aspects, to the cardinal tenets of Bahá'í belief. To some of the principles and ideals animating political and ecclesiastical institutions every conscientious follower of the Faith of Bahá'u'lláh can, no doubt, readily subscribe. With none of these institutions, however, can he identify himself, nor can he unreservedly endorse the creeds, the principles and programs on which they are based.

Shoghi Effendi

7
SEARCH AFTER TRUTH

THE INDEPENDENT INVESTIGATION OF TRUTH

The first teaching of Bahá'u'lláh is the duty incumbent upon all to investigate reality. What does it mean to investigate reality? It means that man must forget all hearsay and examine truth himself, for he does not know whether statements he hears are in accordance with reality or not.

'Abdu'l-Bahá

Warn...the beloved of the one true God, not to view with too critical an eye the sayings and writings of men. Let them rather approach such sayings and writings in a spirit of openmindedness and loving sympathy.

Bahá'u'lláh

Take heed to carefully consider the words of every soul, then hold fast to the proofs which attest the truth. If ye fail to discover truth in a person's words, make them not the object of contention...

The Báb

FREEDOM FROM PREJUDICE AND IMITATION

The essence of all that We have revealed for thee is Justice, is for man to free himself from idle fancy and imitation, discern with the eye of oneness His glorious handiwork, and look into all things with a searching eye.

Bahá'u'lláh

Science must be accepted. No one truth can contradict another truth...Be free from prejudice...You will realize that if the Divine light of truth shone in Jesus Christ it also shone in Moses and in Buddha. The earnest seeker will arrive at this truth. This is what is meant by the 'Search after Truth'.

'Abdu'l-Bahá

He whose father was a Zoroastrian is a Zoroastrian. He whose father was a Buddhist remains a Buddhist. The son of a Muslim continues a Muslim, and so on throughout. Why is this? Because they are slaves and captives of mere imitation. They have not investigated the reality of religion and arrived at its fundamentals and conclusions.

'Abdu'l-Bahá

So long as man persists in his adherence to ancestral forms and imitation of obsolete ceremonials, denying higher revelations of the divine light in the world, strife and contention will destroy the purpose of religion and make love and fellowship impossible.

'Abdu'l-Bahá

SUPERSTITION CLOUDS THE LIGHT OF RELIGION

Alas that humanity is completely submerged in imitations and unrealities, notwithstanding that the truth of divine religion has ever remained the same. Superstitions have obscured the fundamental reality, the world is darkened, and the light of religion is not apparent. This darkness is conductive to differences and dissensions; rites and dogmas are many and various; therefore, discord has arisen among the religious systems, whereas religion is for the unification of mankind. True religion is the source of love and agreement amongst men, the cause of the development of praiseworthy qualities, but the people are holding to the counterfeit and imitation, negligent of the reality which unifies, so they are bereft and deprived of the radiance of religion. They follow superstitions inherited from their fathers and ancestors. To such an extent has this prevailed that they have taken away the heavenly light of divine truth and sit in the darkness of imitations and imaginations. That which was meant to be conducive to life has become the cause of death; that which should have been an evidence of knowledge is now a proof of ignorance; that which was a factor in the sublimity of human nature has proved to be its degradation. Therefore, the realm of the religionist has gradually narrowed and darkened, and the sphere of the materialist has widened and advanced; for the religionist has held to imitation and counterfeit, neglecting and discarding holiness and the sacred reality of religion. When the sun sets, it is the time for bats to fly. They come forth because they are creatures of the night. When the lights of religion become darkened, the materialists appear. They are the bats of night. The decline of religion is their time of activity; they seek the shadows when the world is darkened and clouds have spread over it...

Therefore, we must investigate reality in order that by its light the clouds and darkness may be dispelled.

'Abdu'l-Bahá

BAHÁ'U'LLÁH SUMMONS MANKIND TO CONSIDER HIS REVELATION

Great is the Cause, and great the Announcement! Patiently and calmly ponder thou upon the resplendent signs and the sublime words, and all that hath been revealed in these days, that haply thou mayest fathom the mysteries that are hid in the Books...

Bahá'u'lláh

Blessed are they that judge this impregnable Cause, this glorious Announcement, with fairness and equity.

Bahá'u'lláh

Let him who will, acknowledge the truth of My words; and as to him that willeth not, let him turn aside.

Bahá'u'lláh

THE RESPONSIBILITY OF JOURNALISTS TO OBJECTIVELY MIRROR THE TRUTH

In this day the secrets of the earth are laid bare before the eyes of men. The pages of swiftly-appearing newspapers are indeed the mirror of the world. They reflect the deeds and the pursuits of divers peoples and kindreds. They both reflect them and make them known. They are a mirror endowed with hearing, sight and speech. This is an amazing and potent phenomenon. However, it behoveth the writers thereof to be purged from the promptings of evil passions and desires and to be attired with the raiment of justice and equity. They should enquire into situations as much as possible and ascertain the facts, then set them down in writing.

Bahá'u'lláh

8
THE ONENESS OF RELIGION

THE UNITY OF RELIGION

The religion of God is one religion, but it must ever be renewed...When thou dost plant a tree, its height increaseth day by day. It putteth forth blossoms and leaves and luscious fruits. But after a long time, it doth grow old, yielding no fruitage any more. Then doth the Husbandman of Truth take up the seed from that same tree, and plant it in a pure soil; and lo, there standeth the first tree, even as it was before.

'Abdu'l-Bahá

If the Holy Books were rightly understood, none of this discord and distress would have existed, but love and fellowship would have prevailed instead.

'Abdu'l-Bahá

Thy Lord hath never raised up a prophet in the past who failed to summon the people to His Lord, and today is truly similar to the times of old, were ye to ponder over the verses revealed by God.

The Báb

THE ESSENTIAL UNITY OF THE PROPHETS

Know thou assuredly that the essence of all the Prophets of God is one and the same. Their unity is absolute...They all have but one purpose; their secret is the same secret. To prefer one in honor to another, to exalt certain ones above the rest, is in no wise to be permitted. Every true Prophet hath regarded His Message as fundamentally the same as the Revelation of every other Prophet gone before Him...

But do not therefore attribute to the Masters and Prophets the evil deeds of their followers. If the priests, teachers and people, lead lives which are contrary to the religion they profess to follow, is that the fault of Christ or the other Teachers?

...Bahá'u'lláh spent His life teaching this lesson of Love and Unity. Let us then put away from us all prejudice and intolerance, and strive with all our hearts and souls to bring about understanding and unity...

'Abdu'l-Bahá

THE CONTINUITY OF DIVINE REVELATION

...in every age and dispensation the Prophets of God and His chosen Ones have appeared amongst men...

Can one of sane mind ever seriously imagine that, in view of certain words and meaning of which he cannot comprehend, the portal of God's infinite guidance can ever be closed in the face of men? Can he ever conceive for these Divine Luminaries, these resplendent Lights either a beginning or an end?

Bahá'u'lláh

No breeze can compare with the breeze of Divine Revelation, whilst the Word which is uttered by God shineth and flasheth as the sun amidst the books of men. Happy the man that hath discovered it and recognized it...

Bahá'u'lláh

PROGRESSIVE NATURE OF DIVINE REVELATION

God hath, at all times and under all conditions, been wholly independent of His creatures. He hath cherished and will ever cherish the desire that all men may attain His gardens of Paradise with utmost love, that no one should sadden another, not even for a moment, and that all should dwell within His cradle of protection and security until the Day of Resurrection which marketh the dayspring of the Revelation of Him Whom God will make manifest.

The Lord of the universe hath never raised up a prophet nor hath He sent down a Book unless He hath established His covenant with all men, calling for their acceptance of the next Revelation and the next Book; inasmuch as the outpourings of His bounty are ceaseless and without limits.

The Báb

Know thou assuredly that the essence of all the Prophets of God is one and the same. Their unity is absolute...They all have but one purpose; their secret is the same secret. To prefer one in honor to another, to exalt certain ones above the rest, is in no wise permitted. Every true Prophet hath regarded His Message as fundamentally the same as the Revelation of every other Prophet gone before Him. If any man, therefore, should fail to comprehend this truth, and should consequently indulge in vain and unseemly language, no one whose sight is keen and whose understanding is enlightened would ever allow such idle talk to cause him to waver in his belief.

The measure of the revelation of the Prophets of God in this world, however, must differ. Each and every one of them hath been the Bearer of a distinct Message, and hath been commissioned to reveal Himself through specific acts. It is for this reason that they appear to vary in their greatness...

It is clear and evident, therefore, that any apparent variation in the intensity of their light is not inherent in the light itself, but should rather be attributed to the varying receptivity of an ever-changing world. Every Prophet Whom the Almighty and Peerless Creator hath purposed to send to the people of the earth hath been entrusted with a Message, and charged to act in a manner that would best meet the requirements of the age in which He appeared. God's purpose in sending His Prophets unto men is twofold. The first is to liberate the children of men from the darkness of ignorance, and guide them to the light of true understanding. The second is to ensure the peace and tranquillity of mankind, and provide all the means by which they can be established.

Bahá'u'lláh

THE BASIS FOR THE ONENESS OF HUMANITY

The foundations of the divine religions are one. If we investigate these foundations, we discover much ground for agreement, but if we consider the imitations of forms and ancestral belief, we find points of disagreement and division; for these imitations differ, while the sources and foundations are one and the same. That is to say, the fundamentals are conductive to unity, but imitations are the cause of disunion and dismemberment. Whosoever is lacking in love for humanity or manifests hatred and bigotry toward any part of it violates the foundation and source of his own belief and is holding to forms and imitations.

...The essentials of the divine religion are one reality, indivisible and not multiple. It is one. And when through investigation we find it to be single, we have a basis for the oneness of the world of humanity.

'Abdu'l-Bahá

THE EFFECTS OF SUPERSTITION AND BLIND IMITATION

Although the divine teachings are truth and reality, yet with the passage of time thick clouds envelop and obscure them. These clouds are imitations and superstitions; they are not the fundamentals. Then the Sun of Truth, the Word of God, arises again, shines forth once more in the glory of its power and disperses the enveloping darkness.

For a long time the divine precepts of the effulgent Word were obscured by clouds of superstition and error until Bahá'u'lláh appeared upon the horizon of humanity, rent the shadows, scattered the clouds and revealed anew the foundations of the teachings of God.

'Abdu'l-Bahá

A man is a Jew because his father was a Jew. The Muslim follows implicitly the footsteps of his ancestors in belief and observance. The Buddhist is true to his heredity as a Buddhist. That is to say, they profess religious belief blindly and without investigation, making unity and agreement impossible. It is evident, therefore, that this condition will not be remedied without a reformation in the world of religion. In other words, the fundamental reality of the divine religions must be renewed, reformed, revoiced to mankind.

From the seed of reality religion has grown into a tree which has put forth leaves and branches, blossoms and fruit. After a time this tree has fallen into a condition of decay. The leaves and blossoms have withered and perished; the tree has become stricken and fruitless. It is not reasonable that man should hold to the old tree, claiming that its life forces are undiminished, its fruit unequalled, its existence eternal. The seed of reality must be sown again in human hearts in order that a new tree may grow therefrom and new divine fruits refresh the world. By this means the nations and peoples now divergent in religion will be brought into unity, imitations will be forsaken, and a universal brotherhood in reality itself will be established.

'Abdu'l-Bahá

LEADING MANKIND TO THE PATH OF VIRTUE

All down the ages the prophets of God have been sent into the world to serve the cause of truth-Moses brought the law of truth, and all the prophets of Israel after him sought to spread it.

When Jesus came He lighted the flaming torch of truth, and carried it aloft so that the whole world might be illumined thereby...

Then came Muhammad, who in His time and way spread the knowledge of truth among a savage people; for this has always been the mission of God's elect.

So, at last, when Bahá'u'lláh arose in Persia, this was His most ardent desire, to rekindle the waning light of truth in all lands. All the holy ones of God have tried with heart and soul to spread the light of love and unity throughout the world, so that the darkness of materiality might disappear and the light of spirituality might shine forth among the children of men. Then would hate, slander and murder disappear, and in their stead love, unity and peace would reign.

All the Manifestations of God came with the same purpose, and they have all sought to lead men into the paths of virtue.

'Abdu'l-Bahá

THE LIGHT OF THE HOLY SPIRIT

This Holy Spirit is a mediator between God and His creatures. It is like a mirror facing the sun. As the pure mirror receives light from the sun and transmits this bounty to others, so the Holy Spirit is the mediator of the Holy Light from the Sun of Reality, which it gives to the sanctified realities. It is adorned with all the divine perfections. Every time it appears the world is renewed, and a new cycle is founded. The body of the world of humanity puts on a new garment. It can be compared to the spring; whenever it comes, the world passes from one condition to another. Through the advent of the season of spring the black earth and the fields and wilderness will become verdant and blooming, and all sorts of flowers and sweet-scented herbs will grow; the trees will have new life, and new fruits will appear, and a new cycle is founded.

'Abdu'l-Bahá

THE INAUGURATION OF THE BAHÁ'Í DISPENSATION

Whoso layeth claim to a Revelation direct from God, ere the expiration of a full thousand years, such a man is assuredly a lying impostor. We pray God that He may graciously assist him to retract and repudiate such claim. Should he repent, God will, no doubt, forgive him...Whosoever interpreteth this verse otherwise than its obvious meaning is deprived of the Spirit of God and of His mercy which encompasseth all created things.

Bahá'u'lláh

9
RELATION TO OTHER FAITHS

ALL FAITHS EMANATE FROM ONE HEAVENLY SOURCE

There can be no doubt whatever that the peoples of the world, of whatever race or religion, derive their inspiration from one heavenly Source, and are the subjects of one God. The differences between the ordinances under which they abide should be attributed to the varying requirements and exigencies of the age in which they were revealed. All of them, except a few which are the outcome of human perversity, were ordained of God, and are a reflection of His Will and Purpose.

Bahá'u'lláh

Know of a certainty that in every Dispensation the light of Divine Revelation hath been vouchsafed unto men in direct proportion to their spiritual capacity.

Bahá'u'lláh

FORSAKING SUPERSTITION AND BLIND IMITATION

May fanaticism and religious bigotry be unknown, all humanity enter the bond of brotherhood, souls consort in perfect agreement, the nations of earth at last hoist the banner of truth, and the religions of the world enter the divine temple of oneness, for the foundations of the heavenly religions are one reality. Reality is not divisible; it does not admit multiplicity. All the holy Manifestations of God have proclaimed and promulgated the same reality. They have summoned mankind to reality itself, and reality is one. The clouds and mists of imitations have obscured the Sun of Truth. We must forsake these imitations, dispel these clouds and mists and free the Sun from the darkness of superstition. Then will the Sun of Truth shine most gloriously; then all the inhabitants of the world will be united, the religions will be one, sects and denominations will reconcile, all nationalities will flow together in the recognition of one Fatherhood, and all degrees of humankind will gather in the shelter of the same tabernacle, under the same banner.

'Abdu'l-Bahá

THE UNITY AND PURPOSE OF THE HOLY MANIFESTATIONS

These attributes of God are not and have never been vouchsafed specially unto certain Prophets, and withheld from others. Nay, all the Prophets of God, His well-favoured, His holy, and chosen Messengers, are without exception, the bearers of His names, and the embodiments of His attributes. They only differ in the intensity of their revelation, and the comparative potency of their light...That a certain attribute of God hath not been outwardly manifested by these Essences of Detachment doth in no wise imply that they Who are the Daysprings of God's attributes and the Treasuries of His holy names did not actually possess it. Therefore, these illuminated Souls, these beauteous Countenances have, each and every one of them, been endowed with all the attributes of God, such as sovereignty, dominion, and the like, even though to outward seeming they be shorn of all earthly majesty. To every discerning eye this is evident and manifest; it requireth neither proof nor evidence.

Bahá'u'lláh

The holy Manifestations Who have been the Sources or Founders of the various religious systems were united and agreed in purpose and teaching. Abraham, Moses, Zoroaster, Buddha, Jesus, Muhammad, the Báb and Bahá'u'lláh are one in spirit and reality.

'Abdu'l-Bahá

Blessed souls-whether Moses, Jesus, Zoroaster, Krishna, Buddha, Confucius or Muhammad-were the cause of the illumination of the world of humanity.

'Abdu'l-Bahá

God sent His Prophets into the world to teach and enlighten man, to explain to him the mystery of the Power of the Holy Spirit, to enable him to reflect the light, and so in his turn, to be the source of guidance to others. The Heavenly Books, the Bible, the Qur'án, and the other Holy Writings have been given by God as guides into the paths of Divine virtue, love, justice and peace.

Therefore I say unto you that ye should strive to follow the counsels of these Blessed Books, and so order your lives that ye may, following the examples set before you, become yourselves the saints of the Most High!

'Abdu'l-Bahá

The Message of Krishna is the message of love. All God's prophets have brought the message of love.

'Abdu'l-Bahá

Buddha also established a new religion, and Confucius renewed morals and ancient virtues, but their institutions have been entirely destroyed. The beliefs and rites of the Buddhists and Confucianists have not continued in accordance with their fundamental teachings. The founder of Buddhism was a wonderful soul.

'Abdu'l-Bahá

CONCERNING CHRISTIANITY

Fifty years ago [mid nineteenth century] no one would touch the Christian Bible in Persia. Bahá'u'lláh came and asked, "Why?" They said, "It is not the Word of God." He said, "You must read it with understanding of its meanings, not as those who merely recite its words." Now Bahá'ís all over the East read the Bible and understand its spiritual teaching. Bahá'u'lláh spread the Cause of Christ and opened the book of the Christians and Jews...He proved that all the divine Prophets taught the same reality and that to deny One is to deny the Others, for all are in perfect oneness with God.

'Abdu'l-Bahá

When Christians act according to the teachings of Christ, they are called Bahá'ís. For the foundations of Christianity and the religion of Bahá'u'lláh are one. The difference among them is one of terminology only...The difference between a Christian and a Bahá'í, therefore, is this: There was a former springtime, and there is a springtime now. No other difference exists because the foundations are the same. Whoever acts completely in accordance with the teachings of Christ is a Bahá'í.

'Abdu'l-Bahá

For the Faith of Bahá'u'lláh-if we would faithfully appraise it-can never, and in no aspect of its teachings, be at variance, much less in conflict, with the purpose animating, or the authority invested in, the Faith of Jesus Christ.

Shoghi Effendi

As to the position of Christianity, let it be stated without any hesitation or equivocation that its divine origin is unconditionally acknowledged...The Founder of the Christian Faith is designated by Bahá'u'lláh as the "Spirit of God," is proclaimed as the One Who "appeared out of the breath of the Holy Ghost," and is even extolled as the "Essence of the Spirit." His mother is described as "that veiled and immortal, that most beauteous, countenance," and the station of her Son eulogized as a "station which hath been exalted above the imaginings of all that dwell on earth"...

Shoghi Effendi

THE TRUE GREATNESS OF JESUS CHRIST THE SPIRIT OF GOD

If you reflect upon the essential teachings of Jesus, you will realize that they are the light of the world. Nobody can question their truth. They are the very source of life and the cause of happiness to the human race. The forms and superstitions which appeared and obscured the light did not affect the reality of Christ.

'Abdu'l-Bahá

Verily the body is composed of physical elements, and every composite must needs be decomposed. The spirit, however, is a single essence, fine and delicate, incorporeal, everlasting, and of God. For this reason whoso looketh for Christ in His physical body hath looked in vain, and will be shut away from Him as by a veil. But whoso yearneth to find Him in the spirit will grow from day to day in joy and desire and burning love, in closeness to Him, and in beholding Him clear and plain. In this new and wondrous day, it behoveth thee to seek after the spirit of Christ.

'Abdu'l-Bahá

A great man is a great man, whether born of a human father or not. If being without a father is a virtue, Adam is greater and more excellent than all the Prophets and Messengers, for he had neither father nor mother. That which causes honour and greatness, is the splendour and bounty of the divine perfections.

'Abdu'l-Bahá

A TRIBUTE TO JESUS CHRIST

Know thou that when the Son of Man [Jesus] yielded up His breath to God, the whole creation wept with a great weeping. By sacrificing Himself, however, a fresh capacity was infused into all created things. Its evidences, as witnessed in all the peoples of the earth, are now manifest before thee. The deepest wisdom which the sages have uttered, the profoundest learning which any mind hath unfolded, the arts which the ablest hands have produced, the influence exerted by the most potent of rulers, are but manifestations of the quickening power released by His transcendent, His all-pervasive, and resplendent Spirit.

We testify that when He came into the world, He shed the splendor of His glory upon all created things. Through Him the leper recovered from the leprosy of perversity and ignorance. Through Him, the unchaste and wayward were healed. Through His power, born of Almighty God, the eyes of the blind were opened, and the soul of the sinner sanctified...

He it is Who purified the world. Blessed is the man who, with a face beaming with light, hath turned towards Him.

Bahá'u'lláh

MUHAMMAD, THE APOSTLE OF GOD

As to Muhammad, the Apostle of God, let none among His followers who read these pages, think for a moment that either Islám, or its Prophet, or His Book, or His appointed Successors, or any of His authentic teachings, have been or are to be in any way, or to however slight a degree disparaged...

Shoghi Effendi

In the early days, when Islám was still to outward seeming devoid of authority and power, the friends of the Prophet, who had turned their face toward God, wherever they went, were harassed, persecuted, stoned and vilified. At such a time this blessed verse was sent down from the heaven of divine Revelation. It revealed an irrefutable evidence, and brought the light of an unfailing guidance. It instructed the companions of Muhammad to declare the following unto the infidels and idolators: "Ye oppress and persecute us, and yet, what else have we done except that we have believed in God and in the verses sent down unto us through the tongue of Muhammad, and in those which descended upon the Prophets of old?" By this is meant that their only guilt was to have recognized that the new and wondrous verses of God, which had descended upon Muhammad, as well as those which had been revealed unto the Prophets of old, were all of God, and to have acknowledged and embraced their truth. This is the testimony which the divine King hath taught His servants.

In view of this, is it fair for this people to repudiate these newly-revealed verses which have encompassed both the East and the West, and to regard themselves as the upholders of true belief? Should they not rather believe in Him Who hath revealed these verses?

Bahá'u'lláh

WIDENING THE BASIS OF ALL REVEALED RELIGIONS

The Faith standing identified with the name of Bahá'u'lláh disclaims any intention to belittle any of the Prophets gone before Him, to whittle down any of their teachings, to obscure, however slightly, the radiance of their Revelation, to oust them from the hearts of their followers, to abrogate the fundamentals of their doctrines, to discard any of their revealed Books, or to suppress the legitimate aspirations of their adherents. Repudiating the claim of any religion to be the final revelation of God to man, disclaiming finality for His own Revelation, Bahá'u'lláh inculcated the basic principle of the relativity of religious truth, the continuity of Divine Revelation, the progressiveness of religious experience. His aim is to widen the basis of all revealed religions and to unravel the mysteries of their scriptures. He insists on the unqualified recognition of the unity of their purpose, restates the eternal verities they enshrine, coordinated their functions, distinguishes the essential and the authentic from the non-essential and spurious in their teachings, separates the God-given truths from the priest-prompted superstitions, and on this as a basis proclaims the possibility, and even prophesies the inevitability, of their unification, and the consummation of their highest hopes...

Shoghi Effendi

10
PROMULGATION OF THE FAITH

THE GIFT OF FAITH

It is better to guide one soul than to possess all that is on earth, for as long as that guided soul is under the shadow of the Tree of Divine Unity, he and the one who hath guided him will both be recipients of God's tender mercy, whereas possession of earthly things will cease at the time of death. The path to guidance is one of love and compassion, not of force and coercion. This hath been God's method in the past, and shall continue to be in the future! He causeth him whom He pleaseth to enter the shadow of His Mercy. Verily, He is the Supreme Protector, the All-Generous.

There is no paradise more wondrous for any soul than to be exposed to God's Manifestation in His Day, to hear His verses and believe in them, to attain His presence, which is naught but the presence of God, to sail upon the sea of heavenly kingdom of His good-pleasure, and to partake of the choice fruits of the paradise of His divine Oneness.

The Báb

Take ye good heed that ye may all, under the leadership of Him Who is the Source of Divine Guidance, be enabled to direct your steps aright upon the Bridge, which is sharper than the sword and finer than a hair, so that perchance the things which from the beginning of thy life till the end thou hast performed for the love of God, may not, all at once and unrealized by thyself, be turned to acts not acceptable in the sight of God.

The Báb

TEACHING BY EXAMPLE

Know thou that We have annulled the rule of the sword, as an aid to Our Cause, and substituted for it the power born of the utterance of men...Open, O people, the city of the human heart with the key of your utterance...

Let your acts be a guide unto all mankind, for the professions of most men, be they high or low, differ from their conduct. It is through your deeds that ye can distinguish yourselves from others. Through them the brightness of your light can be shed upon the whole earth.

Bahá'u'lláh

In this Most Great Revelation goodly deeds and a praiseworthy character are regarded as the host of God, likewise is His blessed and holy Word. These hosts are the lodestone of the hearts of men and the effective means for unlocking doors. Of all the weapons in the world this is the keenest.

Bahá'u'lláh

Piety and detachment are even as two most great luminaries of the heaven of teaching. Blessed the one who hath attained unto this supreme station, this habitation of transcendent holiness and sublimity.

Bahá'u'lláh

OBLIGATION TO TEACH ONE'S OWN SELF

Whoso ariseth among you to teach the Cause of his Lord, let him, before all else, teach his own self, that his speech may attract the hearts of them that hear him. Unless he teacheth his own self, the words of his mouth will not influence the heart of the seeker.

Bahá'u'lláh

PLANT SEEDS IN PURE HEARTS

It behoveth every one in this Day of God to dedicate himself to the teaching of the Cause with utmost prudence and steadfastness. Should he discover a pure soil, let him sow the seed of the Word of God, otherwise it would be preferable to observe silence.

Bahá'u'lláh

Grieve thou not at men's failure to apprehend the Truth. Erelong thou shalt find them turning towards God, the Lord of all mankind. We have indeed, through the potency of the Most Sublime Word, encompassed the whole world, and the time is approaching when God will have subdued the hearts of all that dwell on earth.

Bahá'u'lláh

BE UNRESTRAINED AS THE WIND

Be unrestrained as the wind, while carrying the Message of Him Who hath caused the Dawn of the Divine Guidance to break. Consider, how the wind, faithful to that which God hath ordained, bloweth upon all regions of the earth, be they inhabited or desolate. Neither the sight of desolation, nor the evidences of prosperity, can either pain or please it. It bloweth in every direction, as bidden by its Creator. So should be every one that claimeth to be a lover of the one true God.

Bahá'u'lláh

If they arise to teach My cause, they must let the breath of Him Who is the Unconstrained, stir them and must spread it abroad on the earth with high resolve, with hearts that are completely detached from and independent of all things, and with souls that are sanctified from the world and its vanities. It behoveth them to choose as the best provision for their journey reliance upon God, and to clothe themselves with the love of their Lord, the Most Exalted, the All-Glorious. If they do so, their words shall influence their hearers.

Bahá'u'lláh

Proclaim the Cause of thy Lord unto all who are in the heavens and on the earth. Should any man respond to thy call, lay bare before him the pearls of thy wisdom of the Lord, thy God, which His Spirit hath sent down unto thee, and be thou of them that truly believe. And should any one reject thine offer, turn thou away from him, and put thy trust and confidence in the Lord, thy God, the Lord of all worlds.

Bahá'u'lláh

Wherefore we should never grieve over the blindness of the unwitting, the attacks of the foolish, the hostility of the low and base, the heedlessness of the divines, the charges of infidelity brought against us by the empty of mind.

'Abdu'l-Bahá

BREATHING NEW LIFE INTO HUMANITY

Arise for the triumph of My cause, and, through the power of thine utterance, subdue the hearts of men. Thou must show forth that which will ensure the peace and the well-being of the miserable and the downtrodden. Gird up the loins of thine endeavour, that perchance thou mayest release the captive from his chains, and enable him to attain unto true liberty.

Justice is, in this day, bewailing its plight, and Equity groaneth beneath the yoke of oppression. The thick clouds of tyranny have darkened the face of the earth, and enveloped its peoples. Through the movement of Our Pen of glory We have, at the bidding of the omnipotent Ordainer, breathed a new life into every human frame, and instilled into every word a fresh potency. All created things proclaim the evidences of this world-wide regeneration. This is the most great, the most joyful tidings imparted by the Pen of this Wronged One to mankind. Wherefore fear ye, O My well-beloved ones? Who is it that can dismay you? A touch of moisture sufficeth to dissolve the hardened clay out of which this perverse generation is moulded.

Bahá'u'lláh

Now the new age is here and creation is reborn. Humanity hath taken on new life. The autumn hath gone by, and the reviving spring is here. All things are now made new. Arts and industries have been reborn, there are new discoveries in science, and there are new inventions; even the details of human affairs, such as dress and personal effects-even weapons-all these have likewise been renewed. The laws and procedures of every government have been revised. Renewal is the order of the day...

Unless these Teaching are effectively spread among the people, until the old ways, the old concepts, are gone and forgotten, this world of being will find no peace, nor will it reflect the perfections of the Heavenly Kingdom. Strive ye with all your hearts to make the heedless conscious, to waken those who sleep, to bring knowledge to the ignorant, to make the blind to see, the deaf to hear, and restore the dead to life.

'Abdu'l-Bahá

COMPULSION IS ABSOLUTELY FORBIDDEN

It has...been fully established that the Faith of God must be propagated through human perfections, through qualities that are excellent and pleasing, and spiritual behavior. If a soul of his own accord advances toward God he will be accepted at the Threshold of Oneness, for such a one is free of personal considerations, of greed and selfish interests, and he has taken refuge within the sheltering protection of his Lord. He will become known among men as trustworthy and truthful, temperate and scrupulous, high-minded and loyal...In this way the primary purpose in revealing the Divine Law-which is to bring about happiness in the after life and civilization and the refinement of character in this-will be realized. As for the sword, it will only produce a man who is outwardly a believer, and inwardly a traitor and apostate.

'Abdu'l-Bahá

Necessarily there will be some who are defective amongst men, but it is our duty to enable them by kind methods of guidance and teaching to become perfected. Some will be found who are morally sick; they should be treated in order that they may be healed. Others are immature and like children; they must be trained and educated so that they may become wise and mature. Those who are asleep must be awakened; the indifferent must become mindful and attentive. But all this must be accomplished in the spirit of kindness and love and not by strife, antagonism nor in a spirit of hostility and hatred, for this is contrary to the good pleasure of God. That which is acceptable in the sight of God is love. Love is, in reality, the first effulgence of Divinity and the greatest splendor of God.

'Abdu'l-Bahá

Know thou that We have annulled the rule of the sword, as an aid to Our Cause, and substituted for it the power born of the utterance of men...Sow not the seeds of discord among men, and refrain from contending with your neighbor, for your Lord hath committed the world and the cities thereof to the care of the kings of the earth...The things He hath reserved for Himself are the cities of men's hearts, that He may cleanse them from all earthly defilements, and enable them to draw nigh unto the hallowed Spot...Open, O people, the city of the human heart with the key of your utterance.

Bahá'u'lláh

If this Cause be of God, no man can prevail against it; and if it be not of God, the divines amongst you, and they that follow their corrupt desires and such as have rebelled against Him will surely suffice to overpower it.

Bahá'u'lláh

TEACH WITH CONSTANCY

Face ye all nations of the world with the constancy and the endurance of the people of Bahá, that all men may be astounded and ask how this could be, that your hearts are as well-springs of confidence and faith, and as mines so rich in the love of God. Be ye so, that ye shall neither fail nor falter on account of these tragedies in the Holy Land; let not these dread events make you despondent. And if all the believers be put to the sword, and only one be left, let that one cry out in the name of the Lord and tell the joyous tidings; let that one rise up and confront all the peoples of the earth.

'Abdu'l-Bahá

CONCERNING THE NUMBER OF BAHÁ'ÍS

Grieve thou not over the slow advance of the Bahá'í Cause in that land. This is but the early dawn. Consider how, with the Cause of Christ, three hundred years had to go by, before its great influence was made manifest. Today, not sixty years from its birth, the light of this Faith hath been shed around the planet.

'Abdu'l-Bahá

Look ye not upon the fewness of thy numbers, rather, seek ye out hearts that are pure. One consecrated soul is preferable to a thousand other souls. If a small number of people gather lovingly together, with absolute purity and sanctity, with their hearts free of the world, experiencing the emotions of the Kingdom and the powerful magnetic forces of the Divine, and being at one in their happy fellowship, that gathering will exert its influence over all the earth. The nature of that band of people, the words they speak, the deeds they do, will unleash the bestowals of Heaven, and provide a foretaste of eternal bliss.

'Abdu'l-Bahá

THE LIGHT OF ETERNITY

Magnify My cause that I may reveal unto thee the mysteries of My greatness and shine upon thee with the light of eternity.

Humble thyself before Me, that I may graciously visit thee. Arise for the triumph of My cause, that while yet on earth thou mayest obtain the victory.

Make mention of Me on My earth, that in My heaven I may remember thee, thus shall Mine eyes and thine be solaced.

Bahá'u'lláh

EXERCISE PRUDENCE IN ALL THINGS

In these days the Cause of God, the world over, is fast growing in power and, day by day, is spreading further and further to the utmost bounds of the earth. Its enemies, therefore, from all the kindreds and peoples of the world, are growing aggressive, malevolent, envious and bitterly hostile. It is incumbent upon the loved ones of God to exercise the greatest care and prudence in all things, whether great or small, to take counsel together and unitedly resist the onslaught of the stirrers up of strife and the movers of mischief. They must endeavour to consort in a friendly spirit with everyone, must follow moderation in their conduct, must have respect and consideration one for another and show loving-kindness and tender regard to all the peoples of the world. They must be patient and long-suffering, that they may grow to become the divine magnets of the Abhá Kingdom and acquire the dynamic power of the hosts of the realm of high.

The fleeting hours of man's life on earth pass swiftly by and the little that still remaineth shall come to an end, but that which endureth and lasteth for evermore is the fruit that man reapeth from his servitude at the Divine Threshold. Behold the truth of this saying, how abundant and glorious are the proofs thereof in the world of being!

The glory of glories rest upon the people of Bahá!

'Abdu'l-Bahá

TEACHING THE CAUSE WITH WISDOM

Under all conditions, the teaching must be carried forward, but with wisdom. If the work cannot proceed openly, then let them teach in private, and thus engender spirituality and fellowship among the children of men. If, for example, each and every one of the believers would become a true friend to one of the unheeding, and, conducting himself with absolute rectitude, associate with this soul, treat him with the utmost kindness, himself exemplify the divine instructions he hath received, the good qualities and behaviour pattern, and at all times act in accord with the admonitions of God-it is certain that little by little he will succeed in awakening that previously heedless individual, and in changing his ignorance to knowledge of the truth.

Souls are inclined toward estrangement. Steps should first be taken to do away with this estrangement, for only then will the Word take effect. If a believer showeth kindness to one of the neglectful, and, with great love, gradually leadeth him to an understanding of the validity of the Holy Cause, so that he may come to know the fundamentals of God's Faith and the implications thereof-such a one will certainly be transformed, excepting only those seldom-encountered individuals who are even as ashes, whose hearts are 'hard as rocks, or harder still'. [Qur'án 2:69]

If every one of the friends should strive in this way to guide one soul aright, the number will double every year; and this can be accomplished with prudence and wisdom, and no harm whatever would result therefrom.

'Abdu'l-Bahá

...this activity [teaching] should be tempered with wisdom-not that wisdom which requireth one to be silent and forgetful of such an obligation, but rather that which requireth one to display divine tolerance, love, kindness, patience, a goodly character, and holy deeds.

'Abdu'l-Bahá

SPEECH

Follow thou the way of thy Lord, and say not that which the ears cannot bear to hear, for such speech is like luscious food given to small children. However palatable, rare and rich the food may be, it cannot be assimilated by the digestive organs of a suckling child. Therefore unto every one who hath a right, let his settled measure be given.

'Not everything that a man knoweth can be disclosed, nor can everything that he can disclose be regarded as timely, nor can every timely utterance be considered as suited to the capacity of those who hear it.' Such is the consummate wisdom to be observed in thy pursuits.

'Abdu'l-Bahá

When thou art about to begin thine address, turn first to Bahá'u'lláh, and ask for the confirmations of the Holy Spirit, then open thy lips and say whatever is suggested to thy heart; this, however, with the utmost courage, dignity and conviction.

'Abdu'l-Bahá

O peoples of the earth! Haste ye to do the pleasure of God, and war ye valiantly, as it behooveth you to war, for the sake of proclaiming His resistless and immovable Cause. We have decreed that war shall be waged in the path of God with the armies of wisdom and utterance, and of a goodly character and praiseworthy deeds...Beware lest ye shed the blood of any one. Unsheathe the sword of your tongue from the scabbard of utterance, for therewith ye can conquer the citadels of men's hearts. We have abolished the law to wage holy war against each other. God's mercy hath, verily, encompassed all created things, if ye do but understand.

Bahá'u'lláh

Every word is endowed with a spirit, therefore the speaker or expounder should carefully deliver his words at the appropriate time and place, for the impression which each word maketh is clearly evident and perceptible...One word may be likened unto fire, another unto light, and the influence which both exert is manifest in the world...Therefore an enlightened man of wisdom should primarily speak with words as mild as milk, that the children of men may be nurtured and edified thereby and may attain the ultimate goal of human existence which is the station of true understanding and nobility...It behoveth a prudent man of wisdom to speak with utmost leniency and forbearance so that the sweetness of his words may induce everyone to attain that which befitteth man's station.

Bahá'u'lláh

Purge thou thy heart that We may cause fountains of wisdom and utterance to gush out therefrom, thus enabling thee to raise thy voice among all mankind. Unloose thy tongue and proclaim the truth for the sake of the remembrance of thy merciful Lord. Be not afraid of anyone, place thy whole trust in God, the Almighty, the All-knowing.

Bahá'u'lláh

We have ordained that complete victory should be achieved through speech and utterance, that Our servants throughout the earth may thereby become the recipients of divine good...

...Human utterance is an essence which aspireth to exert its influence and needeth moderation. As to its influence, this is conditional upon refinement, which in turn is dependent upon hearts which are detached and pure. As to its moderation, this hath to be combined with tact and wisdom as prescribed in the Holy Scriptures and Tablets.

O My Name! Utterance must needs possess penetrating power. For if bereft of this quality it would fail to exert influence. And this penetrating influence dependeth on the spirit being pure and the heart stainless. Likewise it needeth moderation, without which the hearer would be unable to bear it, rather he would manifest opposition from the very outset. And moderation will be obtained by blending utterance with the tokens of divine wisdom which are recorded in the sacred Books and Tablets. Thus when the essence of one's utterance is endowed with these two requisites it will prove highly effective and will be the prime in transforming the souls of men.

Bahá'u'lláh

FAITH OPENED TO SCIENTISTS AND ACADEMICIANS

Such things have appeared in this Revelation that there is no recourse for either the exponents of science and knowledge or the manifestations of justice and equity other than to recognize them. It is incumbent upon thee, in this day, to arise with celestial power and dissipate, with the aid of knowledge, the doubts of the peoples of the world, so that all men may be sanctified, and direct their steps towards the Most Great Ocean and cleave fast unto that which God hath purposed.

Bahá'u'lláh

11
GOD

And as we reflect, we observe that man is like unto a tiny organism contained within a fruit; this fruit hath developed out of the blossom, the blossom hath grown out of the tree, the tree is sustained by the sap, and the sap formed out of the earth and water. How then can this tiny organism comprehend the nature of the garden, conceive of the gardener and comprehend his being? That is manifestly impossible. Should that organism understand and reflect, it would observe that this garden, this tree, this blossom, this fruit would in no wise have come to exist by themselves in such order and perfection. Similarly the wise and reflecting soul will know of a certainty that this infinite universe with all its grandeur and perfect order could not have come to exist by itself.

'Abdu'l-Bahá

Thou hast asked concerning the fundamentals of religion and its ordinances: Know thou that first and foremost in religion is the knowledge of God. This attaineth its consummation in the recognition of His divine unity, which in turn reacheth its fulfilment in acclaiming that His hallowed and exalted Sanctuary, the Seat of His transcendent majesty, is sanctified from all attributes. And know thou that in this world of being the knowledge of God can never be attained save through the knowledge of Him Who is the Dayspring of divine Reality.

The Báb

THE UNFATHOMABLE ESSENCE

The glory of glories and the most resplendent light rest upon Thee, O my God. Thy majesty is so transcendent that no human imagination can reach it and Thy consummate power is so sublime that the birds of men's hearts and minds can never attain its heights. All beings acknowledge

God

their powerlessness to praise Thee as beseemeth Thy station. Immeasurably exalted art Thou. No one can glorify Thy Being, or fathom the evidences of Thy bounty as it exists in Thine inmost Essence, since Thou alone knowest Thyself as Thou art in Thyself...

Lauded and glorified art Thou. Too exalted is Thy loftiness for the hands of such as are endued with understanding to reach unto Thee, and too profound is Thy fathomless depth for the rivers of men's minds and perceptions to flow out therefrom.

The Báb

Every man of perception who hath scaled the noble heights of detachment, and every man of eloquence who hath attained the most sublime station, beareth witness that Thou art God, the Incomparable, and that Thou hast assigned no associate unto Thyself in the kingdom of creation, nor is there anyone to compare with Thee in the realm of invention. Men of wisdom, who had but a notion of the revelation of Thy glory, conceived a likeness of Thee according to their own understanding, and men of erudition, who had gained but a glimpse of the manifold evidences of Thy loving-kindness and glory, have contrived peers for Thee in conformity with their own imaginations. Glorified, immeasurably glorified art Thou, O Lord! Every man of insight is far astray in his attempt to recognize Thee, and every man of consummate learning is sore perplexed in his search after Thee. Every evidence falleth short of Thine unknowable Essence and every light retreateth and sinketh below the horizon when confronted with but a glimmer of the dazzling splendour of Thy might.

The Báb

The conceptions of the devoutest of mystics, the attainments of the most accomplished amongst men, the highest praise which human tongue or pen can render are all the product of man's finite mind and are conditioned by its limitations...From time immemorial He hath been veiled in the ineffable sanctity of His exalted Self, and will everlastingly continue to be wrapt in the impenetrable mystery of His unknowable Essence. Every attempt to attain to an understanding of His inaccessible Reality hath ended in complete bewilderment, and every effort to approach His exalted Self and envisage His Essence hath resulted in hopelessness and failure.

How bewildering to me, insignificant as I am, is the attempt to fathom the sacred depths of Thy knowledge! How futile my efforts to visualize the magnitude of the power inherent in Thine handiwork-the revelation of Thy creative power! ... How can I claim to have known Thee, when the entire creation is bewildered by Thy mystery, and how can I confess not to have known Thee, when, lo, the whole universe proclaimeth Thy Presence and testifieth to Thy truth? The portals of Thy grace have throughout eternity been open, and the means of access unto Thy Presence made available, unto all created things, and the revelations of Thy matchless Beauty have at all times been imprinted upon the realities of all beings, visible and invisible. Yet, notwithstanding this most gracious favor, this perfect and consummate bestowal, I am moved to testify that Thy court of holiness and glory is immeasurably exalted above the knowledge of all else besides Thee, and the mystery of Thy Presence is inscrutable to every mind except Thine own. No one except Thyself can unravel the secret of Thy nature, and naught else but Thy transcendental Essence can grasp the reality of Thy unsearchable being.

Bahá'u'lláh

Praise be to God, the All-Possessing, the King of incomparable glory, a praise which is immeasurably above the understanding of all created things, and is exalted beyond the grasp of the minds of men. None else besides Him hath ever been able to sing adequately His praise, nor will any man succeed at any time in describing the full measure of His glory. Who is it that can claim to have attained the heights of His exalted Essence, and what mind can measure the depths of His unfathomable mystery? From each and every revelation emanating from the Source of His glory, holy and never-ending evidences of unimaginable splendor have appeared, and out of every manifestation of His invincible power oceans of eternal light have outpoured. How immensely exalted are the wondrous testimonies of His almighty sovereignty, a glimmer of which, if it but touched them, would utterly consume all that are in the heavens and in the earth! How indescribably lofty are the tokens of His consummate power, a single sign of which, however inconsiderable, must transcend the comprehension of whatsoever hath, from the beginning that hath no beginning, been brought into being, or will be created in the future till the end that hath no end.

Bahá'u'lláh

How puny and insignificant is the evanescent drop when compared with the waves and billows of God's limitless and everlasting Ocean, and how utterly contemptible must every contingent and perishable thing appear when brought face to face with the uncreated, the unspeakable glory of the Eternal!

Bahá'u'lláh

He, in truth, hath, throughout eternity, been one in His Essence, one in His attributes, one in His works. Any and every comparison is applicable only to His creatures, and all conceptions of association are conceptions that belong solely to those that serve Him. Immeasurably exalted is His Essence above the descriptions of His creatures. He, alone, occupieth the Seat of transcendent majesty, of supreme and inaccessible glory. The birds of men's hearts, however high they soar, can never hope to attain the heights of His unknowable Essence.

Bahá'u'lláh

To whatever heights the mind of the most exalted of men may soar, however great the depths which the detached and understanding heart can penetrate, such mind and heart can never transcend that which is the creature of their own conceptions and the product of their own thoughts. The meditations of the profoundest thinker, the devotions of the holiest of saints, the highest expressions of praise from either human pen or tongue, are but a reflection of that which hath been created within themselves, through the revelation of the Lord, their God. Whoever pondereth this truth in his heart will readily admit that there are certain limits which no human being can possibly transgress. Every attempt which, from the beginning that hath no beginning, hath been made to visualize and know God is limited by the exigencies of His own creation—a creation which He, through the operation of His own Will and for the purposes of none other but His own Self, hath called into being. Immeasurably exalted is He above the strivings of human mind to grasp His Essence, or of human tongue to describe His mystery. No tie of direct intercourse can ever bind Him to the things He hath created, nor can the most abstruse and most remote allusions of His creatures do justice to His being. Through His world-pervading Will He hath brought into being all created things. He is and hath ever been veiled in the ancient eternity of His own exalted and indivisible Essence, and will everlastingly continue to remain concealed in His inaccessible majesty and glory. All that is in heaven and all that is in the earth have come to exist at His bidding, and by His Will all have stepped out of utter nothingness into the realm of being. How can, therefore, the creature which the Word of God hath fashioned comprehend the nature of Him Who is the Ancient of Days?

Bahá'u'lláh

What has an atom of dust to do with the pure world, and what relation is there between the limited mind and the infinite world? Minds are powerless to comprehend God, and the souls become bewildered in explaining Him.

'Abdu'l-Bahá

CONCERNING DISBELIEF IN GOD

Know thou for a certainty that whoso disbelieveth in God is neither trustworthy nor truthful. This, indeed, is the truth, the undoubted truth...Nothing whatever can deter such a man from evil, nothing can hinder him from betraying his neighbor, nothing can induce him to walk uprightly.

Bahá'u'lláh

THE KNOWLEDGE AND LOVE OF GOD

...that which is the cause of everlasting life, eternal honour, universal enlightenment, real salvation and prosperity, is, first of all, the knowledge of God. It is known that the knowledge of God is beyond all knowledge, and it is the greatest glory of the human world. For, in the existing knowledge of the reality of things there is material advantage, and through it outward civilisation progresses; but the knowledge of God is the cause of spiritual progress and attraction, and through it the perception of truth, the exaltation of humanity, divine civilisation, rightness of morals and illumination, are obtained.

Secondly comes the love of God, the light of which shines in the lamp of the hearts of those who know God; its brilliant rays illuminate the horizon and give to man the life of the Kingdom. In truth, the fruit of human existence is the love of God, for this love is the spirit of life, and the eternal bounty. If the love of God did not exist, the contingent world would be in darkness; if the love of God did not exist, the hearts of men would be dead, and deprived of the sensations of existence; if the love of God did not exist, spiritual union would be lost; if the love of God did not exist, the light of unity would not illuminate humanity...The love of the human world has shone forth from the love of God, and has appeared by the bounty and grace of God.

'Abdu'l-Bahá

GOD IS BEYOND VAIN IMAGININGS

Consider then, how all the peoples of the world are bowing the knee to a fancy of their own contriving, how they have created a creator within their own minds, and they call it the Fashioner of all that is-whereas in truth it is but an illusion. Thus are the people worshipping only an error of perception.

But that Essence of Essences, that Invisible of Invisibles, is sanctified above all human speculation, and never to be overtaken by the mind of man. Never shall that immemorial Reality lodge with the compass of a contingent being. His is another realm, and of that realm no understanding can be won. No access can be gained thereto; all entry is forbidden there. The utmost one can say is that Its existence can be proved, but the conditions of Its existence are unknown.

'Abdu'l-Bahá

GOD IS EXALTED ABOVE TIME AND SPACE

In the world of God there is no past, no future, and no present; all are one.

'Abdu'l-Bahá

The first thing which emanated from God is that universal reality, which the ancient philosophers termed 'First Mind', and which the people of Bahá call the 'First Will'. This emanation, in that which concerns its actions in the world of God, is not limited by time or place; it is without beginning or end; beginning and end in relation to God are one. The pre-existence of God is the pre-existence of essence, and also pre-existence of time, and the phenomenatlity of contingency is essential and not temporal, as we have already explained one day at table.

Though the 'First Mind' is with beginning, it does not become a sharer in the pre-existence of God, for the existence of the universal reality in relation to the existence of God is nothingness, and it has not the power to become an associate of God and like unto Him in pre-existence.

'Abdu'l-Bahá

To every discerning and illumined heart it is evident that God, the unknowable Essence, the divine Being, is immensely exalted beyond every human attribute, such as corporeal existence, ascent and descent, egress and regress. Far be it from His glory that human tongue should adequately recount His praise, or that human heart comprehend His fathomless mystery. He is and hath ever been veiled in the ancient eternity of His Essence, and will remain in His Reality everlastingly hidden from the sight of men...No tie of direct intercourse can possibly bind Him to His creatures. He standeth exalted beyond and above all separation and union, all proximity and remoteness. No sign can indicate His presence or His absence; inasmuch as by a word of His command all that are in heaven and on earth have come to exist, and by His wish, which is the Primal Will itself, all have stepped out of utter nothingness into the realm of being, the world of the visible.

Bahá'u'lláh

12
CREATION

GOD THE CREATOR

Sanctified art Thou, O Lord my God. The tongues of men fall short in extolling Thy glorious handiwork, how much more then would they falter in lauding the majesty of Thy transcendent power; and since human understanding is sore perplexed to fathom the mystery of a single object of Thy creation, how can anyone ever attain the recognition of Thine Own Being?

I have known Thee by Thy making known unto me that Thou art unknowable to anyone save Thyself. I have become apprised by the creation Thou hast fashioned out of sheer non-existence that the way to attain the comprehension of Thine Essence is barred to everyone. Thou art God, besides Whom there is none other God. No one except Thine Own Self can comprehend Thy nature. Thou art without peer or partner. From everlasting Thou hast been alone with no one else besides Thee and unto everlasting Thou wilt continue to be the same, while no created thing shall ever approach Thine exalted position.

The Báb

In every age and cycle He hath, through the splendorous light shed by the Manifestations of His wondrous Essence, recreated all things, so that whatsoever reflecteth in the heavens and on the earth the signs of His glory may not be deprived of the outpourings of His mercy, nor despair of the showers of His favors. How all-encompassing are the wonders of His boundless grace! Behold how they have pervaded the whole of creation. Such is their virtue that not a single atom in the entire universe can be found which doth not declare the evidences of His might, which doth not glorify His holy Name, or is not expressive of the effulgent light of His unity. So perfect and comprehensive is His creation that no mind nor heart, however keen or pure, can ever grasp the nature of the most insignificant of His creatures; much less fathom the mystery of Him Who is the invisible and unknowable Essence.

Bahá'u'lláh

THE BEGINNING WITHOUT A BEGINNING

As regards thine assertions about the beginning of creation, this is a matter on which conceptions vary by reason of the divergencies in men's thought and opinions. Wert thou to assert that it hath ever existed and shall continue to exist, it would be true; or wert thou to affirm the same concept as is mentioned in the sacred Scriptures, no doubt would there be about it, for it hath been revealed by God, the Lord of the worlds. Indeed He was a hidden treasure. This is a station that can never be described nor even alluded to. And in the station of 'I did wish to make Myself known', God was, and His creation had ever existed beneath His shelter from the beginning that hath no beginning, apart from its being preceded by a Firstness which cannot be regarded as firstness and originated by a Cause inscrutable even unto all men of learning.

That which hath been in existence had existed before, but not in the form thou seest today. The world of existence came into being through the heat generated from the interaction between the active force and that which is its recipient. These two are the same, yet they are different. Thus doth the Great Announcement inform thee about this glorious structure. Such as communicate the generating influence and such as receive its impact are indeed created through the irresistible Word of God which is the Cause of the entire creation, while all else besides His Word are but the creatures and the effects thereof...

Know thou, moreover, that the Word of God-exalted be His glory-is higher and far superior to that which the senses can perceive, for it is sanctified from any property or substance. It transcendeth the limitations of known elements and is exalted above all the essential and recognized substances. It became manifest without any syllable or sound and is none but the Command of God which pervadeth all created things. It hath never been withheld from the world of being. It is God's all-pervasive grace, from which all grace doth emanate. It is an entity far removed above all that hath been and shall be...

Verily, the Word of God is the Cause which hath preceded the contingent world-a world which is adorned with the splendors of the Ancient of Days, yet is being renewed and regenerated at all times.

Immeasurably exalted is the God of Wisdom Who hath raised this sublime structure.

Bahá'u'lláh

INFINITE IN ITS RANGE

A drop of the billowing ocean of His endless mercy hath adorned all creation with the ornament of existence, and a breath wafted from His peerless Paradise hath invested all beings with the robe of His sanctity and glory. A sprinkling from the unfathomed deep of His sovereign and all-pervasive Will hath, out of utter nothingness, called into being a creation which is infinite in its range and deathless in its duration. The wonders of His bounty can never cease, and the stream of His merciful grace can never be arrested. The process of His creation hath had no beginning, and can have no end.

Bahá'u'lláh

THE WORLDS OF GOD

So you will find the smallest atoms in the universal system are similar to the greatest beings of the universe. It is clear that they come into existence from one laboratory of might under one natural system, and one universal law...

'Abdu'l-Bahá

Thou hast, moreover, asked Me concerning the nature of the celestial spheres...Every heart is filled with wonder at so bewildering a theme, and every mind is perplexed by its mystery. God, alone, can fathom its import. The learned men, that have fixed at several thousand years the life of this earth, have failed, throughout the long period of their observation, to consider either the number or the age of the other planets. Consider, moreover, the manifold divergencies that have resulted from the theories propounded by these men...

Bahá'u'lláh

Know thou of a truth that the worlds of God are countless in their numbers, and infinite in their range. None can reckon or comprehend them except God, the All-Knowing, the All-Wise...

Verily I say, the creation of God embraceth worlds besides this world, and creatures apart from these creatures. In each of these worlds

He hath ordained things which none can search except Himself, the All-Searching, the All-Wise. Do thou meditate on that which We have revealed unto thee, that thou mayest discover the purpose of God, thy Lord, and the Lord of all worlds.

Bahá'u'lláh

THE DEVELOPMENT OF THE HUMAN SPECIES

In the same way the species existing on this earth are phenomenal, for it is established that there was a time when these species did not exist on the surface of the earth. Moreover, the earth has not always existed, but the world of existence has always been; for the universe is not limited to this terrestrial globe.

'Abdu'l-Bahá

Let us return to our subject that man, in the beginning of his existence and in the womb of the earth, like the embryo in the womb of the mother, gradually grew and developed, and passed from one form to another, from one shape to another, until he appeared with this beauty and perfection, this force and this power. It is certain that in the beginning he had not this loveliness and grace and elegance, and that he only by degrees attained this shape, this form, this beauty, and this grace. There is no doubt that the human embryo did not at once appear in this form...Gradually it passed through various conditions and different shapes, until it attained this form and beauty, this perfection, grace and loveliness. Thus it is evident and confirmed that the development and growth of man on this earth, until he reached his present perfection, resembled the growth and development of the embryo in the womb of the mother: by degrees it passed from condition to condition, from form to form, from one shape to another, for this is according to the requirement of the universal system and Divine Law.

'Abdu'l-Bahá

13
NATURE

The country is the world of the soul, the city is the world of bodies.

Bahá'u'lláh

THE GLORY OF THE CREATOR IS REVEALED

Look at the world and ponder a while upon it. It unveileth the book of its own self before thine eyes and revealeth that which the Pen of thy Lord, the Fashioner, the All-Informed, hath inscribed therein. It will acquaint thee with that which is within it and upon it and will give thee such clear explanations as to make thee independent of every eloquent expounder.

Nature in its essence is the embodiment of My Name, the Maker, the Creator. Its manifestations are diversified by varying causes, and in this diversity there are signs for men of discernment. Nature is God's Will and is its expression in and through the contingent world. It is a dispensation of Providence ordained by the Ordainer, the All-Wise... It is endowed with a power whose reality men of learning fail to grasp. Indeed a man of insight can perceive naught therein save the effulgent splendor of Our Name, the Creator. Say: This is an existence which knoweth no decay, and Nature itself is lost in bewilderment before its revelations, its compelling evidences and its effulgent glory which have encompassed the universe.

Bahá'u'lláh

...observe that the universe is a scroll that discloseth His hidden secrets...And not an atom of all the atoms in existence, not a creature from amongst the creatures but speaketh His praise and telleth of His attributes and names, revealeth the glory of His might...

And whenever thou dost gaze upon creation all entire, and dost observe the very atoms thereof, thou wilt note the rays of the Sun of Truth are shed upon all things and shining within them...Look thou upon trees, upon the blossoms and fruits, even upon the stones. Here too wilt thou behold the Sun's rays shed upon them, clearly visible within them, and manifested by them.

'Abdu'l-Bahá

A REPOSITORY OF WISDOM

Indeed, O Brother, if we ponder each created thing, we shall witness a myriad perfect wisdoms and learn a myriad new and wondrous truths.

Bahá'u'lláh

MAN INHERITED A PRISTINE ENVIRONMENT

We were not in the world of existence, but as soon as we were born, we found everything prepared for our needs and comfort without question on our part. He has given us ...pure atmosphere, refreshing water, gentle breezes and the sun shining above our heads.

'Abdu'l-Bahá

ALL CREATURES SHOULD BE VIEWED WITH THE EYE OF KINDNESS AND MERCY

Look not upon the creatures of God except with the eye of kindliness and mercy, for Our loving providence hath pervaded all created things, and Our grace encompassed the earth and the heavens.

Bahá'u'lláh

TREATMENT OF ANIMALS

The feelings are one and the same, whether ye inflict pain on man or on beast. There is no difference here whatever. And indeed ye do worse to harm an animal, for man hath a language, he can lodge a complaint, he can cry out and moan; if injured he can have recourse to the authorities and these will protect him from his aggressor. But the hapless beast is mute, able neither to express its hurt nor take its case to the authorities. If a man inflict a thousand ills upon a beast, it can neither ward him off with speech nor hale him into court. Therefore is it essential that ye show forth the utmost consideration to the animal, and that ye be even kinder to him than to your fellow man.

Train your children from their earliest days to be infinitely tender and loving to animals. If an animal be sick, let the children try to heal it, if it be hungry, let them feed it, if thirsty, let them quench its thirst, if weary, let them see that it rests.

Most human beings are sinners, but the beasts are innocent. Surely those without sin should receive the most kindness and love...

'Abdu'l-Bahá

EVERYTHING IS INTERCONNECTED

Now concerning nature, it is but the essential properties and the necessary relations inherent in the realities of things. And though these infinite realities are diverse in their character yet they are in the utmost harmony and closely connected together. As one's vision is broadened and the matter observed carefully, it will be made certain that every reality is but an essential requisite of other realities.

'Abdu'l-Bahá

CREATION IS SUBJECTED TO GOD'S PHYSICAL LAWS

Nature is that condition, that reality, which in appearance consists in life and death, or in other words, in the composition and decomposition of all things.

This Nature is subjected to an absolute organisation, to determined laws, to a complete order and a finished design, from which it will never depart; to such a degree, indeed, that if you look carefully and with keen sight, from the smallest invisible atom up to such large bodies of the world of existence as the globe of the sun or the other great stars and luminous spheres, whether you regard their arrangement, their composition, their form or their movement, you will find that all are in the highest degree of organisation, and are under one law from which they will never depart...

Hence it is evident that Nature in its own essence is in the grasp of the power of God, who is the Eternal Almighty One: He holds Nature within accurate regulations and laws, and rules over it.

'Abdu'l-Bahá

14
LOVE

In the garden of thy heart plant naught but the rose of love...
Bahá'u'lláh

LOVE THE FOREMOST TEACHING

The essence of Bahá'u'lláh's Teaching is all-embracing love, for love includeth every excellence of humankind. It causeth every soul to go forward.
'Abdu'l-Bahá

Love is the fundamental principle of God's purpose for man, and He has commanded us to love each other even as He loves us...
'Abdu'l-Bahá

Love is greater than peace, for peace is founded upon love. Love is the object point of peace, and peace is an outcome of love. Until love is attained, peace cannot be; but there is a so-called peace without love. The love which is from God is the fundamental. This love is the object of all human attainment, the radiance of heaven, the light of man.
'Abdu'l-Bahá

What a power is love! It is the most wonderful, the greatest of all living powers...
'Abdu'l-Bahá

THE MOST GLORIOUS LIGHT

Know thou of a certainty that Love is the secret of God's holy Dispensation, the manifestation of the All-Merciful, the fountain of spiritual outpourings. Love is heaven's kindly light... Love is the cause of God's revelation unto man, the vital bond inherent, in accordance with the divine creation, in the realities of things. Love is the one means that ensureth true felicity both in this world and the next. Love is the light that guideth in darkness, the living link that uniteth God with man, that assureth the progress of every illumined soul. Love is the most great law that ruleth this mighty and heavenly cycle, the unique power that bindeth together the divers elements of this material world, the supreme magnetic force that directeth the movements of the spheres in the celestial realms. Love revealeth with unfailing and limitless power the mysteries latent in the universe. Love is the spirit of life unto the adorned body of mankind, the establisher of true civilization in this mortal world, and the shedder of imperishable glory upon every high-aiming race and nation...

Strive to become the manifestations of the love of God, the lamps of divine guidance shining amongst the kindreds of the earth with the light of love and concord. All hail to the revealers of this glorious light!

'Abdu'l-Bahá

THE QUINTESSENTIAL BOND FOR ALL EXISTENCE

We declare that love is the cause of the existence of all phenomena and that the absence of love is the cause of disintegration or nonexistence. Love is the conscious bestowal of God, the bond of affiliation in all phenomena.

'Abdu'l-Bahá

THE SOURCE OF ADVANCEMENT

If love and agreement are manifest in a single family, that family will advance, become illumined and spiritual; but if enmity and hatred exist within it, destruction and dispersion are inevitable. This is, likewise, true of a city. If those who dwell within it manifest a spirit of accord and fellowship, it will progress steadily and human conditions become brighter, whereas through enmity and strife it will be degraded and its inhabitants scattered. In the same way, the people of a nation develop and advance toward civilization and enlightenment through love and accord and are disintegrated by war and strive. Finally, this is true of humanity itself in the aggregate. When love is realized and the ideal spiritual bonds unite the hearts of men, the whole human race will be uplifted, the world will continually grow more spiritual and radiant and the happiness and tranquillity of mankind be immeasurably increased.

'Abdu'l-Bahá

All down the ages we see how blood has stained the surface of the earth; but now a ray of greater light has come, man's intelligence is greater, spirituality is beginning to grow, and a time is surely coming when the religions of the world will be at peace. Let us leave the discordant arguments concerning outward forms, and let us join together to hasten forward the Divine Cause of unity, until all humanity knows itself to be one family, joined together in love.

'Abdu'l-Bahá

THINK LOVING THOUGHTS

I charge you all that each one of you concentrate all the thoughts of your heart on love and unity. When a thought of war comes, oppose it by a stronger thought of peace. A thought of hatred must be destroyed by a more powerful thought of love. Thoughts of war bring destruction to all harmony, well-being, restfulness and content.

Thoughts of love are constructive of brotherhood, peace, friendship, and happiness.

'Abdu'l-Bahá

THE SPIRIT OF LOVE

Shed the light of a boundless love on every human being whom you meet, whether of your country, your race, your political party, or of any other nation, colour or shade of political opinion. Heaven will support you while you work in this in-gathering of the scattered peoples of the world beneath the shadow of the almighty tent of unity...

One must never consider one's own feebleness, it is the strength of the Holy Spirit of Love, which gives the power to teach. The thought of our own weakness could only bring despair. We must look higher than all earthly thoughts; detach ourselves from every material idea, crave for the things of the spirit; fix our eyes on the everlasting bountiful Mercy of the Almighty, who will fill our souls with the gladness of joyful service to His command 'Love One Another'.

'Abdu'l-Bahá

A pure heart is as a mirror; cleanse it with the burnish of love and severance from all save God, that the true sun may shine within it and the eternal morning dawn.

Bahá'u'lláh

Grant, I beseech Thee, O Thou Who art the Everlasting King and the Sovereign Protector of all men, that I may be enabled to manifest that which shall cause the hearts and souls of men to soar in the limitless immensity of Thy love, and to commune with Thy Spirit.

Bahá'u'lláh

15
THE PROPHETS

Blessed souls-whether Moses, Jesus, Zoroaster, Krishna, Buddha, Confucius or Muhammad-were the cause of the illumination of the world of humanity.

'Abdu'l-Bahá

PORTALS OF GOD'S GRACE

God...hath ordained that in every age and dispensation a pure and stainless Soul be made manifest in the kingdoms of earth and heaven. Unto this subtle, this mysterious and ethereal Being He hath assigned a twofold nature; the physical, pertaining to the world of matter, and the spiritual, which is born of the substance of God Himself...Led by the light of unfailing guidance, and invested with supreme sovereignty, they are commissioned to use the inspiration of Their words, the effusions of Their infallible grace and the sanctifying breeze of Their Revelation for the cleansing of every longing heart and receptive spirit from the dross and dust of earthly cares and limitations. Then, and only then, will the Trust of God, latent in the reality of man, emerge, as resplendent as the rising Orb of Divine Revelation, from behind the veil of concealment, and implant the ensign of its revealed glory upon the summits of men's hearts.

Bahá'u'lláh

LUMINARIES OF INFINITE SPLENDOUR

It is clear and evident to thee that all the Prophets are the Temples of the Cause of God, Who have appeared clothed in divers attire. If thou wilt observe with discriminating eyes, thou wilt behold them all abiding in the same tabernacle, soaring in the same heaven, seated upon the same throne, uttering the same speech, and proclaiming the same Faith. Such is

The Prophets

the unity of those Essences of being, those Luminaries of infinite and immeasurable splendour.

Bahá'u'lláh

EXPONENTS OF THE UNKNOWABLE ESSENCE

To every discerning and illuminated heart it is evident that God, the unknowable Essence, the Divine Being, is immensely exalted beyond every human attribute such as corporeal existence, ascent and descent, egress and regress. Far be it from His glory that human tongue should adequately recount His praise, or that human heart comprehend His fathomless mystery...

The door of the knowledge of the Ancient of Days being thus closed in the face of all beings, the Source of infinite grace...hath caused those luminous Gems of Holiness to appear out of the realm of the spirit, in the noble form of the human temple, and be made manifest unto all men, that they may impart unto the world the mysteries of the unchangeable Being, and tell of the subtleties of His imperishable Essence.

These sanctified Mirrors, these Day Springs of ancient glory, are, one and all, the Exponents on earth of Him Who is the central Orb of the universe, its Essence and ultimate Purpose. From Him proceed their knowledge and power; from Him is derived their sovereignty. The beauty of their countenance is but a reflection of His image, and their revelation a sign of His deathless glory. They are the Treasuries of Divine knowledge, and the Repositories of celestial wisdom. Through them is transmitted a grace that is infinite, and by them is revealed the Light that can never fade...

Bahá'u'lláh

THE EMBODIMENTS OF HOLY ATTRIBUTES

These Tabernacles of Holiness, these Primal Mirrors which reflect the light of unfading glory, are but expressions of Him Who is the Invisible of the Invisibles. By the revelation of these Gems of Divine virtue all the names and attributes of God...are made manifest...

These attributes of God are not, and have never been vouchsafed specially unto certain Prophets, and withheld from others. Nay, all the Prophets of God, His well-favored, His holy and chosen Messengers are, without exception, the bearers of His names, and the embodiments of His attributes. They only differ in the intensity of their revelation, and the comparative potency of their light...

Bahá'u'lláh

From that which hath been said it becometh evident that all things, in their inmost reality, testify to the revelation of the names and attributes of God within them. Each according to its capacity, indicateth, and is expressive of, the knowledge of God...Man, the noblest and most perfect of all created things, excelleth them all in the intensity of this revelation, and is a fuller expression of its glory. And of all men, the most accomplished, the most distinguished and the most excellent are the Manifestations of the Sun of Truth...Human tongue can never befittingly sing their praise, and human speech can never unfold their mystery. These Tabernacles of holiness, these primal Mirrors which reflect the light of unfading glory, are but expressions of Him Who is the Invisible of the Invisibles. By the revelation of these gems of divine virtue all the names and attributes of God, such as knowledge and power, sovereignty and dominion, mercy and wisdom, glory, bounty and grace, are made manifest.

Bahá'u'lláh

THE TWO STATIONS OF THE MANIFESTATIONS OF GOD

The Manifestations of God have each a twofold station. One is the station of pure abstraction and essential unity...

The other station is the station of distinction, and pertaineth to the world of creation, and to the limitations thereof. In this respect, each Manifestation of God hath a distinct individuality, a definitely prescribed mission, a predestined revelation, and specially designated limitations. Each one of them is known by a different name, is characterized by a special attribute, fulfils a definite mission, and is entrusted with a particular Revelation...

Bahá'u'lláh

It is because of this difference in their station and mission that the words and utterances flowing from these Well-springs of divine knowledge appear to diverge and differ. Otherwise, in the eyes of them that are initiated into the mysteries of divine wisdom, all their utterances are in reality but the expressions of one Truth. As most of the people have failed to appreciate those stations to which We have referred, they therefore feel perplexed and dismayed at the varying utterances pronounced by Manifestations that are essentially one and the same.

The Prophets

It hath ever been evident that all these divergences of utterance are attributable to differences of station. Thus, viewed from the standpoint of their oneness and sublime detachment, the attributes of Godhead, Divinity, Supreme Singleness, and Inmost Essence, have been and are applicable to those Essences of being, inasmuch as they all abide on the throne of divine Revelation, and are established upon the seat of divine Concealment. Through their appearance the Revelation of God is made manifest, and by their countenance the Beauty of God is revealed. Thus it is that the accents of God Himself have been heard uttered by these manifestations of the divine Being.

Viewed in the light of their second station-the station of distinction, differentiation, temporal limitations, characteristics and standards,-they manifest absolute servitude, utter destitution and complete self-effacement. Even as He saith: "I am the servant of God. I am but a man like you."

...Were any of the all-embracing Manifestations of God to declare: "I am God!" He verily speaketh the truth, and no doubt attacheth thereto. For it hath been repeatedly demonstrated that through their Revelation, their attributes and names, the Revelation of God, His name and His attributes, are made manifest in the world... Thus in moments in which these Essences of being were deep immersed beneath the oceans of ancient and everlasting holiness, or when they soared to the loftiest summits of divine mysteries, they claimed their utterance to be the Voice of divinity, the Call of God Himself. Were the eye of discernment to be opened, it would recognize that in this very state, they have considered themselves utterly effaced and non-existent in the face of Him Who is the All-Pervading, the Incorruptible. Methinks, they have regarded themselves as utter nothingness, and deemed their mention in that Court an act of blasphemy. For the slightest whisperings of self within such a Court, is an evidence of self-assertion and independent existence. In the eyes of them that have attained unto that Court, such a suggestion is itself a grievous transgression. How much more grievous would it be, were aught else to be mentioned in that Presence, were man's heart, his tongue, his mind, or his soul, to be busied with anyone but the Well-Beloved, were his eyes to behold any countenance other than His beauty, were his ear to be inclined to any melody but His voice, and were his feet to tread any way but His way.

In this day the breeze of God is wafted, and His Spirit hath pervaded all things. Such is the outpouring of His grace that the pen is stilled and the tongue is speechless.

By virtue of this station, they have claimed for themselves the Voice of Divinity and the like, whilst by virtue of their station of Messengership, they have declared themselves the Messengers of God. In every instance they have voiced an utterance that would conform to the requirements of the occasion, and have ascribed all these declarations to Themselves, declarations ranging from the realm of divine Revelation to the realm of creation, and from the domain of Divinity even unto the domain of earthly existence. Thus it is that whatsoever be their utterance, whether it pertain to the realm of Divinity, Lordship, Prophethood, Messengership, Guardianship, Apostleship or Servitude, all is true, beyond the shadow of a doubt. Therefore, these sayings which We have quoted in support of Our argument must be attentively considered, that the divergent utterances of the Manifestations of the Unseen and Daysprings of Holiness may cease to agitate the soul and perplex the mind.

Those words uttered by the Luminaries of Truth must needs be pondered...

Bahá'u'lláh

DIVINE PHYSICIANS

The Prophets of God should be regarded as physicians whose task is to foster the well-being of the world and its peoples, that, through the spirit of oneness, they may heal the sickness of a divided humanity...No man, however acute his perception, can ever hope to reach the heights which the wisdom and understanding of the Divine Physician have attained. Little wonder, then, if the treatment prescribed by the physician in this day should not be found to be identical with that which he prescribed before. How could it be otherwise when the ills affecting the sufferer necessitate at every stage of his sickness a special remedy?

Bahá'u'lláh

VEILS COVERING THE DIVINE LUMINARIES

It is evident that the changes brought about in every Dispensation constitute the dark clouds that intervene between the eye of man's understanding and the Divine Luminary which shineth forth from the day spring of the Divine Essence. Consider how men for generations have been blindly imitating their fathers, and have been trained according to such ways and manners as have been laid down by the dictates of their Faith. Were these men, therefore, to discover suddenly that a Man, Who hath been living in their midst, Who, with respect to every human limitation hath been their equal, had risen to abolish every established principle imposed by their Faith-principles by which for centuries they have been disciplined, and every opposer and denier of which they have come to regard as infidel, profligate and wicked,-they would of a certainty be veiled and hindered from acknowledging His truth. Such things are as "clouds" that veil the eyes of those whose inner being hath not tasted...detachment, nor drunk from...the knowledge of God. Such men, when acquainted with those circumstances, become so veiled that, without the least question, they pronounce the Manifestation of God as infidel, and sentence Him to death. You must have heard of such things taking place all down the ages, and are now observing them in these days.

That which is preeminent above all other gifts, is incorruptible in nature, and pertaineth to God Himself, is the gift of Divine Revelation. Every bounty conferred by the Creator upon man, be it material or spiritual, is subservient unto this. It is, in its essence, and will ever so remain, the Bread which cometh down from Heaven. It is God's supreme testimony, the clearest evidence of His truth, the sign of His consummate bounty, the token of His all-encompassing mercy, the proof of His most loving providence, the symbol of His most perfect grace.

Bahá'u'lláh

It behoveth us, therefore, to make the utmost endeavor, that, by God's invisible assistance, these dark veils, these clouds of Heaven-sent trials, may not hinder us from beholding the beauty of His shining Countenance, and that we may recognize Him only by His own Self.

Bahá'u'lláh

THE WISDOM OF VEILING THEIR ASCENDANCY

He Who is the Day Spring of Truth is, no doubt, fully capable of rescuing from such remoteness wayward souls and of causing them to draw nigh unto His court and attain His Presence...His purpose, however, is to enable the pure in spirit and the detached in heart to ascend, by virtue of their own innate powers, unto the shores of the Most Great Ocean, that thereby they who seek the Beauty of the All-Glorious may be distinguished and separated from the wayward and perverse...

That the Manifestation of Divine justice...have when they appeared amongst men always been destitute of all earthly dominion and shorn of the means of worldly ascendancy, should be attributed to this same principle of separation and distinction which animateth the Divine Purpose. Were the Eternal Essence to manifest all that is latent within Him, were He to shine in the plenitude of his glory, none would be found to question His power or repudiate His truth. Nay, all created things would be so dazzled and thunderstruck by the evidences of His light as to be reduced to utter nothingness. How, then, can the godly be differentiated under such circumstances from the froward?

This principle hath operated in each of the previous Dispensations and been abundantly demonstrated...It is for this reason that, in every age, when a new manifestation hath appeared and a fresh revelation of God's transcendent power was vouchsafed unto men, they that misbelieved in Him, deluded by the appearance of the peerless and everlasting Beauty in the garb of mortal men, have failed to recognize Him...They have even arisen to decimate the ranks of the faithful and to exterminate such as believed in Him.

Bahá'u'lláh

THE PROPHETS AS ICONOCLASTS

The divine Manifestations have been iconoclastic in Their teachings, uprooting error, destroying false religious beliefs and summoning mankind anew to the fundamental oneness of God. All of Them have, likewise, proclaimed the oneness of the world of humanity. The essential teaching of Moses was the law of Sinai, the Ten Commandments. Christ renewed and again revealed the commands of the one God and precepts of human action. In Muhammad, although the circle was wider, the intention of His teaching was likewise to uplift and unify humanity in the knowledge of the one God. In the Báb the circle was again very much enlarged, but the essential teaching was the same. The Books of Bahá'u'lláh number more than one hundred. Each one is an evident proof sufficient for mankind; each one from foundation to apex proclaims the essential unity of God and humanity, the love of God, the abolition of war and the divine standard of peace. Each one also inculcates divine morality, the manifestation of lordly graces-in every word a book of meanings. For the Word of God is collective wisdom, absolute knowledge and eternal truth.

'Abdu'l-Bahá

THE PROPHETS AND THE LEADERS OF RELIGION

Leaders of Religion, in every age, have hindered their people from attaining the shores of eternal salvation, inasmuch as they held the reins of authority in their mighty grasp. Some for the lust of leadership, others through want of knowledge and understanding, have been the cause of the deprivation of the people. By their sanction and authority, every Prophet of God hath drunk from the chalice of sacrifice, and winged His flight unto the heights of glory. What unspeakable cruelties they that have occupied the seats of authority and learning have inflicted upon the true Monarchs of the world, those Gems of divine virtue! Content with a transitory dominion, they have deprived themselves of an everlasting sovereignty. Thus, their eyes beheld not the light of the countenance of the Well-Beloved...

Bahá'u'lláh

16
PRAYER, REFLECTION & WORSHIP

WORSHIP GOD WITHOUT FEAR OF PUNISHMENT OR HOPE OF REWARD

Worship thou God in such wise that if thy worship lead thee to the fire, no alteration in thine adoration would be produced, and so likewise if thy recompense should be paradise. Thus and thus alone should be the worship which befitteth the one True God. Shouldst thou worship Him because of fear, this would be unseemly in the sanctified Court of His presence, and could not be regarded as an act by thee dedicated to the Oneness of His Being. Or if thy gaze should be on paradise, and thou shouldst worship Him while cherishing such a hope, thou wouldst make God's creation a partner with Him, notwithstanding the fact that paradise is desired by men.

...That which is worthy of His Essence is to worship Him for His sake, without fear of fire, or hope of paradise.

Although when true worship is offered, the worshipper...entereth the paradise of God's good-pleasure, yet such should not be the motive of his act. However, God's favour and grace ever flow in accordance with the exigencies of His inscrutable wisdom.

The most acceptable prayer is the one offered with the utmost spirituality and radiance; its prolongation hath not been and is not beloved by God. The more detached and the purer the prayer, the more acceptable is it in the presence of God.

The Báb

WORSHIP SHOULD LEAD TO EXULTATION AND NOT TO LASSITUDE

Pride not yourselves on much reading of the verses or on a multitude of pious acts by night and day; for were a man to read a single verse with joy and radiance it would be better for him than to read with lassitude all the Holy Books of God, the Help in Peril, the Self-Subsisting. Read ye the sacred verses in such measure that ye be not overcome by languor and despondency. Lay not upon your souls that which will weary them and weigh them down, but rather what will lighten and uplift them, so that they may soar on the wings of Divine verses towards the Dawning-place of His manifest signs; this will draw you nearer to God, did ye but comprehend.

Bahá'u'lláh

One hour's reflection is preferable to seventy years of pious worship...

Bahá'u'lláh

NEVER PAY LIP SERVICE WHILE PRAISING GOD

The reason why privacy hath been enjoined in moments of devotion is this, that thou mayest give thy best attention to the remembrance of God, that thy heart may at all times be animated with His Spirit, and not be shut out as by a veil from thy Best Beloved. Let not thy tongue pay lip service in praise of God while thy heart be not attuned to the exalted Summit of Glory, and the Focal Point of communion...For He is the Source of all goodness, and unto Him revert all thing.

The Báb

THE LAW OF PRAYER

...in every Dispensation the law concerning prayer hath been emphasized and universally enforced...The traditions established the fact that in all Dispensations the law of prayer hath constituted a fundamental element of the Revelation of all the Prophets of God-a law the form and the manner of which hath been adapted to the varying requirements of every age.

Bahá'u'lláh

REMEMBERING ONE'S PARENTS

It is seemly that the servant should, after each prayer, supplicate God to bestow mercy and forgiveness upon his parents. Thereupon God's call will be raised: 'Thousand upon thousand of what thou hast asked for thy parents shall be thy recompense!' Blessed is he who remembereth his parents when communing with God.

The Báb

MEDITATION

Bahá'u'lláh says there is a sign in every phenomenon: the sign of the intellect is contemplation and the sign of contemplation is silence, because it is impossible for a man to do two things at one time-he cannot both speak and meditate.

It is an axiomatic fact that while you meditate you are speaking with your own spirit. In that state of mind you put certain questions to your spirit and the spirit answers: the light breaks forth and the reality is revealed.

You cannot apply the name 'man' to any being void of this faculty of meditation; without it he would be a mere animal...

The spirit of man is itself informed and strengthened during meditation; through it affairs of which man knew nothing are unfolded before his views...

Meditation is the key for opening the doors of mysteries. In that state man abstracts himself: in that subjective mood he is immersed in the ocean of spiritual life and can unfold the secrets of things-in-themselves...

This faculty of meditation frees man from the animal nature, discerns the reality of things, puts man in touch with God.

This faculty brings forth from the invisible plane the sciences and arts. Through the meditative faculty inventions are made possible, colossal undertakings are carried out...

'Abdu'l-Bahá

A SAMPLE OF TOPICS FOR MEDITATION AND CONTEMPLATION

...contemplate the manifest signs of the universe, and ...penetrate the hidden mysteries of the soul. Gazing with the eye of God, ...perceive within every atom a door that leadeth...to the station of absolute certitude.

Bahá'u'lláh

Consider the rational faculty with which God hath endowed the essence of man...

Wert thou to ponder in thine heart, from now until the end that hath no end, and with all the concentrated intelligence and understanding which the greatest minds have attained in the past or will attain in the future, this divinely ordained and subtle Reality, this sign of the revelation of the All-Abiding, All-Glorious God, thou wilts fail to comprehend its mystery or to appraise its virtue. Having recognized thy powerlessness to attain to an adequate understanding of that Reality which abideth within thee, thou wilt readily admit the futility of such efforts as may be attempted by thee, or by any of the created things, to fathom the mystery of the Living God, the Day Star of unfading glory, the Ancient of everlasting days. This confession of helplessness which mature contemplation must eventually impel every mind to make is in itself the acme of human understanding, and marketh the culmination of man's development.

Bahá'u'lláh

If any man were to meditate on that which the Scriptures, sent down from the heaven of God's holy Will, have revealed, he would readily recognize that their purpose is that all men shall be regarded as one soul...

Bahá'u'lláh

This Revelation is endowed with such a power that it will act as the lodestone for all nations and kindreds of the earth. Should one pause to meditate attentively he would recognize that no place is there, nor can there be, for anyone to flee to.

Bahá'u'lláh

Do thou meditate on that which We have revealed unto thee, that thou mayest discover the purpose of God, thy Lord, and the Lord of all worlds. In these words the mysteries of Divine Wisdom have been treasured.

Bahá'u'lláh

Meditate on what the poet hath written: "Wonder not, if my Best-Beloved be closer to me than mine own self; wonder at this, that I, despite such nearness, should still be so far from Him".

Bahá'u'lláh

Judge ye fairly the Cause of God, your Creator, and behold that which hath been sent down from the Throne on high, and meditate thereon with innocent and sanctified hearts. Then will the truth of this Cause appear unto you as manifest as the sun in its noon-tide glory...

Bahá'u'lláh

Reflect a while, and consider how they who are the loved ones of God must conduct themselves, and to what heights they must soar.

Bahá'u'lláh

Human utterance is an essence which aspireth to exert its influence and needeth moderation. As to its influence, this is conditional upon refinement which in turn is dependent upon hearts which are detached and pure. As to its moderation, this hath to be combined with tact and wisdom as prescribed in the Holy Scriptures and Tablets. Meditate upon that which hath streamed forth from the heaven of the Will of thy Lord, He Who is the Source of all grace, that thou mayest grasp the intended meaning which is enshrined in the sacred depths of the Holy Writings.

Bahá'u'lláh

Let God be all-sufficient for thee. Commune intimately with His Spirit, and be thou of the thankful.

Bahá'u'lláh

THE EFFECTS OF PRAYER

Intone, O My servant, the verses of God that have been received by thee, as intoned by them who have drawn nigh unto Him, that the sweetness of thy melody may kindle thine own soul, and attract the hearts of all men. Whoso reciteth, in the privacy of his chamber, the verses revealed by God, the scattering angels of the Almighty shall scatter abroad the fragrance of the words uttered by his mouth, and shall cause the heart of every righteous man to throb. Though he may, at first, remain unaware of its effect, yet the virtue of the grace vouchsafed unto him must needs sooner or later exercise its influence upon his soul. Thus have the mysteries of the Revelation of God been decreed by virtue of the Will of Him Who is the Source of power and wisdom.

Bahá'u'lláh

Although the reality of Divinity is sanctified and boundless, the aims and needs of the creatures are restricted. God's grace is like the rain that cometh down from heaven: the water is not bounded by the limitations of form, yet on whatever place it poureth down, it taketh on limitations-dimensions, appearance, shape-according to the characteristics of that place. In a square pool, the water, previously unconfined, becometh a square; in a six-sided pool it becometh a hexagon, in an eight-sided pool an octagon, and so forth. The rain itself hath no geometry, no limits, no form, but it taketh on one form or another, according to the restrictions of its vessel. In the same way, the Holy Essence of the Lord God is boundless, immeasurable, but His graces and splendours become finite in the creature, because of their limitation, wherefore the prayers of given persons will receive favourable answers in certain cases.

'Abdu'l-Bahá

SERVICE IS ALSO PRAYER

In the Bahá'í Cause arts, sciences and all crafts are worship...Briefly, all effort and exertion put forth by man from the fullness of his heart is worship, if it is prompted by the highest motives and the will to do service to humanity. This is worship: to serve mankind and to minister to the needs of the people. Service is prayer. A physician ministering to the sick, gently, tenderly, free from prejudice and believing in the solidarity of the human race, he is giving praise.

'Abdu'l-Bahá

THE DYNAMICS OF PRAYER

These five steps were suggested to an individual believer by Shoghi Effendi as a way of arriving at a solution with the aid of prayer. Although these steps are most helpful, it should be remembered that they are notes of a conversation and not necessarily the exact words of Shoghi Effendi, as such they have no binding authority.

1st Step

Pray and meditate about it. Use the prayers of the Manifestations as they have the greatest power. Then remain in the silence of contemplation for a few minutes.

2nd Step

Arrive at a decision and hold this. This decision is usually born during the contemplation. It may seem almost impossible of accomplishment but if it seems to be an answer to a prayer or a way of solving the problem, then immediately take the next step.

3rd Step

Have determination to carry the decision through. Many fail here. The decision, building into determination, is blighted and instead becomes a wish or a vague longing. When determination is born, immediately take the next step.

4th Step
Have faith and confidence that the power will flow through you, the right way will appear, the door will open, the right thought, the right message, the right principle, or the right book will be given to you. Have confidence and the right thing will come to your need. Then, as you rise from prayer, take at once the 5th Step.

5th Step
Act as though it had all been answered. Then act with tireless, ceaseless energy. And as you act, you, yourself, will become a magnet, which will attract more power to your being, until you become an unobstructed channel for the Divine power to flow through you.

Many pray but do not remain for the last half of the first step. Some who meditate arrive at a decision, but fail to hold it. Few have the determination to carry the decision through, still fewer have the confidence that the right thing will come to their need. But how many remember to act as though it had all been answered? How true these words, "Greater than the prayer is the spirit in which it is uttered" and greater than the way it is uttered is the spirit in which it is carried out.

Shoghi Effendi

17
SELECTION OF BAHA'I PRAYERS

O my God! O my God! Unite the hearts of Thy servants, and reveal to them Thy great purpose. May they follow Thy commandments and abide in Thy law. Help them, O God, in their endeavour, and grant them strength to serve Thee. O God! Leave them not to themselves, but guide their steps by the light of Thy knowledge, and cheer their hearts by Thy love. Verily, Thou art their Helper and their Lord.

Bahá'u'lláh

O Lord! Unto Thee I repair for refuge and toward all Thy signs I set my heart.

O Lord! Whether travelling or at home, and in my occupation or in my work, I place my whole trust in Thee.

Grant me then Thy sufficing help so as to make me independent of all things, O Thou Who art unsurpassed in Thy mercy!

Bestow upon me my portion, O Lord, as Thou pleaseth, and cause me to be satisfied with whatsoever Thou has ordained for me. Thine is the absolute authority to command.

The Báb

Vouchsafe unto me, O my God, the full measure of Thy love and Thy good-pleasure, and through the attractions of Thy resplendent light enrapture our hearts, O Thou Who art the Supreme Evidence and the All-Glorified. Send down upon me, as a token of Thy grace, Thy vitalizing breezes, throughout the day-time and in the night season, O lord of bounty.

No deed have I done, O my God, to merit beholding Thy face, and I know of a certainty that were I to live as long as the world lasts I would fail to accomplish any deed such as to deserve this favour, inasmuch as the station of a servant shall ever fall short of access to Thy holy precincts, unless Thy bounty should reach me and Thy tender mercy pervade me and Thy loving-kindness encompass me.

All praise be unto Thee, O Thou besides Who there is none other God. Graciously enable me to ascend unto Thee, to be granted the honour of dwelling in Thy nearness and to have communion with Thee alone. No God is there but Thee.

Indeed shouldst Thou desire to confer blessing upon a servant Thou wouldst blot out from the realm of his heart every mention or disposition except Thine Own mention; and shouldst Thou ordain evil for a servant by reason of that which his hands have unjustly wrought before Thy face, Thou wouldst test him with the benefits of this world and of the next that he might become preoccupied therewith and forget Thy remembrance.

The Báb

O God, my God! Shield Thy trusted servants from the evils of self and passion, protect them with the watchful eye of Thy loving-kindness from all rancor, hate and envy, shelter them in the impregnable stronghold of Thy care and, safe from the darts of doubtfulness, make them the manifestations of Thy glorious signs, illumine their faces with the effulgent rays shed from the Day-spring of Thy divine unity, gladden their hearts with the verses revealed from Thy holy Kingdom, strengthen their loins by Thine all-swaying power that cometh from Thy realm of glory. Thou art the All-Bountiful, the Protector, the Almighty, the Gracious.

'Abdu'l-Bahá

I am aware, O Lord, that my trespasses have covered my face with shame in Thy presence, and have burdened my back before Thee, have intervened between me and Thy beauteous countenance, have compassed me from every direction and have hindered me on all sides from gaining access unto the revelations of Thy celestial power.

O Lord! If Thou forgivest me not, who is there then to grant pardon, and if Thou hast no mercy upon me who is capable of showing compassion? Glory be unto Thee, Thou didst create me when I was non-existent and Thou didst nourish me while I was devoid of any understanding. Praise be unto Thee, every evidence of bounty proceedeth from Thee and every token of grace emanateth from the treasuries of Thy decree.

The Báb

I beg Thee to forgive me, O my Lord, for every mention but the mention of Thee, and for every praise but the praise of Thee, and for every delight but delight in Thy nearness, and for every pleasure but the pleasure of communion with Thee, and for every joy but the joy of Thy love and of Thy good-pleasure, and for all things pertaining unto me which bear no relationship unto Thee, O Thou Who art the Lord of lords, He Who provideth the means and unlocketh the doors.

The Báb

O my God, O my Lord, O my Master! I beg Thee to forgive me for seeking any pleasure save Thy love, or any comfort except Thy nearness, or any delight besides Thy good-pleasure, or any existence other than communion with Thee.

The Báb

O God! Refresh and gladden my spirit. Purify my heart. Illumine my powers. I lay all my affairs in Thy hand. Thou art my Guide and my Refuge. I will no longer be sorrowful and grieved; I will be a happy and joyful being. O God! I will no longer be full of anxiety, nor will I let trouble harass me. I will not dwell on the unpleasant things of life.

O God! Thou art more friend to me than I am to myself. I dedicate myself to Thee, O Lord.

'Abdu'l-Bahá

Glory be to Thee, O God, for Thy manifestation of love to mankind! O Thou Who art our Life and Light, guide Thy servants in Thy way, and make us rich in Thee and free from all save Thee.

O God, teach us Thy Oneness and give us a realization of Thy Unity, that we may see no one save Thee. Thou art the Merciful and the Giver of bounty!

O God, create in the hearts of Thy beloved the fire of Thy love, that it may consume the thought of everything save Thee.

Reveal to us, O God, Thine exalted eternity-that Thou hast ever been and wilt ever be, and that there is no God save Thee. Verily, in Thee will we find comfort and strength.

Bahá'u'lláh

18
PLACES OF WORSHIP

Blessed is the spot, and the house, and the place, and the city, and the heart, and the mountain, and the refuge, and the cave, and the valley, and the land, and the sea, and the island, and the meadow where mention of God hath been made, and His praise glorified.

Bahá'u'lláh

Whensoever a company of people shall gather in a meeting place, shall engage in glorifying God, and shall speak with one another of the mysteries of God, beyond any doubt the breathings of the Holy Spirit will blow gently over them, and each shall receive a share thereof.

'Abdu'l-Bahá

DAWNING PLACE OF THE REMEMBRANCE OF GOD (Mashriqu'l-Adhkár)

O people of the world! Build ye houses of worship throughout the lands in the name of Him Who is the Lord of all religions. Make them as perfect as is possible in the world of being, and adorn them with that which befitteth them, not with images and effigies. Then, with radiance and joy, celebrate therein the praise of your Lord, the Most Compassionate. Verily, by His remembrance the eye is cheered and the heart is filled with light.

Bahá'u'lláh

Blessed is he who, at the hour of dawn, centring his thoughts on God, occupied with His remembrance, and supplicating His forgiveness, directeth his steps to the Mashriqu'l-Adhkár and, entering therein, seateth himself in silence to listen to the verses of God, the Sovereign, the Mighty, the All-Praised. Say: The Mashriqu'l-Adhkár is each and every building which hath been erected in cities and villages for the celebration of My praise. Such is the name by which it hath been designated before the throne of glory, were ye of those who understand.

They who recite the verses of the All-Merciful in the most melodious of tones will perceive in them that with which the sovereignty of earth and heaven can never be compared. From them they will inhale the divine fragrance of My worlds-worlds which today none can discern save those who have been endowed with vision through this sublime, this beauteous Revelation. Say: These verses draw hearts that are pure unto those spiritual worlds that can neither be expressed in words nor intimated by allusion. Blessed be those who hearken.

Bahá'u'lláh

Teach your children the verses revealed from the heaven of majesty and power, so that, in most melodious tones, they may recite the Tablets of the All-Merciful in the alcoves within the Mashriqu'l-Adhkár. Whoever hath been transported by the rapture born of the adoration for My Name, the Most Compassionate, will recite the verses of God in such wise as to captivate the hearts of those yet wrapped in slumber. Well is it with him who hath quaffed the Mystic Wine of everlasting life from the utterance of his merciful Lord in My Name-a Name through which every lofty and majestic mountain hath been reduced to dust.

Bahá'u'lláh

THE FUNCTION OF THE HOUSE OF WORSHIP

Among the institutes of the Holy Books is that of the foundation of places of Worship...In brief, the original purpose of temples and houses of worship is simply that of unity-places of meeting where various peoples, different races and souls of every capacity may come together in order that love and agreement should be manifest between them. This is why Bahá'u'lláh has commanded that a place of worship be built for all religionists of the world; that all religions, races and sects may come together within its universal shelter; that the proclamation of the oneness of mankind shall go forth from its open courts of holiness-the announcement that humanity is the servant of God and that all are submerged in the ocean of His mercy. It is the Mashriqu'l-Adhkár [house of worship, lit., Dawning Place of the Remembrance of God].

'Abdu'l-Bahá

Thou hast asked about places of worship and the underlying reason therefor. The wisdom in raising up such buildings is that at a given hour, the people should know it is time to meet, and all should gather together, and, harmoniously attuned one to another, engage in prayer; with the result that out of this coming together, unity and affection shall grow and flourish in the human heart.

'Abdu'l-Bahá

Although to outward seeming the Mashriqu'l-Adhkár is a material structure, yet it hath a spiritual effect. It forgeth bonds of unity from heart to heart; it is a collective centre for men's souls. Every city in which, during the days of the Manifestation, a temple was raised up, hath created security and constancy and peace, for such buildings were given over to the perpetual glorification of God, and only in the remembrance of God can the heart find rest. Gracious God! The edifice of the House of Worship hath a powerful influence on every phase of life. Experience hath, in the east, clearly shown this to be a fact. Even if, in some small village, a house was designated as the Mashriqu'l-Adhkár, it produced a marked effect; how much greater would be the impact of one especially raised up.

'Abdu'l-Bahá

The Mashriqu'l-Adhkár is one of the most vital institutions in the world, and it hath many subsidiary branches. Although it is a House of Worship, it is also connected with a hospital, a drug dispensary, a traveller's hospice, a school for orphans, and a university for advanced studies. Every Mashriqu'l-Adhkár is connected with these five things...Make these matters known to the beloved of the Lord, so that they will understand how very great is the importance of this 'Dawning-Point of the Remembrance of God.' The Temple is not only a place for worship; rather, in every respect is it complete and whole.

'Abdu'l-Bahá

19
THE STATION OF MAN

THE POTENTIAL FOR GREATNESS

Great is the station of man. Great must also be his endeavours for the rehabilitation of the world and the well-being of nations. I beseech the One true God to graciously confirm thee in that which beseemeth man's station.

Bahá'u'lláh

How lofty is the station which man, if he but choose to fulfill his high destiny, can attain! To what depths of degradation he can sink, depths which the meanest of creatures have never reached! Seize, O friends, the chance which this Day offereth you, and deprive not yourselves of the liberal effusions of His grace.

Bahá'u'lláh

Man must be lofty in endeavor. He must seek to become heavenly and spiritual...

'Abdu'l-Bahá

Success or failure, gain or loss, must, therefore, depend upon man's own exertions. The more he striveth, the greater will be his progress.

Bahá'u'lláh

The greatest bestowal of God to man is the capacity to attain human virtues.

'Abdu'l-Bahá

Look not at your own capacities, for the divine bestowal can transform a drop into an ocean; it can make a tiny seed a lofty tree.

'Abdu'l-Bahá

How resplendent the luminaries of knowledge that shine in an atom, and how vast the oceans of wisdom that surge within a drop! To a supreme degree is this true of man, who, among all created things, hath been invested with the robe of such gifts, and hath been singled out for the glory of such distinction. For in him are potentially revealed all the attributes and names of God to a degree that no other created being hath excelled or surpassed.

Bahá'u'lláh

Having created the world and all that liveth and moveth therein, He, through the direct operation of His unconstrained and sovereign Will, chose to confer upon man the unique distinction and capacity to know Him and to love Him-a capacity that must needs be regarded as the generating impulse and the primary purpose underlying the whole of creation... Upon the inmost reality of each and every created thing He hath shed the light of one of His names, and made it a recipient of the glory of one of His attributes. Upon the reality of man, however, He hath focused and radiance of all of His names and attributes, and made it a mirror of His own Self. Alone of all created things man hath been singled out for so great a favor, so enduring a bounty.

Bahá'u'lláh

THE DUAL NATURE OF MAN

In man there are two natures; his spiritual or higher nature and his material or lower nature. In one he approaches God, in the other he lives for the world alone. Signs of both these natures are to be found in men. In his material aspect he expresses untruth, cruelty and injustice; all these are the outcome of his lower nature. The attributes of his Divine nature are shown forth in love, mercy, kindness, truth and justice, one and all being expressions of his higher nature. Every good habit, every noble quality belongs to man's spiritual nature, whereas all his imperfections and sinful actions are born of his material nature. If a man's Divine nature dominates his human nature, we have a saint.

'Abdu'l-Bahá

The Almighty hath not created in men the claws and teeth of ferocious animals, nay rather hath the human form been fashioned and set with the most comely attributes and adorned with the most perfect virtues. The honour of this creation and the worthiness of this garment therefore require man to have love and affinity for his own kind, nay rather, to act towards all living creatures with justice and equity...

...But the sublime achievements of man reside in those qualities and attributes that exclusively pertain to the angels of the Supreme Concourse. Therefore, when praiseworthy qualities and high morals emanate from man, he becometh a heavenly being...

In short, man is endowed with two natures: one tendeth towards moral sublimity and intellectual perfection, while the other turneth to bestial degradation and carnal imperfections. If ye travel the countries of the globe ye shall observe on one side the remains of ruin and destruction, while on the other ye shall see the signs of civilization and development. Such desolation and ruin are the result of war, strife and quarrelling, while all development and progress are fruits of the lights of virtue, co-operation and concord.

'Abdu'l-Bahá

THE GIFT OF INTELLECT

First and foremost among these favors, which the Almighty hath conferred upon man, is the gift of understanding. His purpose in conferring such a gift is none other except to enable His creature to know and recognize the one true God-exalted be His glory. This gift giveth man the power to discern the truth in all things, leadeth him to that which is right, and helpeth him to discover the secrets of creation.

Bahá'u'lláh

The reality of man is his thought, not his material body. The thought force and the animal force are partners. Although man is part of the animal creation, he possesses a power of thought superior to all other created beings.

If a man's thought is constantly aspiring towards heavenly subjects then does he become saintly; if on the other hand his thought does not soar, but is directed downwards to centre itself upon the things of this world, he grows more and more material until he arrives at a state little better than that of a mere animal.

'Abdu'l-Bahá

The power of the intellect is one of God's greatest gifts to men, it is the power that makes him a higher creature than the animal. For whereas, century by century and age by age man's intelligence grows and becomes keener, that of the animal remains the same. They are no more intelligent today than they were a thousand years ago! Is there a greater proof than this needed to show man's dissimilarity to the animal creation?

'Abdu'l-Bahá

CREATED IN THE IMAGE OF GOD

Man is the microcosm; and the infinite universe, the macrocosm. The mysteries of the greater world, or macrocosm, are expressed or revealed in the lesser world, the microcosm. Likewise, the greater world, the macrocosm, is latent and miniatured in the lesser world, or microcosm, of man. This constitutes the universality or perfection of virtues potential in mankind. Therefore, it is said that man has been created in the image and likeness of God.

Let us now discover more specifically how he is the image and likeness of God and what is the standard or criterion by which he can be measured and estimated. This standard can be no other that the divine virtues which are revealed in him. Therefore, every man imbued with divine qualities, who reflects heavenly moralities and perfections, who is the expression of ideal and praiseworthy attributes, is, verily, in the image and likeness of God. If a man possesses wealth, can we call him an image and likeness of God? Or is human honor and notoriety the criterion of divine nearness? Can we apply the test of racial color and say that man of a certain hue-white, black, yellow, red-is the true image of his Creator? We must conclude that color is not the standard and estimate of judgement and that it is of no importance, for color is accidental in nature. The spirit and intelligence of man is essential, and that is the manifestation of divine virtues, the merciful bestowals of God, the eternal life and baptism through the Holy Spirit.

'Abdu'l-Bahá

THE SPIRITUAL STATION OF MAN

We exhort you, O peoples of the world, to observe that which will elevate your station...Henceforward everyone should utter that which is meet and seemly, and should refrain from slander, abuse and whatever causeth sadness in men...Lofty is the station of man, were he to hold fast to righteousness and truth and to remain firm and steadfast in the Cause.

Bahá'u'lláh

The Station of Man

Then it is clear that the honour and exaltation of man must be something more than material riches; material comforts are only a branch, but the root of the exaltation of man is the good attributes and virtues which are the adornments of his reality. These are the divine appearances, the heavenly bounties, the sublime emotion, the love and knowledge of God; universal wisdom, intellectual perception, scientific discoveries, justice, equity, truthfulness, benevolence, natural courage, and innate fortitude; the respect for rights and the keeping of agreements and covenants; rectitude in all circumstances; serving the truth under all conditions; the sacrifice of one's life for the good of all people; kindness and esteem for all nations: obedience to the teachings of God; service in the Divine Kingdom; the guidance of the people, and the education of the nations and races. This is the prosperity of the human world! This is the exaltation of man in the world! This is eternal life and heavenly honour!

'Abdu'l-Bahá

THE SHORTCOMINGS OF MAN

Nothing is more fruitful for man than the knowledge of his own shortcomings. The Blessed Perfection says, "I wonder at the man who does not find his own imperfections."

'Abdu'l-Bahá

If a man kills another, no matter what the cause may be, he is pronounced a murderer, imprisoned or executed; but the brutal oppressor who has slain one hundred thousand is idolized as a hero, conqueror or military genius. A man steals a small sum of money; he is called a thief and sent to the penitentiary; but the military leader who invades and pillages a whole kingdom is acclaimed a heroic and mighty man of valor. How base and ignorant is man!

'Abdu'l-Bahá

If animals are savage and ferocious, it is simply a means for their subsistence and preservation. They are deprived of that degree of intellect which can reason and discriminate between right and wrong, just and injustice; they are justified in their actions and not responsible. When man is ferocious and cruel toward his fellowman, it is not for subsistence or safety. His motive is selfish advantage and willful wrong. It is neither seemly nor befitting that such a noble creature, endowed with intellect and lofty thoughts, capable of wonderful achievement and discoveries in sciences and arts, with potential for even higher perceptions and the accomplishment of divine purposes in life, should seek the blood of his fellowmen upon the field of battle. Man is the temple of God. He is not a human temple. If you destroy a house, the owner of that house will be grieved and wrathful. How much greater is the wrong when man destroys a building planned and erected by God! Undoubtedly, he deserves the judgement and wrath of God.

'Abdu'l-Bahá

This physical world of man is subject to the power of the lusts, and sin is the consequence of this power of the lusts, for it is not subject to the laws of justice and holiness. The body of man is a captive of nature; it will act in accordance with whatever nature orders. It is therefore certain that sins such as anger, jealousy, dispute, covetousness, avarice, ignorance, prejudice, hatred, pride, and tyranny exist in the physical world. All these brutal qualities exist in the nature of man. A man who has not had a spiritual education is a brute.

'Abdu'l-Bahá

A single falsehood brings reproach and censure, but the wiles of politicians and diplomats excite the admiration and praise of a nation.

'Abdu'l-Bahá

THAT WHICH BESEEMETH THE STATION OF MAN

It ill beseemeth the station of man to commit tyranny; rather it behooveth him to observe equity and be attired with the raiment of justice under all conditions.

Bahá'u'lláh

Man is like unto a tree. If he be adorned with fruit, he hath been and will ever be worthy of praise and commendation. Otherwise a fruitless tree is but fit for fire. The fruits of the human tree are exquisite, highly desired and dearly cherished. Among them are upright character, virtuous deeds and a goodly utterance. The springtime for earthly trees occurreth once every year, while the one for human trees appeareth in the Days of God...The Water for these trees is the living water of the sacred Words uttered by the Beloved of the world. In one instant are such trees planted and in the next their branches shall, through the outpourings of the showers of divine mercy, have reached the skies. A dried-up tree, however, hath never been nor will be worth of any mention.

Bahá'u'lláh

Observe equity in your judgement, ye men of understanding heart! He that is unjust in his judgement is destitute of the characteristics that distinguish man's station.

Bahá'u'lláh

Sow not, O people, the seeds of dissension amongst men, and contend not with your neighbor. Be patient under all conditions, and place your whole trust and confidence in God. Aid ye your Lord with the sword of wisdom and of utterance. This indeed well becometh the station of man.

Bahá'u'lláh

20
THE SOUL

INDEPENDENT OF THE BODY

The spirit, or human soul, is the rider; and the body is only the steed.
'Abdu'l-Bahá

Spirit is the lamp; mind is the light which shines from the lamp. Spirit is the tree, and the mind is the fruit.
'Abdu'l-Bahá

Know thou that the soul of man is exalted above and is independent of all infirmities of body or mind. That a sick person showeth signs of weakness is due to the hindrances that interpose themselves between his soul and his body, for the soul itself remaineth unaffected by any bodily ailments. Consider the light of the lamp. Though an external object may interfere with its radiance, the light itself continueth to shine with undiminished power. In like manner, every malady afflicting the body of man is an impediment that preventeth the soul from manifesting its inherent might and power. When it leaveth the body, however, it will evince such ascendancy, and reveal such influence as no force on earth can equal. Every pure, every refined and sanctified soul will be endowed with tremendous power, and shall rejoice with exceeding gladness.
 Consider the lamp which is hidden under a bushel. Though its light be shining, yet, its radiance is concealed from men. Likewise, consider the sun which hath been obscured by the clouds. Observe how its splendor appeareth to have diminished, when in reality the source of that light hath remained unchanged. The soul of man should be likened unto this sun, and all things on earth should be regarded as his body. So long as no external impediment interveneth between them, the body will, in its entirety, continue to reflect the light of the soul, and to be sustained by its

power. As soon as, however, a veil interposeth itself between them, the brightness of that light seemeth to lessen.

...The soul of man is the sun by which his body is illumined, and from which it draweth its sustenance, and should be so regarded.

Bahá'u'lláh

See how dark and narrow is the physical world of man's body, and what a prey it is to diseases and ills. On the other hand, how fresh and bright is the realm of the human spirit. Judge thou from this metaphor how the world of the Kingdom hath shone down, and how its laws have been made to work in this nether realm. Although the spirit is hidden from view, still its commandments shine out like rays of light upon the world of the human body. In the same way, although the Kingdom of heaven is hidden from the sight of this unwitting people, still, to him who seeth with the inner eye, it is plain as day.

'Abdu'l-Bahá

THE NATURE OF THE SOUL

Thou hast asked Me concerning the nature of the soul. Know, verily, that the soul is a sign of God, a heavenly gem whose reality the most learned of men hath failed to grasp, and whose mystery no mind, however acute, can ever hope to unravel. It is the first among all created things to declare the excellence of its Creator, the first to recognize His glory, to cleave to his truth, and to bow down in adoration before Him. If it be faithful to God, it will reflect His light, and will, eventually, return unto Him...

Verily I say, the human soul is, in its essence, one of the signs of God, a mystery among His mysteries. It is one of the mighty signs of the Almighty, the harbinger that proclaimeth the reality of all the worlds of God. Within it lieth concealed that which the world is now utterly incapable of apprehending...

Bahá'u'lláh

Know that, although the human soul has existed on the earth for prolonged times and ages, yet it is phenomenal. As it is a divine sign, when once it has come into existence it is eternal. The spirit of man has a beginning, but it has no end; it continues eternally.

'Abdu'l-Bahá

Man-the true man-is soul, not body; though physically man belongs to the animal kingdom, yet his soul lifts him above the rest of creation.

Behold how the light of the sun illuminates the world of matter: Even so doth the divine light shed its rays in the kingdom of the soul. The soul it is which makes the human creature a celestial entity!

'Abdu'l-Bahá

In explaining these intellectual realities, one is obliged to express them by sensible figures, because in exterior existence there is nothing that is not material. Therefore to explain the reality of the spirit, its condition, its station, one is obliged to give explanations under the forms of sensible things, because in the external world all that exists is sensible.

'Abdu'l-Bahá

AFTER SEPARATION FROM THE BODY

As to thy question regarding discoveries made by the soul after it hath put off its human form...once he hath departed this life, he will behold, in that world whatsoever was hidden from him here: but there he will look upon and comprehend all things with his inner eye. There will he gaze on his fellows and his peers, and those in the ranks above him, and those below. As for what is meant by the equality of souls in the all-highest realm, it is this: the souls of the believers, at the time when they first become manifest in the world of the body, are equal, and each is sanctified and pure. In this world, however, they will begin to differ one from another, some achieving the highest station, some a middle one, others remaining at the lowest stage of being. Their equal status is at the beginning of their existence; the differentiation followeth their passing away.

'Abdu'l-Bahá

Take thou the step of the spirit, so that, swift as the twinkling of an eye, thou mayest flash through the wilds of remoteness and bereavement, attain the Ridván of everlasting reunion, and in one breath commune with the heavenly Spirits. For with human feet thou canst never hope to traverse these immeasurable distances, nor attain thy goal. Peace be upon him whom the light of truth guideth unto all truth, and who, in the name of God, standeth in the path of His Cause, upon the shore of true understanding.

Bahá'u'lláh

21
LIFE AFTER DEATH

RETURNING TO THE RADIANT LIGHT OF GOD

The spirit of holiness beareth unto thee the joyful tidings of reunion; wherefore dost thou grieve? The spirit of power confirmeth thee in His cause; why dost thou veil thyself? The light of His countenance doth lead thee; how canst thou go astray?

Bahá'u'lláh

I have made death a messenger of joy to thee. Wherefore dost thou grieve? I made the light to shed on thee its splendour. Why dost thou veil thyself therefrom?

Bahá'u'lláh

With the joyful tidings of light I hail thee: rejoice! To the court of holiness I summon thee; abide therein that thou mayest live in peace for evermore.

Bahá'u'lláh

Say, this earthly life shall come to an end, and everyone shall expire and return unto my Lord God Who will reward with the choicest gifts the deeds of those who endure with patience. Verily God assigneth the measure of all created things as He willeth, by virtue of His behest; and those who conform to the good-pleasure of your Lord, they are indeed among the blissful.

The Báb

DEATH IS LIFE

Death proffereth unto every confident believer the cup that is life indeed. It bestoweth joy, and is the bearer of gladness. It conferreth the gift of everlasting life.

Bahá'u'lláh

Didst thou behold immortal sovereignty, thou wouldst strive to pass from this fleeting world. But to conceal the one from thee and to reveal the other is a mystery which none but the pure in heart can comprehend.

Bahá'u'lláh

Sorrow not if, in these days and on this earthly plane, things contrary to your wishes have been ordained and manifested by God, for days of blissful joy, of heavenly delight, are assuredly in store for you. Worlds, holy and spiritually glorious, will be unveiled to your eyes. You are destined by Him, in this world and hereafter, to partake of their benefits, to share in their joys, and to obtain a portion of their sustaining grace. To each and every one of them you will, no doubt, attain.

Bahá'u'lláh

IMMORTALITY

Just as the conception of faith hath existed from the beginning that hath no beginning, and will endure till the end that hath no end, in like manner will the true believer eternally live and endure. His spirit will everlastingly circle round the Will of God. He will last as long as God, Himself, will last...Death can never invade that holy seat. Thus have We entrusted thee with the signs of Thy Lord, that thou mayest persevere in thy love for Him, and be of them that comprehend this truth.

Bahá'u'lláh

The rewards of the other world are peace, the spiritual graces, the various spiritual gifts in the Kingdom of God, the gaining of the desires of the heart and the soul, and the meeting of God in the world of eternity. In the same way the punishment of the other world-that is to say, the torments of the other world-consist in being deprived of the special, divine blessings and the absolute bounties, and falling into the lowest degree of existence. He who is deprived of these divine favors, although he continues after death, is considered as dead by the people of truth.

'Abdu'l-Bahá

SOUL AFTER SEPARATION FROM THE BODY

Thou hast, moreover, asked Me concerning the state of the soul after its separation from the body. Know thou, of a truth, that if the soul of man hath walked in the ways of God, it will, assuredly, return and be gathered to the glory of the Beloved. By the righteousness of God! It shall attain a station such as no pen can depict, or tongue describe. The soul that hath remained faithful to the Cause of God, and stood unwaveringly firm in His Path, shall, after his ascension, be possessed of such power that all the worlds which the Almighty hath created can benefit through him...

Bahá'u'lláh

Hear no evil, and see no evil, abase not thyself, neither sigh and weep. Speak no evil, that thou mayest not hear it spoken unto thee, and magnify not the faults of others that thine own faults may not appear great; and wish not the abasement of anyone, that thine own abasement be not exposed. Live then the days of thy life, that are less than a fleeting moment, with thy mind stainless, thy heart unsullied, thy thoughts pure, and thy nature sanctified, so that, free and content, thou mayest put away this mortal frame, and repair unto the mystic paradise and abide in the eternal kingdom for evermore.

Bahá'u'lláh

As to the soul of man after death, it remains in the degree of purity to which it has evolved during life in the physical body, and after it is freed from the body, it remains plunged in the ocean of God's mercy.

From the moment the soul leaves the body and arrives in the heavenly world, its evolution is spiritual, and that evolution is: The approaching unto God.

...The soul does not evolve from degree to degree as a law-it only evolves nearer to God, by the mercy and bounty of God.

'Abdu'l-Bahá

The differences and distinction between men will naturally become realized after their departure from this mortal world. But this distinction is not in respect to place, but in respect to the soul and conscience. For the Kingdom of God is sanctified (or free) from time and place; it is another world and another universe.

'Abdu'l-Bahá

Your questions, however, can be answered only briefly, since there is no time for a detailed reply. The answer to the first question: the souls of the children of the Kingdom, after their separation from the body, ascend unto the realm of everlasting life. But if ye ask as to the place, know ye that the world of existence is a single world, although its stations are various and distinct...

As to the second question: the tests and trails of God take place in this world, not in the world of the Kingdom.

The answer to the third question is this, that in the other world the human reality doth not assume a physical form, rather doth it take on a heavenly form, made up of elements of that heavenly realm.

And the answer to the fourth question: the centre of the Sun of Truth is in the supernal world-the Kingdom of God. Those souls who are pure and unsullied, upon the dissolution of their elemental frames, hasten away to the world of God, and that world is within this world. The people of this world, however, are unaware of that world, and are even as the mineral and the vegetable that know nothing of the world of the animal and the world of man.

'Abdu'l-Bahá

A LIFE REVIEW

Bring thyself to account each day ere thou art summoned to a reckoning; for death, unheralded, shall come upon thee and thou shalt be called to give account for thy deeds.

Bahá'u'lláh

This mortal life is sure to perish; its pleasures are bound to fade away and ere long ye shall return unto God, distressed with pangs of remorse, for presently ye shall be roused from your slumber, and ye shall soon find yourselves in the presence of God and will be asked of your doings.

The Báb

BAHÁ'U'LLÁH ADDRESSES THE OPPRESSORS

Know ye that the world and its vanities and its embellishments shall pass away. Nothing will endure except God's Kingdom...The days of your life shall roll away, and all the things with which ye are occupied and of which ye boast yourselves shall perish, and ye shall, most certainly, be summoned by a company of His angels to appear at the spot where the limbs of the entire creation shall be made to tremble, and the flesh of every oppressor to creep. Ye shall be asked of the things your hands have wrought in this, your vain life, and shall be repaid for your doings. This is the day that shall inevitably come upon you, the hour that none can put back.

Bahá'u'lláh

GOD HAS NEVER CREATED AN EVIL SPIRIT

God has never created an evil spirit; all such ideas and nomenclature are symbols expressing the mere human or earthly nature of man. It is an essential condition of the soil of earth that thorns, weeds and fruitless trees may grow from it. Relatively speaking, this is evil; it is simply the lower state and baser product of nature.

'Abdu'l-Bahá

THE DENIAL OF THE MATERIALISTS

God, the Exalted, hath placed these signs in men, to the end that philosophers may not deny the mysteries of the life beyond nor belittle that which hath been promised them. For some hold to reason and deny whatever the reason comprehendeth not, and yet weak minds can never grasp the matters which we have related, but only the Supreme Intelligence can comprehend them.

Bahá'u'lláh

The inability of the materialistic mind to grasp the idea of the Life Eternal is no proof of the non-existence of that life.
 The comprehension of that other life depends on our spiritual birth!
 My prayer for you is that your spiritual faculties and aspirations may daily increase, and that you will never allow the material senses to veil from your eyes the glories of the Heavenly Illumination.

'Abdu'l-Bahá

THOUGHTS OF ANNIHILATION ARE DESTRUCTIVE

The concept of annihilation is a factor in human degradation, a cause of human debasement and lowliness, a source of human fear and abjection. It has been conductive to the dispersion and weakening of human thought, whereas the realization of existence and continuity has upraised man to sublimity of ideals, established the foundations of human progress and stimulated the development of heavenly virtues; therefore, it behooves man to abandon thoughts of nonexistence and death, which are absolutely imaginary, and see himself ever-living, everlasting in the divine purpose of his creation. He must turn away from ideas which degrade the human soul so that day by day and hour by hour he may advance upward and higher to spiritual perception of the continuity of the human reality. If he dwells upon the thought of nonexistence, he will become utterly incompetent; with weakened willpower his ambition for progress will be lessened and the acquisition of human virtues will cease.

Therefore, you must thank God that He has bestowed upon you the blessing of life and existence in the human kingdom. Strive diligently to acquire virtues befitting your degree and station. Be as lights of the world which cannot be hid and which have no setting in horizons of darkness. Ascend to the zenith of an existence which is never beclouded by the fears and forebodings of nonexistence. When man is not endowed with inner perception, he is not informed of these important mysteries. The retina of outer vision, though sensitive and delicate, may, nevertheless, be a hindrance to the inner eye which alone can perceive. The bestowals of God which are manifest in all phenomenal life are sometimes hidden by intervening veils of mental and moral vision which render man spiritually blind and incapable, but when those scales are removed and the veils rent asunder, then the great signs of God will become visible, and he will witness the eternal light filling the world.

'Abdu'l-Bahá

REINCARNATION REJECTED

...this material world has not such value or such excellence that man, after having escaped from this cage, will desire a second time to fall into this snare. No, through the eternal Bounty the worth and true ability of man becomes apparent and visible by traversing the degrees of existence, and not by returning. When the shell is once opened, it will be apparent and evident whether it contains a pearl or worthless matter. When once the plant has grown it will bring forth either thorns or flowers; there is no need for it to grow up again. Besides, advancing and moving in the worlds in a direct order according to the natural law, is the cause of existence; and a movement contrary to the system and law of nature is the cause of non-existence. The return of the soul after death is contrary to the natural movement, and opposed to divine system...

...the spirit is an incorporeal being, and does not enter and come forth, but is only connected with the body, as the sun is with the mirror. If it were thus, and the spirit by returning to this material world could pass through the degrees, and attain to essential perfection, it would be better if God prolonged the life of the spirit in the material world, until it had acquired perfections and graces; it then would not be necessary for it to taste of the cup of death, or to acquire a second life.

The idea that existence is restricted to this perishable world, and the denial of the existence of divine worlds, originally proceeded from the imaginations of certain believers in reincarnation; but the divine worlds are infinite. If the divine worlds culminated in this material world, creation would be futile: nay, existence would be pure child's play. The result of these endless beings, which is the noble existence of man, would come and go for a few days in the perishable dwelling, and after receiving punishments and rewards, at last all would become perfect. The divine creation and the infinite existing beings would be perfected and completed, and then the Divinity of the Lord, and the names and qualities of God, on behalf of these spiritual beings, would, as regards their effect, result in laziness and inaction! 'Glory to thy Lord, the Lord who is sanctified from all their descriptions.'

Such were the limited minds of the former philosophers, like Ptolemy and the others who believed and imagined that the world, life, and existence, were restricted to this terrestrial globe, and that this boundless space was confined within the nine spheres of heaven, and that all were empty and void. Consider how greatly their thoughts were limited and how weak their minds. Those who believe in reincarnation think that the spiritual worlds are restricted to the worlds of human imagination...What an ignorant supposition! For, in this universe of God, which appears in the most complete perfection, beauty, and grandeur, the luminous stars of the material universe are innumerable! Then we must reflect how limitless and infinite are the spiritual worlds, which are the essential foundations...

'Abdu'l-Bahá

22
SELF

Let your vision be world-embracing, rather than confined to your own self.

Bahá'u'lláh

KNOW THYSELF

Could ye apprehend with what wonders of My munificence and bounty I have willed to entrust your souls, ye would, of a truth, rid yourselves of attachment to all created things, and would gain a true knowledge of your own selves-a knowledge which is the same as the comprehension of Mine own Being.

Bahá'u'lláh

THE PRISON OF SELF

Deliver your souls, O people, from the bondage of self...

Bahá'u'lláh

Free thyself from the fetters of this world, and loose thy soul from the prison of self. Seize thy chance, for it will come to thee no more.

Bahá'u'lláh

Arise, O people, and, by the power of God's might, resolve to gain the victory over your own selves, that haply the whole earth may be freed and sanctified from its servitude to the gods of its idle fancies-gods that have inflicted such loss upon, and are responsible for the misery of, their wretched worshipers.

Bahá'u'lláh

Behold, all the people are imprisoned within the tomb of self, and lie buried beneath the nethermost depths of worldly desire! Wert thou to attain to but a dewdrop of the crystal waters of divine knowledge, thou wouldst readily realize that true life is not the life of the flesh but the life of the spirit. For the life of the flesh is common to both men and animals, whereas the life of the spirit is possessed only by the pure in heart who have quaffed from the ocean of faith and partaken of the fruit of certitude. This life knoweth no death, and this existence is crowned by immortality.

Bahá'u'lláh

HUMBLENESS

Know ye not why We created you all from the same dust? That no one should exalt himself over the other. Ponder at all times in your hearts how ye were created. Since We have created you all from one same substance it is incumbent on you to be even as one soul, to walk with the same feet, eat with the same mouth and dwell in the same land, that from your inmost being, by your deeds and actions, the signs of oneness and the essence of detachment may be made manifest. Such is My counsel to you, O concourse of light! Heed ye this counsel that ye may obtain the fruit of holiness from the tree of wondrous glory.

Bahá'u'lláh

...man should know his own self and recognize that which leadeth unto loftiness or lowliness, glory or abasement, wealth or poverty.

Bahá'u'lláh

OVERLOOKING THE FAULTS OF OTHERS

The tongue I have designed for the mention of Me, defile it not with detraction. If the fire of self overcome you, remember your own faults and not the faults of My creatures, inasmuch as every one of you knoweth his own self better than he knoweth others.

Bahá'u'lláh

Breathe not the sins of others so long as thou art thyself a sinner. Shouldst thou transgress this command, accursed wouldst thou be, and to this I bear witness.

Bahá'u'lláh

Thine eye is My trust, suffer not the dust of vain desires to becloud its luster. Thine ear is a sign of My bounty, let not the tumult of unseemly motives turn it away from My Word that encompasseth all creation. Thine heart is My treasury, allow not the treacherous hand of self to rob thee of the pearls which I have treasured therein. Thine hand is a symbol of My loving-kindness, hinder it not from holding fast unto My guarded and hidden Tablets...Be as resigned and submissive as the earth, that from the soil of your being there may blossom the fragrant, the holy and multicolored hyacinths of My knowledge. Be ablaze as the fire, that ye may burn away the veils of heedlessness and set aglow, through the quickening energies of the love of God, the chilled and wayward heart. Be light and untrammeled as the breeze, that ye may obtain admittance into the precincts of My court, My inviolable Sanctuary.

Bahá'u'lláh

HE WHO OVERCOMES EGOTISM WILL BE SUPPORTED BY THE GOD

Whensoever ye behold a person whose entire attention is directed toward the Cause of God; whose only aim is this, to make the Word of God to take effect; who, day and night, with pure intent, is rendering service to the Cause; from whose behaviour not the slightest trace of egotism or private motives is discerned-who rather, wandereth distracted in the wilderness of the love of God, and drinketh only from the cup of the knowledge of God, and is utterly engrossed in spreading the sweet savours of God, and is enamoured of the holy verses of the Kingdom of God-know ye for a certainty that this individual will be supported and reinforced by heaven; that like unto the morning star, he will forever gleam brightly out of the skies of eternal grace. But if he show the slightest taint of selfish desires and self love, his efforts will lead to nothing...

'Abdu'l-Bahá

23
DEEDS & ACTIONS

VIRTUOUS ACTS THE ADORNMENT OF THE PEOPLE OF BAHÁ

Adorn yourselves with the raiment of goodly deeds. He whose deeds attain unto God's good pleasure is assuredly of the people of Bahá and is remembered before His throne. Assist ye the Lord of all creation with works of righteousness, and also through wisdom and utterance.

Bahá'u'lláh

GUIDANCE BY DEEDS

Guidance hath ever been given by words, and now it is given by deeds. Every one must show forth deeds that are pure and holy, for words are the property of all alike, whereas such deeds as these belong only to Our loved ones. Strive then with heart and soul to distinguish yourselves by your deeds. In this wise We counsel you in this holy and resplendent tablet.

Bahá'u'lláh

...advance into the vast immensity of the realm of God, and abide ye in the meads of sanctity and of detachment, that the fragrance of your deeds may lead the whole of mankind to the ocean of God's unfading glory.

Bahá'u'lláh

TURN TOWARDS YOUR NEIGHBOR

Forget your own selves, and turn your eyes towards your neighbor. Bend your energies to whatever may foster the education of men. Nothing is, or can ever be, hidden from God. If ye follow in His way, His incalculable and imperishable blessings will be showered upon you.

Bahá'u'lláh

Be fair to yourselves and to others, that the evidences of justice may be revealed, through your deeds, among Our faithful servants. Beware lest ye encroach upon the substance of your neighbor. Prove yourselves worthy of his trust and confidence in you, and withhold not from the poor the gifts which the grace of God hath bestowed upon you. He, verily, shall recompense the charitable, and doubly repay them for what they have bestowed. No God is there but Him. All creation and its empire are His. He bestoweth His gifts on whom He will, and from whom He will He withholdeth them. He is the Great Giver, the Most Generous, the benevolent.

Let truthfulness and courtesy be your adorning. Suffer not yourselves to be deprived of the robe of forbearance and justice, that the sweet savors of holiness may be wafted from your hearts upon all created things. Say: Beware, O people of Bahá, lest ye walk in the ways of them whose words differ from their deeds. Strive that ye may be enabled to manifest to the peoples of the earth the signs of God, and to mirror forth His commandments. Let your acts be a guide unto all mankind, for the professions of most men, be they high or low, differ from their conduct. It is through your deeds that ye can distinguish yourselves from others. Through them the brightness of your light can be shed upon the whole earth. Happy is the man that heedeth My counsel.

Bahá'u'lláh

CHARITY A PRINCE AMONG DEEDS

Charity is pleasing and praiseworthy in the sight of God and is regarded as a prince among goodly deeds.

Bahá'u'lláh

Today there is no result or fruit greater than guiding the people. Undoubtedly the friends of God, upon such a day, must leave tangible philanthropic or ideal traces that should reach all mankind and not pertain only to the Bahá'ís. In this wonderful dispensation, philanthropic affairs are for all humanity without exception, because it is the manifestation of the mercifulness of God. Therefore, my hope is that the friends of God, every one of them, may become as the mercy of God to all mankind.

'Abdu'l-Bahá

AVOIDANCE OF HYPOCRISY & EGOTISM

Holy words and pure and goodly deeds ascend unto the heaven of celestial glory. Strive that your deeds may be cleansed from the dust of self and hypocrisy and find favour at the court of glory; for erelong the assayers of mankind shall, in the holy presence of the Adored One, accept naught but absolute virtue and deeds of stainless purity. This is the day-star of wisdom and of divine mystery that hath shone above the horizon of the divine will. Blessed are they that turn thereunto.

Bahá'u'lláh

Praise be to God that whatever is essential for the believers in this Revelation to be told has been revealed. Their duties have been clearly defined, and the deeds they are expected to perform have been plainly set forth in Our Book. Now is the time for them to arise and fulfil their duty. Let them translate into deeds the exhortations We have given them. Let them beware lest the love they bear God, a love that glows so brightly in their hearts, cause them to transgress the bounds of moderation, and to overstep the limits We have set for them.

Bahá'u'lláh

24
TRIALS & DIFFICULTIES

GRIEVE NOT

Should prosperity befall thee, rejoice not, and should abasement come upon thee, grieve not, for both shall pass away and be no more.

Bahá'u'lláh

Lament not in your hours of trial, neither rejoice therein; seek ye the Middle Way which is the remembrance of Me in your afflictions and reflection over that which may befall you in the future.

Bahá'u'lláh

FEAR NOT

If poverty overtake thee, be not sad; for in time the Lord of wealth shall visit thee. Fear not abasement, for glory shall one day rest on thee.

Bahá'u'lláh

HAVE PATIENCE

For everything there is a sign. The sign of love is fortitude under My decree and patience under My trials.

Bahá'u'lláh

It is easy to approach the Kingdom of Heaven, but hard to stand firm and staunch with it, for the tests are rigorous, and heavy to bear.

'Abdu'l-Bahá

THROUGH TESTS WE LEARN AND GROW

Men who suffer not, attain no perfection. The plant most pruned by the gardeners is that one which, when the summer comes, will have the most beautiful blossoms and the most abundant fruit.

'Abdu'l-Bahá

Tribulation is a horizon unto My Revelation. The day star of grace shineth above it, and sheddeth a light which neither the clouds of men's idle fancy nor the vain imaginations of the aggressor can obscure.

Bahá'u'lláh

The mind and spirit of man advance when he is tried by suffering. The more the ground is ploughed the better the seed will grow, the better the harvest will be. Just as the plough furrows the earth deeply, purifying it of weeds and thistles, so suffering and tribulation free man from the petty affairs of this worldly life until he arrives at a state of complete detachment. His attitude in this world will be that of divine happiness. Man is, so to speak, unripe: the heat of the fire of suffering will mature him. Look back to the times past and you will find that the greatest men have suffered most.

'Abdu'l-Bahá

My calamity is My providence, outwardly it is fire and vengeance, but inwardly it is light and mercy. Hasten thereunto that thou mayest become an eternal light and an immortal spirit.

Bahá'u'lláh

25
MATERIALISM

TRUE HAPPINESS

Happy the days that have been consecrated to the remembrance of God, and blessed the hours which have been spent in praise of Him Who is the All-Wise. By My life! Neither the pomp of the mighty, nor the wealth of the rich, nor even the ascendancy of the ungodly will endure. All will perish, at a word from Him. He, verily, is the All-Powerful, the All-Compelling, the Almighty. What advantage is there in the earthly things which men possess? That which shall profit them, they have utterly neglected. Erelong, they will awake from their slumber, and find themselves unable to obtain that which hath escaped them in the days of their Lord, the Almighty, the All-Praised. Did they but know it, they would renounce their all, that their names may be mentioned before His throne. They, verily, are accounted among the dead.

Bahá'u'lláh

Be not content with the ease of a passing day, and deprive not thyself of everlasting rest. Barter not the garden of eternal delight for the dust-heap of a mortal world. Up from thy prison ascend unto the glorious meads above, and from thy mortal cage wing thy flight unto the paradise of the Placeless.

Bahá'u'lláh

Know ye from what heights your Lord, the All-Glorious, is calling? Think ye that ye have recognized the Pen wherewith your Lord, the Lord of all names, commandeth you? Nay, by My life! Did ye but know it, ye would renounce the world, and would hasten with your whole hearts to the presence of the Well-Beloved. Your spirits would be so transported by His Word as to throw into commotion the Greater World-how much more this small and petty one! Thus have the showers of My bounty been poured down from the heaven of My loving-kindness, as a token of My grace, that ye may be of the thankful.

Bahá'u'lláh

A VAIN & EMPTY SHOW

The world is but a show, vain and empty, a mere nothing, bearing the semblance of reality. Set not your affections upon it. Break not the bond that uniteth you with your Creator, and be not of those that have erred and strayed from His ways. Verily I say, the world is like the vapor in a desert, which the thirsty dreameth to be water and striveth after it with all his might, until when he cometh unto it, he findeth it to be mere illusion.

Bahá'u'lláh

Disencumber yourselves of all attachment to this world and the vanities thereof. Beware that ye approach them not, inasmuch as they prompt you to walk after your own lusts and covetous desires, and hinder you from entering the straight and glorious Path...

Whatsoever deterreth you, in this Day, from loving God is nothing but the world. Flee it, that ye may be numbered with the blest. Should a man wish to adorn himself with the ornaments of the earth, to wear its apparels, or partake of the benefits it can bestow, no harm can befall him, if he alloweth nothing whatever to intervene between him and God, for God hath ordained every good thing, whether created in the heavens or in the earth, for such of His servants as truly believe in Him. Eat ye, O people, of the good things which God hath allowed you, and deprive not yourselves from His wondrous bounties. Render thanks and praise unto Him, and be of them that are truly thankful.

Bahá'u'lláh

PRESERVING A LOFTY STATION

Suffer not your idle fancies, your evil passions, your insincerity and blindness of heart to dim the luster, or stain the sanctity, of so lofty a station. Ye are even as the bird which soareth, with the full force of its mighty wings and with complete and joyous confidence, through the immensity of the heavens, until, impelled to satisfy its hunger, it turneth longingly to the water and clay of the earth below it, and, having been entrapped in the mesh of its desire, findeth itself impotent to resume its flight to the realms whence it came. Powerless to shake off the burden weighing on its sullied wings, that bird, hitherto an inmate of the heavens, is now forced to seek a dwelling-place upon the dust. Wherefore, O My servants, defile not your wings with the clay of waywardness and vain desires, and suffer them not to be stained with the dust of envy and hate, that ye may not be hindered from soaring in the heavens of My divine knowledge.

Bahá'u'lláh

FLEETING WORLD

If ye be seekers after this life and the vanities thereof, ye should have sought them while ye were still enclosed in your mothers' wombs, for at that time ye were continually approaching them, could ye but perceive it. Ye have, on the other hand, ever since ye were born and attained maturity, been all the while receding from the world and drawing closer to dust. Why, then, exhibit such greed in amassing the treasures of the earth, when your days are numbered and your chance is well-nigh lost? Will ye not, then, O heedless ones, shake off your slumber?

Bahá'u'lláh

Rejoice not in the things ye possess; tonight they are yours, tomorrow others will possess them...Can ye claim that what ye own is lasting or secure?...The days of your life flee away as a breath of wind, and all your pomp and glory shall be folded up as were the pomp and glory of those gone before you...Neither the pomp of the mighty, nor the wealth of the rich, nor even the ascendancy of the ungodly will endure...Erelong, they will awake from their slumber, and find themselves unable to obtain that which hath escaped them in the days of their Lord, the Almighty, the All-Praised. Did they but know it, they would renounce their all, that their names may be mentioned before His throne.

Bahá'u'lláh

Abandon not for that which perisheth an everlasting dominion, and cast not away celestial sovereignty for a worldly desire. This is the river of everlasting life that hath flowed from the well-spring of the pen of the merciful; well is it with them that drink!

Bahá'u'lláh

If thine heart be set upon this eternal, imperishable dominion, and this ancient, everlasting life, forsake this mortal and fleeting sovereignty...Busy not thyself with this world, for with fire We test the gold, and with gold We test Our servants.

Bahá'u'lláh

Exultest thou over the treasures thou dost possess, knowing they shall perish? Rejoicest thou in that thou rulest a span of earth, when the whole world, in the estimation of the people of Bahá, is worth as much as the black in the eye of a dead ant? Abandon it unto such as have set their affections upon it, and turn thou unto Him Who is the Desire of the world. Whither are gone the proud and their palaces? Gaze thou into their tombs, that thou mayest profit by this example, inasmuch as We made it a lesson unto every beholder.

Bahá'u'lláh

Night hath succeeded day, and day hath succeeded night, and the hours and moments of your lives have come and gone, and yet none of you hath, for one instant, consented to detach himself from that which perisheth. Bestir yourselves, that the brief moments that are still yours may not be dissipated and lost. Even as the swiftness of lighting your days shall pass, and your bodies shall be laid to rest beneath a canopy of dust. What can ye then achieve? How can ye atone for your past failure?

Bahá'u'lláh

SANCTIFIED HEARTS

He hath chosen out of the whole world the hearts of His servants, and made them each a seat for the revelation of His glory. Wherefore, sanctify them from every defilement, that the things for which they were created may be engraven upon them. This indeed is a token of God's bountiful favor.

Bahá'u'lláh

Covetousness hath hindered you from giving a hearing ear unto the sweet voice of Him Who is the All-Sufficing. Wash it away from your hearts, that His Divine secret may be made known unto you. Behold Him manifest and resplendent as the sun in all its glory.

Bahá'u'lláh

Some men's lives are solely occupied with the things of this world; their minds are so circumscribed by exterior manners and traditional interests that they are blind to any other realm of existence, to the spiritual significance of all things! They think and dream of earthly fame, of material progress. Sensuous delights and comfortable surroundings bound their horizon, their highest ambitions centre in successes of worldly conditions and circumstances! They curb not their lower propensities; they eat, drink, and sleep! Like the animal, they have no thought beyond their own physical well-being. It is true that these necessities must be despatched. Life is a load which must be carried on while we are on earth, but the cares of the lower things of life should not be allowed to monopolize all the thoughts and aspirations of a human being. The heart's ambitions should ascend to a more glorious goal, mental activity should rise to higher levels! Men should hold in their souls the vision of celestial perfection, and there prepare a dwelling-place for the inexhaustible bounty of the Divine Spirit.

'Abdu'l-Bahá

THE DARKNESS OF A MATERIAL WORLD

Observe how darkness has overspread the world. In every corner of the earth there is strife, discord and warfare of some kind. Mankind is submerged in the sea of materialism and occupied with the affairs of this world. They have no thought beyond earthly possessions and manifest no desire save the passions of this fleeting, mortal existence. Their utmost purpose is the attainment of material livelihood, physical comforts and worldly enjoyments such as constitute the happiness of the animal world rather than the world of man.

...In fact, the animal's happiness is greater, for its wants are fewer and its means of livelihood easier to acquire. Although it is necessary for man to strive for material needs and comforts, his real need is the acquisition of the bounties of God.

'Abdu'l-Bahá

You see all round you proofs of the inadequacy of material things-how joy, comfort, peace and consolation are not to be found in the transitory things of the world. Is it not then foolishness to refuse to seek these treasures where they may be found? The doors of the spiritual Kingdom are open to all, and without is absolute darkness.

'Abdu'l-Bahá

In cities like New York the people are submerged in the sea of materialism. Their sensibilities are attuned to material forces, their perceptions purely physical.

'Abdu'l-Bahá

SPIRITUAL PROGRESS

It may be that man who has every material benefit, and who lives surrounded by all the greatest comfort modern civilization can give him, is denied the all important gift of the Holy Spirit.

It is indeed a good and praiseworthy thing to progress materially, but in so doing, let us not neglect the more important spiritual progress, and close our eyes to the Divine light shinning in our midst.

'Abdu'l-Bahá

Material or physical association is based upon earthly interests, but divine fellowship owes its existence to the breaths of the Holy Spirit. Spiritual brotherhood may be likened to the light, while the souls of humankind are as lanterns.

'Abdu'l-Bahá

The point is this: that to gain control over physical bodies is an extremely easy matter, but to bring spirits within the bonds of serenity is a most arduous undertaking.

'Abdu'l-Bahá

26
FAMILY

ALL FAMILY MEMBERS HAVE RIGHTS

According to the teachings of Bahá'u'lláh the family, being a human unit, must be educated according to the rules of sanctity. All the virtues must be taught the family. The integrity of the family bond must be constantly considered, and the rights of the individual members must not be transgressed. The rights of the son, the father, the mother-none of them must be transgressed, none of them must be arbitrary. Just as the son has certain obligations to his father, the father, likewise, has certain obligations to his son. The mother, the sister and other members of the household have their certain prerogatives. All these rights and prerogatives must be conserved, yet the unity of the family must be sustained. The injury of one shall be considered the injury of all; the comfort of each, the comfort of all; the honor of one, the honor of all.

'Abdu'l-Bahá

MARRIAGE IS A SPIRITUAL BOND

Among the people of Bahá, however, marriage must be a union of the body and of the spirit as well, for here both husband and wife are aglow with the same wine, both are enamoured of the same matchless Face, both live and move through the same spirit, both are illumined by the same glory. This connection between them is a spiritual one, hence it is a bond that will abide forever. Likewise do they enjoy strong and lasting ties in the physical world as well, for if the marriage is based both on the spirit and the body, that union is a true one, hence it will endure. If, however, the bond is physical and nothing more, it is sure to be only temporary, and must inexorably end in separation.

When, therefore, the people of Bahá undertake to marry, the union must be a true relationship, a spiritual coming together as well as a physical one, so that throughout every phase of life, and in all the worlds of God, their union will endure; for this real oneness is a gleaming out of the love of God.

In the same way, when any souls grow to be true believers, they will attain a spiritual relationship with one another, and show forth a tenderness which is not of this world. They will, all of them, become elated from a draught of divine love, and that union of theirs, that connection, will also abide forever. Souls, that is, who will consign their own selves to oblivion, strip from themselves the defects of humankind, and unchain themselves from human bondage, will beyond any doubt be illumined with the heavenly splendours of oneness, and will all attain unto real union.

'Abdu'l-Bahá

INDIVIDUAL CHOICE & PARENTAL CONSENT

As for the question regarding marriage under the Law of God; first thou must choose one who is pleasing to thee, and then the matter is subject to the consent of father and mother. Before thou makest thy choice, they have no right to interfere.

'Abdu'l-Bahá

BECOME ACQUAINTED WITH THE CHARACTER OF THE OTHER

Bahá'í marriage is the commitment of the two parties one to the other, and their mutual attachment of mind and heart. Each must, however, exercise the utmost care to become thoroughly acquainted with the character of the other, that the binding covenant between them may be a tie that will endure forever. Their purpose must be this: to become loving companions and comrades and at one with each other for time and eternity...

The true marriage of Bahá'ís is this, that husband and wife should be united both physically and spiritually, that they may ever improve the spiritual life of each other, and may enjoy everlasting unity throughout all the worlds of God. This is Bahá'í marriage.

'Abdu'l-Bahá

27
CHILD DEVELOPMENT

AGE DOESN'T GUARANTEE DEVELOPMENT

How many an aged person is ignorant and confused! For growth and development depend on one's powers of intellect and reason, not on one's age or length of days.

'Abdu'l-Bahá

CHARACTER TRAINING MUST BEGIN WELL BEFORE PUBERTY

The root cause of wrongdoing is ignorance, and we must therefore hold fast to the tools of perception and knowledge. Good character must be taught. Light must be spread afar, so that, in the school of humanity, all may acquire the heavenly characteristics of the spirit, and see for themselves beyond any doubt that there is no fiercer hell, no more fiery abyss, than to possess a character that is evil and unsound; no more darksome pit nor loathsome torment than to show forth qualities which deserve to be condemned.

The individual must be educated to such a high degree that he would rather have his throat cut than tell a lie, and would think it easier to be slashed with a sword or pierced with a spear than to utter calumny or be carried away by wrath...

It is extremely difficult to teach the individual and refine his character once puberty is passed. By then, as experience hath shown, even if every effort be exerted to modify some tendency of his, it all availeth nothing. He may, perhaps, improve somewhat today; but let a few days pass and he forgetteth, and turneth backward to his habitual condition and accustomed ways. Therefore it is in early childhood that a firm foundation must be laid. While the branch is green and tender it can easily be made straight.

'Abdu'l-Bahá

THE PARAMOUNT ROLE OF MOTHERS

O ye loving mothers, know ye that in God's sight, the best of all ways to worship Him is to educate the children and train them in all the perfections of humankind; and no nobler deed than this can be imagined.

'Abdu'l-Bahá

So long as the mother faileth to train her children, and start them on a proper way of life, the training which they receive later will not take its full effect.

'Abdu'l-Bahá

Every child is potentially the light of the world-and at the same time its darkness; wherefore must the question of education be accounted as of primary importance. From his infancy, the child must be nursed at the breast of God's love, and nurtured in the embrace of His knowledge, that he may radiate light, grow in spirituality, be filled with wisdom and learning, and take on the characteristics of the angelic host.

'Abdu'l-Bahá

Let the mothers consider that whatever concerneth the education of children is of the first importance. Let them put forth every effort in this regard, for when the bough is green and tender it will grow in whatever way ye train it. Therefore it is incumbent upon the mothers to rear their little ones even as a gardener tendeth his young plants. Let them strive by day and by night to establish within their children faith...and all good qualities and traits. Whensoever a mother seeth that her child hath done well, let her praise and applaud him and cheer his heart; and if the slightest undesirable trait should manifest itself, let her counsel the child and punish him, and use means based on reason, even a slight verbal chastisement should this be necessary. It is not, however, permissible to strike a child, or vilify him, for the child's character will be totally perverted if he be subjected to blows or verbal abuse.

'Abdu'l-Bahá

FROM WEAKNESS TO STRENGTH

Christ has addressed the world, saying, "Except ye be converted, and become as little children, ye shall not enter into the kingdom of heaven"- that is, men must become pure in heart to know God...The hearts of all children are the utmost purity. They are mirrors upon which no dust has fallen. But this purity is on account of weakness and innocence, not on account of any strength and testing...They have neither hypocrisy nor deceit. This is on account of the child's weakness, whereas the man becomes pure through his strength. Through the power of intelligence he becomes simple; through the great power of reason and understanding and not through the power of weakness he comes sincere. When he attains to the state of perfection, he will receive these qualities; his heart becomes purified, his spirit enlightened, his soul is sensitized and tender- all through his great strength. This is the difference between the perfect man and the child. Both have the underlying qualities of simplicity and sincerity-the child through the power of weakness and the man through the power of strength.

'Abdu'l-Bahá

BAHÁ'Í CHILD DEVELOPMENT

For the inner reality of man is a demarcation line between the shadow and the light, a place where the two seas meet...With education it can achieve all excellence; devoid of education it will stay on, at the lowest point of imperfection.

While the children are yet in their infancy feed them from the breast of heavenly grace, foster them in the cradle of all excellence, rear them in the embrace of bounty. Give them the advantage of every useful kind of knowledge. Let them share in every new and rare and wondrous craft and art. Bring them up to work and strive, and accustom them to hardship. Teach them to dedicate their lives to matters of great import, and inspire them to undertake studies that will benefit mankind.

'Abdu'l-Bahá

Bahá'í is not just a name but a truth. Every child must be trained in the things of the spirit, so that he may embody all the virtues and become a source of glory to the Cause of God. Otherwise, the mere word Bahá'í, if it yield no fruit, will come to nothing.

Strive then to the best of thine ability to let these children know that a Bahá'í is one who embodieth all the perfections, that he must shine out like a lighted taper-not be darkness upon darkness and yet bear the name Bahá'í.

'Abdu'l-Bahá

28
EDUCATION

THE FUNCTION OF EDUCATION

Education makes the ignorant wise, the tyrant just, promotes happiness, strengthens the mind, develops the will and makes fruitless trees of humanity fruitful.

'Abdu'l-Bahá

Man is the supreme Talisman. Lack of a proper education hath, however, deprived him of that which he doth inherently possess...Regard man as a mine rich in gems of inestimable value. Education can, alone, cause it to reveal its treasures, and enable mankind to benefit therefrom...If the learned and worldly-wise men of this age were to allow mankind to inhale the fragrance of fellowship and love, every understanding heart would apprehend the meaning of true liberty, and discover the secret of undistrubed peace and absolute composure.

Bahá'u'lláh

Man undeveloped by education is savage, animalistic, brutal. Laws and regulations, schools, colleges and universities have for their purpose the training of man and his uplift from the dark borderland of the animal kingdom.

'Abdu'l-Bahá

BAHÁ'Í EDUCATION

There are certain pillars which have been established as the unshakeable supports of the Faith of God. The mightiest of these is learning and the use of the mind, the expansion of consciousness, and insight into the realities of the universe and the hidden mysteries of Almighty God.

To promote knowledge is thus an inescapable duty imposed on every one of the friends of God. It is incumbent upon that Spiritual Assembly, that assemblage of God, to exert every effort to educate the children, so that from infancy they will be trained in Bahá'í conduct and the ways of God, and will, even as young plants, thrive and flourish in the soft-flowing waters that are the counsels and admonitions of the Blessed Beauty [Bahá'u'lláh].

'Abdu'l-Bahá

O ye young Bahá'í children, ye seekers after true understanding and knowledge! A human being is distinguished from an animal in a number of ways. First of all, he is made in the image of God, in the likeness of the Supernal Light, even as the Torah saith, 'Let us make man in our image, after our likeness.' This divine image betokeneth all the qualities of perfection whose lights, emanating from the Sun of Truth, illumine the realities of men, and are among the perfect attributes that lie within wisdom and knowledge. Ye must therefore put forth a mighty effort, striving by night and day and resting not for a moment, to acquire an abundant share of all the sciences and arts, that the Divine Image, which shineth out from the Sun of Truth, may illumine the mirror of the hearts of men.

'Abdu'l-Bahá

The heart of 'Abdu'l-Bahá longeth, in its love, to find that Bahá'í young people, each and all, are known throughout the world for their intellectual attainments. There is no question but that they will exert all their efforts, their energies, their sense of pride, to acquire the sciences and arts.

'Abdu'l-Bahá

EDUCATING CHILDREN TO SERVE HUMANITY

At the outset of every endeavour, it is incumbent to look to the end of it. Of all the arts and sciences, set the children to studying those which will result in advantage to man, will ensure his progress and elevate his rank. Thus the noisome odours of lawlessness will be dispelled, and thus through the high endeavours of the nation's leaders, all will live cradled, secure and in peace.

...The learned of the day must direct the people to acquire those branches of knowledge which are of use, that both the learned themselves and the generality of mankind may derive benefits therefrom.

Bahá'u'lláh

THE SIGNIFICANCE OF EDUCATION AND TRAINING

The education and training of children is among the most meritorious acts of humankind and draweth down the grace and favour of the All-Merciful, for education is the indispensable foundation of all human excellence and alloweth man to work his way to the heights of abiding glory. If a child be trained from his infancy, he will...drink in the crystal waters of the spirit and of knowledge, like a young tree amid the rilling brooks. And certainly he will gather to himself the bright rays of the Sun of Truth, and through its light and heat will grow ever fresh and fair in the garden of life.

Therefore must the mentor be a doctor as well: that is, he must, in instructing the child, remedy its faults; must give him learning, and at the same time rear him to have a spiritual nature. Let the teacher be a doctor to the character of the child, thus will he heal the spiritual ailments of the children of men.

If, in this momentous task, a mighty effort be exerted, the world of humanity will shine out with other adornings, and shed the fairest light.

'Abdu'l-Bahá

Never, through training and cultivation, will the colocynth and the bitter tree change into the Tree of Blessedness. That is to say, education cannot alter the inner essence of a man, but it doth exert tremendous influence, and with this power it can bring forth from the individual whatever perfections and capacities are deposited with him. A grain of wheat, when cultivated by the farmer, will yield a whole harvest, and a seed, through the gardener's care, will grow into a great tree. Thanks to a teacher's loving efforts, the children of the primary school may reach the highest levels of achievement; indeed, his benefactions may lift some child of small account to an exalted throne. Thus is it clearly demonstrated that by their essential nature, minds vary as to their capacity, while education also playeth a great role and exerteth a powerful effect on their development.

'Abdu'l-Bahá

THE IMPORTANCE OF CHARACTER TRAINING

As to the organization of the schools: if possible the children should all wear the same kind of clothing, even if the fabric is varied. It is preferable that the fabric as well should be uniform; if, however, this is not possible, there is no harm done. The more cleanly the pupils are, the better; they should be immaculate. The school must be located in a place where the air is delicate and pure. The children must be carefully trained to be most courteous and well-behaved. They must be constantly encouraged and made eager to gain all the summits of human accomplishment, so that from their earliest years they will be taught to have high aims, to conduct themselves well, to be chaste, pure, and undefiled, and will learn to be of powerful resolve and firm of purpose in all things. Let them not jest and trifle, but earnestly advance unto their goals, so that in every situation they will be found resolute and firm.

Training in morals and good conduct is far more important than book learning. A child that is cleanly, agreeable, of good character, well-behaved-even though he be ignorant-is preferable to a child that is rude, unwashed, ill-natured, and yet becoming deeply versed in all the sciences and arts. The reason for this is that the child who conducts himself well, even though he be ignorant, is of benefit to others, while an ill-natured, ill-behaved child is corrupted and harmful to others, ever though he be learned. If, however, the child be trained to be both learned and good, the result is light upon light.

'Abdu'l-Bahá

SPEECH EDUCATION ENCOURAGED

Encourage ye the school children, from their earliest years, to deliver speeches of high quality, so that in their leisure time they will engage in giving cogent and effective talks, expressing themselves with clarity and eloquence.

'Abdu'l-Bahá

THE EDUCATION OF BOYS AND GIRLS IS OBLIGATORY

Unto every Father hath been enjoined the instruction of his son and daughter in the art of reading and writing and in all that hath been laid down in the Holy Tablet. He that putteth away that which is commanded unto him, the Trustees are then to take from him that which is required for their instruction if he be wealthy and, if not, the matter devolveth upon the House of Justice. Verily have We made it a shelter for the poor and needy. He that bringeth up his son or the son of another, it is as though he hath brought up a son of Mine; upon him rest My glory, My loving-kindness, My mercy, that have compassed the world.

Bahá'u'lláh

It is for this reason that, in this new cycle, education and training are recorded in the Book of God as obligatory and not voluntary. That is, it is enjoined upon the father and mother, as a duty, to strive with all effort to train the daughter and the son, to nurse them from the breast of knowledge and to rear them in the bosom of sciences and arts.

'Abdu'l-Bahá

Bahá'u'lláh has announced that inasmuch as ignorance and lack of education are barriers of separation among mankind, all must receive training and instruction. Through this provision the lack of mutual understanding will be remedied and the unity of mankind furthered and advanced. Universal education is a universal law. It is, therefore, incumbent upon every father to teach and instruct his children according to his possibilities. If he is unable to educate them, the body politic, the representative of the people, must provide the means for their education.

'Abdu'l-Bahá

Everyone, whether man or woman, should hand over to a trusted person a portion of what he or she earneth through trade, agriculture or other occupation, for the training and education of children, to be spent for this purpose with the knowledge of the Trustees of the House of Justice.

Bahá'u'lláh

Should the father fail in his duty he must be compelled to discharge his responsibility, and should he be unable to comply, let the House of Justice take over the education of the children. This is one of the stringent and inescapable commandments to neglect which would draw down the wrathful indignation of Almighty God.

'Abdu'l-Bahá

THE STATURE OF MEN AND WOMEN OF LEARNING

O people of God! Righteous men of learning who dedicate themselves to the guidance of others and are freed and well guarded from the promtings of a base and covetous nature are, in the sight of Him Who is the Desire of the world, stars of the heaven of true knowledge. It is essential to treat them with deference.

Bahá'u'lláh

...Socrates who was indeed wise, accomplished and righteous. He practised self-denial, repressed his appetites for selfish desires and turned away from material pleasures. He withdrew to the mountains where he dwelt in a cave. He dissuaded men from worshipping idols and taught them the way of God, the Lord of Mercy, until the ignorant rose up against him. They arrested him and put him to death in prison. Thus relateth to thee this swift-moving Pen. What a penetrating vision into philosophy this eminent man had! He is the most distinguished of all philosophers and was highly versed in wisdom. We testify that he is one of the heroes in this field and an outstanding champion dedicated unto it. He had a profound knowledge of such sciences as were current amongst men as well as of those which were veiled from their minds. Methinks he drank one draught when the Most Great Ocean overflowed with gleaming and life-giving waters. He it is who perceived a unique, a tempered, and a pervasive nature in things, bearing the closest likeness to the human spirit, and he discovered this nature to be distinct from the substance of things in their refined form...

...A true philosopher would never deny God nor His evidences, rather would he acknowledge His glory and overpowering majesty which overshadow all created things. Verily We love those men of knowledge who have brought to light such things as promote the best interests of humanity, and We aided them through the potency of Our behest, for well are We able to achieve Our purpose.

Bahá'u'lláh

29
SCIENCE

THE ACQUISITION OF SCIENCE IS CONSIDERED WORSHIP

...in accordance with the divine teachings the acquisition of sciences and the perfection of arts are considered acts of worship. If a man engageth with all his power in the acquisition of sciences or in the perfection of an art, it is as if he has been worshipping God in churches and temples...What bounty greater than this that science should be considered as an act of worship and art as service to the Kingdom of God.

'Abdu'l-Bahá

NO CONTRADICTION BETWEEN TRUE RELIGION AND SCIENCE

If we say religion is opposed to science, we lack knowledge of either true science or true religion, for both are founded upon the premises and conclusions of reason, and both must bear its test.

'Abdu'l-Bahá

There is no contradiction between true religion and science. When a religion is opposed to science it becomes mere superstition: that which is contrary to knowledge is ignorance.

How can a man believe to be a fact that which science has proved to be impossible? If he believes in spite of his reason, it is rather ignorant superstition than faith...

Now, all questions of morality contained in the spiritual, immutable law of every religion are logically right. If religion were contrary to logical reason then it would cease to be a religion and be merely a tradition. Religion and science are the two wings upon which the human soul can progress. It is not possible to fly with one wing alone! Should a man try to fly with the wing of religion alone he would quickly fall into the quagmire of superstition, whilst on the other hand, with the wing of science alone he would also make no progress, but fall into the despairing slough of materialism. All religions of the present day have fallen into superstitious practices, out of harmony alike with the true principles of the teaching they represent and with the scientific discoveries of the time. Many religious leaders have grown to think that the importance of religion lies mainly in the adherence to a collection of certain dogmas and the practice of rites and ceremonies! Those whose souls they profess to cure are taught to believe likewise, and these cling tenaciously to the outward forms, confusing them with the inward truth.

Now, these forms and rituals differ in the various churches and amongst the different sects, and even contradict one another; giving rise to discord, hatred, and disunion. The outcome of all this dissension is the belief of many cultured men that religion and science are contradictory terms, that religion needs no powers of reflection, and should in no wise be regulated by science, but must of necessity be opposed, the one to the other. The unfortunate effect of this is that science has drifted apart from religion, and religion has become a mere blind and more or less apathetic following of the precepts of certain religious teachers, who insist on their own favourite dogmas being accepted even when they are contrary to science. This is foolishness, for it is quite evident that science is the light, and being so, religion truly so-called does not oppose knowledge.

'Abdu'l-Bahá

RELIGION MUST STAND THE TEST OF REASON

Religion must stand the analysis of reason. It must agree with scientific fact and proof so that science will sanction religion and religion fortify science. Both are indissolubly welded and joined in reality. If statements and teachings of religion are found to be unreasonable and contrary to science, they are outcomes of superstition and imagination.

'Abdu'l-Bahá

Every religion which is not in accordance with established science is superstition. Religion must be reasonable. If it does not square with reason, it is superstition and without foundation. It is like a mirage, which deceives man by leading him to think it is a body of water. God has endowed man with reason that he may perceive what is true.

'Abdu'l-Bahá

THE SPIRITUAL ASPECT OF RELIGION IS IN ACCORDANCE WITH SCIENCE

The true principles of all religions are in conformity with the teachings of science.

The Unity of God is logical, and this idea is not antagonistic to the conclusions arrived at by scientific study.

All religions teach that we must do good, that we must be generous, sincere, truthful, law-abiding, and faithful; all this is reasonable, and logically the only way in which humanity can progress.

All religious laws conform to reason, and are suited to the people for whom they are framed, and for the age in which they are to be obeyed. Religion has two main parts:
1. The Spiritual.
2. The Practical.

The spiritual part never changes. All the Manifestations of God and His Prophets have taught the same truths and given the same spiritual law. They all teach the one code of morality. There is no division in the truth. The Sun has sent forth many rays to illumine human intelligence, the light is always the same.

The practical part of religion deals with exterior forms and ceremonies, and with modes of punishment for certain offences. This is the material side of the law, and guides the customs and manners of the people...

It is therefore evident that whilst the spiritual law never alters, the practical rules must change their application with the necessities of the time. The spiritual aspect of religion is the greater, and more important of the two, and this is the same for all time, it never changes! It is the same, yesterday, today, and for ever!

'Abdu'l-Bahá

WING'S TO MAN'S LIFE

Arts, crafts and sciences uplift the world of being, and are conducive to its exaltation. Knowledge is as wings to man's life, and a ladder for his ascent. Its acquisition is incumbent upon everyone. The knowledge of such sciences, however, should be acquired as can profit the peoples of the earth, and not those which begin with words and end with words. Great indeed is the claim of scientists and craftsmen on the peoples of the world...In truth, knowledge is a veritable treasure for man, and a source of glory, of bounty, of joy, of exaltation, of cheer and gladness unto him.

Bahá'u'lláh

Before long, material science and learning, as well as the knowledge of God, will make such progress, and will show forth such wonders, that the beholders will be amazed. Then the mystery of this verse in Isaiah, 'For the earth shall be full of the knowledge of the Lord,' will be completely evident.

'Abdu'l-Bahá

Happy are those who spend their days in gaining knowledge, in discovering the secrets of nature, and in penetrating the subtleties of pure truth! Woe to those who are contented with ignorance, whose hearts are gladdened by thoughtless imitation, who have fallen into the lowest depths of ignorance and foolishness, and who have wasted their lives!

'Abdu'l-Bahá

THE NOBLEST VIRTUE OF ALL

The highest praise is due to men who devote their energies to science, and the noblest center is a center wherein the sciences and arts are taught and studied.

'Abdu'l-Bahá

Although to acquire the sciences and arts is the greatest glory of mankind, this is so only on condition that man's river flow into the mighty sea, and draw from God's ancient source His inspiration. When this cometh to pass, then every teacher is as a shoreless ocean, every pupil a prodigal fountain of knowledge.

'Abdu'l-Bahá

The virtues of humanity are many, but science is the most noble of them all. The distinction which man enjoys above and beyond the station of the animal is due to this paramount virtue. It is a bestowal of God; it is not material; it is divine. Science is an effulgence of the Sun of Reality, the power of investigating and discovering the verities of the universe, the means by which man finds a pathway to God. All the powers and attributes of man are human and hereditary in origin-outcomes of nature's processes-except the intellect, which is supernatural. Through intellectual and intelligent inquiry science is the discoverer of all things.

It unites present and past, reveals the history of bygone nations and events, and confers upon man today the essence of all human knowledge and attainment throughout the ages. By intellectual processes and logical deductions of reason this superpower in man can penetrate the mysteries of the future and anticipate its happenings.

Science is the first emanation from God toward man. All created beings embody the potentiality of material perfection, but the power of intellectual investigation and scientific acquisition is a higher virtue specialized to man alone...The development and progress of a nation is according to the measure and degree of that nation's scientific attainments. Through this means its greatness is continually increased, and day by day the welfare and prosperity of its people are assured.

'Abdu'l-Bahá

THE MIRROR OF REALITY

Science may be likened to a mirror wherein the images of the mysteries of outer phenomena are reflected. It brings forth and exhibits to us in the arena of knowledge all the product of the past. It links together past and present. The philosophical conclusions of bygone centuries, the teaching of the Prophets and wisdom of former sages are crystallized and reproduced in the scientific advancement of today. Science is the discoverer of the past. From its premises of past and present we deduce conclusions as to the future. Science is the governor of nature and its mysteries, the one agency by which man explores the institutions of material creation.

...God has conferred upon and added to man a distinctive power-the faculty of intellectual investigation into the secrets of creation, the acquisition of higher knowledge-the greatest virtue of which is scientific enlightenment.

'Abdu'l-Bahá

30
PREJUDICE

THE BREEDING-GROUND OF TRAGEDY

For a period of 6,000 years history informs us about the world of humanity. During these 6,000 years the world of humanity has not been free from war, strife, murder and bloodthirstiness. In every period war has been waged in one country or another and that war was due to either religious prejudice, racial prejudice, political prejudice or patriotic prejudice. It has therefore been ascertained and proved that all prejudices are destructive of human edifice. As long as these prejudices persist, the struggle for existence must remain dominant, and bloodthirstiness and rapacity continue. Therefore, even as was the case in the past, the world of humanity cannot attain illumination except through the abandonment of prejudices and the acquisition of the morals of the Kingdom.

'Abdu'l-Bahá

Ye observe how the world is divided against itself, how many a land is red with blood and its very dust is caked with human gore. The fires of conflict have blazed so high that never in early times, not in the Middle Ages, not in recent centuries hath there ever been such a hideous war, a war that is even as millstones, taking for grain the skulls of men. Nay, even worse, for flourishing countries have been reduced to rubble, cities have been levelled with the ground, and many a once prosperous village hath been turned into ruin. Fathers have lost their sons, and sons their fathers. Mothers have wept away their hearts over dead children. Children have been orphaned, women left to wander, vagrants without a home. From every aspect, humankind hath sunken low. Loud are the piercing cries of fatherless children; loud the mother's anguished voices, reaching to the skies.

And the breeding-ground of all these tragedies is prejudice: prejudice of race and nation, of religion, of political opinion; and the root cause of prejudice is blind imitation of the past-imitation in religion, in racial attitudes, in national bias, in politics. So long as this aping of the past persisteth, just so long will the foundations of the social order be blown to the four winds, just so long will humanity be continually exposed to direct peril.

'Abdu'l-Bahá

DISTINCTIONS AND BOUNDARIES RESULT FROM HUMAN IGNORANCE

The surface of the earth is one home; humanity is one family and household. Distinctions and boundaries are artificial, human.

'Abdu'l-Bahá

Man declares a river to be a boundary line between two countries, calling this side French and the other side German, whereas the river was created for both and is a natural artery for all. Is it not imagination and ignorance which impels man to violate the divine intention and make the very bounties of God the cause of war, bloodshed and destruction?...Enmity is human disobedience; God Himself is love.

'Abdu'l-Bahá

Prejudice of all kinds-whether religious, racial, patriotic or political-are destructive of divine foundations in man. All the warfare and bloodshed in human history have been the outcome of prejudice...the earth's surface is one wide native land or home for all races of humankind. Racial prejudice or separation into nations such as French, German, American and so on is unnatural and proceeds from human motive and ignorance.

'Abdu'l-Bahá

RACE IS UNIMPORTANT

Therefore, be it known that color or race is of no importance. He who is the image and likeness of God, who is the manifestation of the bestowals of God, is acceptable at the threshold of God-whether his color be white, black or brown; it matters not. Man is not man simply because of bodily attributes. The standard of divine measure and judgement is his intelligence and spirit.

Therefore, let this be the only criterion and estimate, for this is the image and likeness of God. A man's heart may be pure and white though his outer skin be black; or his heart be dark and sinful though his racial color is white. The character and purity of the heart is of all importance. The heart illumined by the light of God is nearest and dearest to God, and inasmuch as God has endowed man with such favor that he is called the image of God, this is truly a supreme perfection of attainment, a divine station which is not to be sacrificed by the mere accident of color.

'Abdu'l-Bahá

God maketh no distinction between white and black. If the hearts are pure both are acceptable unto Him. God is no respecter of persons on account of either color or race.

'Abdu'l-Bahá

In the clustered jewels of the races may the blacks be as sapphires and rubies and the whites as diamonds and pearls. The composite beauty of humanity will be witnessed in their unity and blending. How glorious the spectacle of real unity among mankind! How conductive to peace, confidence and happiness if races and nations were united in fellowship and accord!

In physical bodies, in the law of growth, in sense endowment, intelligence, patriotism, language, citizenship, civilization and religion you are one and the same. A single point of distinction exists-that of racial color. God is not pleased with-neither should any reasonable or intelligent man be willing to recognize-inequality in the races because of this distinction.

But there is need of a superior power to overcome human prejudice, a power which nothing in the world of mankind can withstand and which will overshadow the effect of all other forces at work in the human conditions. That irresistible power is the love of God.

'Abdu'l-Bahá

REJECTING PREJUDICE

Do not listen to anything that is prejudiced, for self-interest prompts men to be prejudiced. They are thoughtful only of their own will and purposes. They live and move in darkness.

'Abdu'l-Bahá

Imitation destroys the foundation of religion, extinguishes the spirituality of the human world, transforms heavenly illumination into darkness and deprives man of the knowledge of God. It is the cause of the victory of materialism and infidelity over religion; it is the denial of Divinity and the law of revelation; it refuses Prophethood and rejects the Kingdom. When materialists subject imitations to the intellectual analysis of reason, they find them to be mere superstition; therefore, they deny religion...

Therefore, it is evident that the Prophets of God have come to unite the children of men and not to disperse them, to establish the law of love and not enmity. Consequently, we must lay aside all prejudice-whether it be religious, racial, political or patriotic; we must become the cause of the unification of the human race. Strive for universal peace, seek the means of love, and destroy the basis of disagreement so that this material world may become divine, the world of matter become the realm of the Kingdom and humanity attain to the world of perfection.

'Abdu'l-Bahá

31
THE EQUALITY OF WOMEN

WOMEN MUST BE TREATED WITH JUSTICE, EQUITY, KINDNESS AND LOVE

All should know, and in this regard attain the splendours of the sun of certitude, and be illumined thereby: Women and men have been and will always be equal in the sight of God. The Dawning Place of the Light of God sheddeth its radiance upon all with the same effulgence. Verily God created women for men, and men for women. The most beloved of people before God are the most steadfast and those who have surpassed others in their love for God, exalted be His glory.

The friends of God must be adorned with the ornament of justice, equity, kindness and love. As they do not allow themselves to be the object of cruelty and transgression, in like manner they should not allow such tyranny to visit the handmaidens of God. He, verily, speaketh the truth and commandeth that which benefitteth His servants and handmaidens. He is the Protector of all in this world and the next.

Bahá'u'lláh

GOD IS NEITHER MALE NOR FEMALE

To every discerning and illuminated heart it is evident that God, the unknowable Essence, the Divine Being, is immensely exalted beyond every human attribute, such as corporeal existence...

Bahá'u'lláh

"MAN" IN THE BAHÁ'Í WRITINGS GENERALLY REFERS TO MEN AND WOMEN COLLECTIVELY

Man is a generic term applying to all humanity...In Persian and Arabic there are two distinct words translated into English as man: one meaning

The Equality of Women

man and woman collectively, the other distinguishing man as male from the female. The first word and its pronoun are generic, collective; the other is restricted to the male.

'Abdu'l-Bahá

THE HAPPINESS OF THE WORLD IS DEPENDENT UPON THE EQUALITY OF WOMEN

To accept and observe a distinction which God has not intended in creation is ignorance and superstition. The fact which is to be considered, however, is that woman, having formerly been deprived, must now be allowed equal opportunities with man for education and training. There must be no difference in their education. Until the reality of equality between man and woman is fully established and attained, the highest social development of mankind is not possible. Even granted that woman is inferior to man in some degree of capacity or accomplishment, this or any other distinction would continue to be productive of discord and trouble. The only remedy is education, opportunity; for equality means equal qualification. In brief, the assumption of superiority by man will continue to be depressing to the ambition of woman, as if her attainment to equality was creationally impossible; woman's aspiration toward advancement will be checked by it, and she will gradually become hopeless. On the contrary, we must declare that her capacity is equal, even greater than man's. This will inspire her with hope and ambition, and her susceptibilities for advancement will continually increase. She must not be told and taught that she is weaker and inferior in capacity and qualification. If a pupil is told that his intelligence is less than his fellow pupils, it is a very great drawback and handicap to his progress. He must be encouraged to advance by the statement, "You are most capable, and if you endeavor, you will attain the highest degree."

It is my hope that the banner of equality may be raised throughout the five continents where as yet it is not fully recognized and established. In this enlightened world of the West woman has advanced an immeasurable degree beyond the women of the Orient. And let it be known once more that until woman and man recognize and realize equality, social and political progress here or anywhere will not be possible. For the world of humanity consists of two parts or members: one is woman; the other is man. Until these two members are equal in strength, the oneness of humanity cannot be established, and the happiness and felicity of mankind will not be a reality. God willing, this is to be so.

'Abdu'l-Bahá

WOMEN HAVE BEEN HINDERED BY LACK OF OPPORTUNITY

In this day man must investigate reality impartially and without prejudice in order to reach the true knowledge and conclusions. What, then, constitutes the inequality between man and woman? Both are human. In powers and function each is the complement of the other. At most it is this: that woman has been denied the opportunities which man has so long enjoyed, especially the privilege of education. But even this is not always a shortcoming. Shall we consider it an imperfection and not always a shortcoming. Shall we consider it an imperfection and weakness in her nature that she is not proficient in the school of military tactics, that she cannot go forth to the field of battle and kill, that she is not able to handle a deadly weapon? Nay, rather, is it not a compliment when we say that in hardness of heart and cruelty she is inferior to man? The woman who is asked to arm herself and kill her fellow creatures will say, "I cannot." Is this to be considered a fault and lack of qualification as man's equal? Yet be it known that if woman had been taught and trained in the military science of slaughter, she would have been the equivalent of man even in this accomplishment. But God forbid! May woman never attain this proficiency; may she never wield weapons of war, for the destruction of humanity is not a glorious achievement. The upbuilding of a home, the bringing of joy and comfort into human hearts are truly glories of mankind. Let not a man glory in this, that he can kill his fellow creatures; nay, rather, let him glory in this, that he can love them.

'Abdu'l-Bahá

In reality, God has created all mankind, and in the estimation of God there is no distinction as to male and female. The one whose heart is pure is acceptable in His sight, be that one man or woman...

...every influential undertaking of the human world wherein woman has been a participant has attained importance. This is historically true and beyond disproof even in religion. Jesus Christ had twelve disciples and among His followers a woman know as Mary Magdalene. Judas Iscariot had become a traitor and hypocrite, and after the crucifixion the remaining eleven disciples were wavering and undecided. It is certain from the evidence of the Gospels that the one who comforted them and reestablished their faith was Mary Magdalene.

The world of humanity consists of two parts: male and female. Each is the complement of the other. ... Just as physical accomplishment is complete with two hands, so man and woman, the two parts of the social body, must be perfect. It is not natural that either should remain undeveloped; and until both are perfected, the happiness of the human world will not be realized.

The most momentous question of this day is international peace and arbitration, and universal peace is impossible without universal suffrage....

It has been objected by some that woman is not equally capable with man and that she is deficient by creation. This is pure imagination. The difference in capability between man and woman is due entirely to opportunity and education. Heretofore woman has been denied the right and privilege of equal development. If equal opportunity be granted her, there is no doubt she would be the peer of man.

'Abdu'l-Bahá

THE IMPORTANCE OF EDUCATION

The status of woman in former times was exceedingly deplorable, for it was the belief of the Orient that it was best for woman to be ignorant. It was considered preferable that she should not know reading or writing in order that she might not be informed of events in the world. Woman was considered to be created for rearing children and attending to the duties of the household. If she pursued educational courses, it was deemed contrary to chastity; hence women were made prisoners of the household. The houses did not even have windows opening upon the outside world. Bahá'u'lláh destroyed these ideas and proclaimed the equality of man and woman. He made woman respected by commanding that all women be educated, that there be no difference in the education of the two sexes and that man and woman share the same rights. In the estimation of God there is no distinction of sex. One whose thought is pure, whose education is superior, whose scientific attainments are greater, whose deeds of philanthropy excel, be that one man or woman, white or colored, is entitled to full rights and recognition; there is no differentiation whatsoever.

'Abdu'l-Bahá

Women must especially devote her energies and abilities toward the industrial and agricultural sciences, seeking to assist mankind in that which is most needful. By this means she will demonstrate capability and ensure recognition of equality in the social and economic equation...

In this day there are women among the Bahá'ís who far outshine men. They are wise, talented, well-informed, progressive, most intelligent and the light of men. They surpass men in courage. When they speak in meetings, the men listen with great respect. Furthermore, the education of women is of greater importance than the education of men, for they are the mother of the race, and mothers rear the children.

'Abdu'l-Bahá

WOMEN ARE VITAL TO WORLD PEACE

In past ages humanity has been defective and inefficient because it has been incomplete. War and its ravages have blighted the world; the education of woman will be a mighty step toward its abolition and ending, for she will use her whole influence against war. Woman rears the child and educates the youth to maturity. She will refuse to give her sons for sacrifice upon the field of battle. In truth, she will be the greatest factor in establishing universal peace and international arbitration. Assuredly, woman will abolish warfare among mankind. Inasmuch as human society consists of two parts, the male and female, each the complement of the other, the happiness and stability of humanity cannot be assured unless both are perfected. Therefore, the standard and status of man and woman must become equalized.

'Abdu'l-Bahá

Therefore, strive to show in the human world that women are most capable and efficient, that their hearts are more tender and susceptible than the hearts of men, that they are more philanthropic and responsive toward the needy and suffering, that they are inflexibly opposed to war and are lovers of peace. Strive that the ideal of international peace may become realized through the efforts of womankind, for man is more inclined to war than woman, and a real evidence of woman's superiority will be her service and efficiency in the establishment of universal peace.

'Abdu'l-Bahá

32
WORK AND OCCUPATION

WORK SHOULD CONTRIBUTE TO THE QUALITY OF LIFE

Our purpose is that all men may cleave unto that which will reduce unnecessary labor and exertion, so that their days may be befittingly spent and ended.

Bahá'u'lláh

To engage in some profession is highly commendable, for when occupied with work one is less likely to dwell on the unpleasant aspects of life. God willing thou mayest experience joy and radiance, gladness and exultation in any city or land where thou mayest happen to sojourn.

Bahá'u'lláh

WORK DONE IN THE SPIRIT OF SERVICE IS ELEVATED TO THE STATUS OF WORSHIP

It is enjoined upon every one of you to engage in some form of occupation, such as crafts, trades and the like. We have graciously exalted your engagement in such work to the rank of worship unto God, the True One. Ponder ye in your hearts the grace and the blessings of God and render thanks unto Him at eventide and at dawn. Waste not your time in idleness and sloth. Occupy yourselves with that which profiteth yourselves and others. Thus hath it been decreed in this Tablet from whose horizon the day-star of wisdom and utterance shineth resplendent.

Bahá'u'lláh

Consecrate and devote yourselves to the betterment and service of all the human race...

...God is the helper of those souls whose aim is to serve humanity and whose efforts and endeavors are devoted to the good and betterment of all mankind.

'Abdu'l-Bahá

OCCUPATION PRESCRIBED PREOCCUPATION DISCOURAGED

Bahá'u'lláh has even said that occupation and labor are devotion. All humanity must obtain a livelihood by sweat of the brow and bodily exertion, at the same time seeking to lift the burden of others, striving to be the source of comfort to souls and facilitating the means of living. This in itself is devotion to God. Bahá'u'lláh has thereby encouraged action and stimulated service. But the energies of the heart must not be attached to these things; the soul must not be completely occupied with them. Though the mind is busy, the heart must be attracted toward the Kingdom of God in order that the virtues of humanity may be attained from every direction and source.

'Abdu'l-Bahá

33
ECONOMICS

THE ELIMINATION OF EXTREMES OF WEALTH AND POVERTY

It is evident that under present systems and conditions of government the poor are subject to the greatest need and distress while others more fortunate live in luxury and plenty far beyond their actual necessities. This inequality of portion and privilege is one of the deep and vital problems of human society.

'Abdu'l-Bahá

Every human being has the right to live; they have a right to rest, and to a certain amount of well-being. As a rich man is able to live in his palace surrounded by luxury and the greatest comfort, so should a poor man be able to have the necessaries of life. Nobody should die of hunger; everybody should have sufficient clothing; one man should not live in excess while another has no possible means of existence.

Let us try with all the strength we have to bring about happier conditions, so that no single soul may be destitute.

'Abdu'l-Bahá

ABSOLUTE EQUALITY IS IMPOSSIBLE

Among the results of the manifestation of spiritual forces will be that the human world will adapt itself to a new social form, the justice of God will become manifest throughout human affairs, and human equality will be universally established. ...the poor of the world will be rewarded and assisted fully, and there will be a readjustment in the economic conditions of mankind so that in the future there will not be the abnormally rich nor the abject poor. The rich will enjoy the privilege of this new economic condition as well as the poor, for owing to certain provisions and restrictions they will not be able to accumulate so much as to be burdened by its management, while the poor will be relieved from the stress of want and misery. The rich will enjoy his palace, and the poor will have his comfortable cottage.

The essence of the matter is that divine justice will become manifest in human conditions and affairs, and all mankind will find comfort and enjoyment in life. It is not meant that all will be equal, for inequality in degree and capacity is a property of nature. Necessarily there will be rich people and also those who will be in want of their livelihood, but in the aggregate community there will be equalization and readjustment of values and interests. In the future there will be no very rich nor extremely poor. There will be an equilibrium of interest, and a condition will be established which will make both rich and poor comfortable and content.

'Abdu'l-Bahá

What could be better before God than thinking of the poor?...Therefore, you must assist the poor as much as possible, even by sacrifice of yourself. No deed of man is greater before God than helping the poor. Organize in an effort to help them and prevent increase of poverty...

Difference of capacity in human individuals is fundamental. It is impossible for all to be alike, all to be equal, all to be wise. Bahá'u'lláh has revealed principles and laws which will accomplish the adjustment of varying human capacities. He has said that whatsoever is possible of accomplishment in human government will be effected through these principles. When the laws He has instated are carried out, there will be no millionaires possible in the community and likewise no extremely poor...Therefore, taxation will be proportionate to capacity and production, and there will be no poor in the community.

'Abdu'l-Bahá

THE OBLIGATION TO THE POOR

O YE RICH THAT PRIDE YOURSELVES ON MORTAL RICHES!

Know ye in truth that wealth is a mighty barrier between the seeker and his desire, the lover and his beloved. The rich, but for a few, shall in no wise attain the court of His presence nor enter the city of content and resignation. Well is it then with him, who, being rich, is not hindered by his riches from the eternal kingdom, nor deprived by them of imperishable dominion. By the Most Great Name! The splendour of such a wealthy man shall illuminate the dwellers of heaven even as the sun enlightens the people of the earth!

Bahá'u'lláh

O YE RICH ONES ON EARTH!

The poor in your midst are My trust; guard ye My trust, and be not intent only on your own ease.

Bahá'u'lláh

O SON OF PASSION!

Cleanse thyself from the defilement of riches and in perfect peace advance into the realm of poverty; that from the well-spring of detachment thou mayest quaff the wine of immortal life.

Bahá'u'lláh

O SON OF MAN!

Bestow My wealth upon My poor, that in heaven thou mayest draw from stores of unfading splendour and treasures of imperishable glory.

Bahá'u'lláh

SOCIAL ORDER TO BE LEGISLATED

The Bahá'í Cause covers all economic and social questions under the heading and ruling of its laws. The essence of the Bahá'í spirit is that, in order to establish a better social order and economic condition, there must be allegiance to the laws and principles of government. Under the laws which are to govern the world, the socialists may justly demand human rights but without resort to force and violence. The governments will enact these laws, establishing just legislation and economics in order that all humanity may enjoy a full measure of welfare and privilege; but this will always be according to legal protection and procedure. Without legislative administration, rights and demands fail, and the welfare of the common wealth cannot be realized. Today the method of demand is the strike and resort to force, which is manifestly wrong and destructive of human foundations. Rightful privilege and demand must be set forth in laws and regulations.

While thousands are considering these questions, we have more essential purposes...The Bahá'ís will bring about this improvement and betterment but not through sedition and appeal to physical force-not through warfare, but welfare...

Show what love is, what kindness is, what true severance is and generosity. This is the important thing for you to do. Act in accordance with the teachings of Bahá'u'lláh. All His Books will be translated...Let your deeds be the real translation of their meaning. Economic questions will not attract hearts. The love of God alone will attract them. Economic question are most interesting; but the power which moves, controls and attracts the hearts of men is the love of God.

'Abdu'l-Bahá

STRIKES

You have questioned me about strikes. This question is and will be for a long time the subject of great difficulties. Strikes are due to two causes. One is the extreme sharpness and rapacity of the capitalists and the manufacturers; the other, the excesses, the avidity and ill-will of the workmen and artisans. It is therefore necessary to remedy these two causes.

But the principal cause of these difficulties lies in the laws of the present civilization; for they lead to a small number of individuals accumulating incomparable fortunes, beyond their needs, whilst the greater number remains destitute, stripped and in the greatest misery. This is contrary to justice, to humanity, to equity; it is the height of inequity, the opposite to what causes divine satisfaction...

Consider an individual who has amassed treasures by colonising a country for his profit: he has obtained an incomparable fortune, and has secured profits and incomes which flow like a river, whilst a hundred thousand unfortunate people, weak and powerless, are in need of a mouthful of bread. There is neither equality nor brotherhood. So you see that general peace and joy are destroyed, the welfare of humanity is partially annihilated, and that collective life is fruitless. Indeed, fortune, honours, commerce, industry are in the hands of some industrials, whilst other people are submitted to quite a series of difficulties and to limitless troubles: they have neither advantages nor profits, nor comforts, nor peace.

Then rules and laws should be established to regulate the excessive fortunes of certain private individuals, and limit the misery of millions of the poor masses; thus a certain moderation would be obtained. However, absolute equality is just as impossible, for absolute equality in fortunes, honours, commerce, agriculture, industry would end in a want of comfort, in discouragement, in disorganisation of the means of existence, and in universal disappointment: the order of the community would be quite destroyed. Thus, there is a great wisdom in the fact that equality is not imposed by law: it is, therefore, preferable for moderation to do its work. The main point is, by means of laws and regulations to hinder the constitution of the excessive fortunes of certain individuals, and to protect the essential needs of the masses...

Therefore, laws and regulations should be established which would permit the workmen to receive from the factory owner their wages and a share in the fourth or the fifth part of the profits, according to the wants of the factory; or in some other way the body of workmen and manufacturers should share equitably the profits and advantages...

When matters will be thus fixed, the owner of the factory will no longer put aside daily a treasure which he has absolutely no need of, (without taking into consideration that if the fortune is disproportionate, the capitalist succumbs under a formidable burden, and gets into the greatest difficulties and troubles; the administration of an excessive fortune is very difficult, and exhausts man's natural strength). And, the workmen and artisans will no longer be in the greatest misery and want, they will no longer be submitted to the worst privations at the end of their life...

It would be well, with regard to the social rights of manufacturers, workmen and artisans, that laws be established, giving moderate profits to manufacturers, and to workmen the necessary means of existence and security for the future. Thus, when they become feeble and cease working, get old and helpless, and die leaving children under age, these children will not be annihilated by excess of poverty. And it is from the income of the factory itself, to which they have a right, that they will derive a little of the means of existence...

The interference of courts of justice and of the Government in difficulties pending between manufacturers and workmen is legal, for the reason that current affairs between workmen and manufacturers cannot be compared with ordinary affairs between private persons, which do not concern the public, and with which the Government should not occupy itself. In reality, although they appear to be matters between private persons, these difficulties between patrons and workmen produce a general detriment; for commerce, industry, agriculture and the general affairs of the country are all intimately linked together. If one of these suffers an abuse, the detriment affects the mass. Thus the difficulties between workmen and manufacturers become a cause of general detriment.

The court of justice and the Government have therefore the right of interference. When a difficulty occurs between two individuals with reference to private rights, it is necessary for a third to settle the question: this is the part of the Government: then the question of strikes-which cause troubles in the country and are often connected with excessive vexations of the workmen, as well as with the rapacity of manufacturers-how could it remain neglected?

'Abdu'l-Bahá

34
DEALING WITH CRIME

THE DIFFERENCES BETWEEN MATERIAL & DIVINE CIVILIZATION

As to the difference between that material civilization now prevailing, and the divine civilization which will be one of the benefits to derive from the House of Justice, it is this: material civilization, through the power of punitive and retaliatory laws, restraineth the people from criminal acts; and notwithstanding this, while laws to retaliate against and punish a man are continually proliferating, as ye can see, no laws exist to reward him. In all the cities of Europe and America, vast buildings have been erected to serve as jails for the criminals.

Divine civilization, however, so traineth every member of society that no one, with the exception of a negligible few, will undertake to commit a crime. There is thus a great difference between the prevention of crime through measures that are violent and retaliatory, and so training the people, and enlightening them, and spiritualizing them, that without any fear of punishment or vengeance to come, they will shun all criminal acts. They will, indeed, look upon the very commission of a crime as a great disgrace and in itself the harshest of punishments. They will become enamoured of human perfections, and will consecrate their lives to whatever will bring light to the world and will further those qualities which are acceptable at the Holy Threshold of God.

See then how wide is the difference between material civilization and divine. With force and punishment, material civilization seeketh to restrain the people from mischief, from inflicting harm on society and committing crimes. But in a divine civilization, the individual is so conditioned that with no fear of punishment, he shunneth the perpetration of crimes, seeth the crime itself as the severest of torments, and with alacrity and joy, setteth himself to acquiring the virtues of humankind, to furthering human progress, and to spreading light across the world.

'Abdu'l-Bahá

PUNISHMENT

There are two sorts of retributory punishments. One is vengeance, the other chastisement. Man has not the right to take vengeance, but the community has the right to punish the criminal; and this punishment is intended to warn and to prevent, so that no other person will dare to commit a like crime. This punishment is for the protection of man's rights, but it is not vengeance; vengeance appeases the anger of the heart by opposing one evil to another. This is not allowable; for man has not the right to take vengeance. But if criminals were entirely forgiven, the order of the world would be upset. So punishment is one of the essential necessities for the safety of communities, but he who is oppressed by a transgressor has not the right to take vengeance: on the contrary, he should forgive and pardon, for this is worthy of the world of man.

The communities must punish the oppressor, the murderer, the malefactor, so as to warn and restrain others from committing like crimes. But the most essential thing is that the people must be educated in such a way that no crimes will be committed; for it is possible to educate the masses so effectively that they will avoid and shrink from perpetrating crimes, so that the crime itself will appear to them as the greatest chastisement, the utmost condemnation and torment. Therefore no crimes which require punishment will be committed.

We must speak of things that are possible of performance in this world. There are many theories and high ideas on this subject, but they are not practicable; consequently we must speak of things that are feasible.

For example, if some one oppresses, injures, and wrongs another, and the wronged man retaliates, this is vengeance, and is censurable...No, rather he must return good for evil, and not only forgive, but also, if possible, be of service to his oppressor. This conduct is worthy of man: for what advantage does he gain by vengeance? The two actions are equivalent; if one action is reprehensible, both are reprehensible. The only difference is that one was committed first, the other later.

But the community has the right of defence and of self-protection; moreover, the community has no hatred nor animosity for the murderer:

Dealing with Crime

it imprisons or punishes him merely for the protection and security of others. It is not for the purpose of taking vengeance upon the murderer, but for the purpose of inflicting a punishment by which the community will be protected. If the community and the inheritors of the murdered one were to forgive and return good for evil, the cruel would be continually ill-treating others, and assassinations would continually occur. Vicious people, like wolves, would destroy the sheep of God. The community has no ill-will and rancour in the infliction of punishment, and it does not desire to appease the anger of the heart; its purpose is by punishment to protect others, so that no atrocious actions may be committed.

Thus when Christ said: 'Whosoever shall smite thee on the right cheek, turn to him the left one also,' it was for the purpose of teaching men not to take personal revenge. He did not mean that if a wolf should fall upon a flock of sheep and wish to destroy it, that the wolf should be encouraged to do so. No, if Christ had known that a wolf had entered the fold and was about to destroy the sheep, most certainly he would have prevented it.

As forgiveness is one of the attributes of the Merciful One, so also justice is one of the attributes of the Lord. The tent of existence is upheld upon the pillar of justice, and not upon forgiveness. The continuance of mankind depends upon justice and not upon forgiveness. So if, at present, the law of pardon were practised in all countries, in a short time the world would be disordered, and the foundations of human life would crumble...

Some people are like bloodthirsty wolves: if they see no punishment forthcoming, they will kill men merely for pleasure and diversion...

Then what Christ meant by forgiveness and pardon is not that, when nations attack you, burn your homes, plunder your goods, assault your wives, children, and relatives, and violate your honour, you should be submissive in the presence of these tyrannical foes, and allow them to perform all their cruelties and oppressions. No, the words of Christ refer to the conduct of two individuals towards each other...

One thing remains to be said: it is that the communities are day and night occupied in making penal laws, and in preparing and organising instruments and means of punishment. They build prisons, make chains and fetters, arrange places of exile and banishment, and different kinds of hardships and tortures, and think by these means to discipline criminals; whereas, in reality, they are causing destruction of morals and perversion of characters. The community, on the contrary, ought day and night to strive and endeavour with the utmost zeal and effort to accomplish the education of men, to cause them day by day to progress and to increase in science and knowledge, to acquire virtues, to gain good morals and to avoid vices, so that crimes may not occur. At the present time the contrary prevails; the community is always thinking of enforcing the penal laws, and of preparing means of punishment, instruments of death and chastisement, places for imprisonment and banishment; and they expect crimes to be committed. This has a demoralising effect.

But if the community would endeavour to educate the masses, day by day knowledge and sciences would become good, and morals normal; in one word, in all these classes of perfections there would be progress, and there would be fewer crimes...

Therefore the communities must think of preventing crimes, rather than of rigorously punishing them.

'Abdu'l-Bahá

35
HEALTH AND NUTRITION

HEALTH THE GREATEST OF ALL GIFTS

Although ill health is one of the unavoidable conditions of man, truly it is hard to bear. The bounty of good health is the greatest of all gifts.

'Abdu'l-Bahá

THE SIMPLE LIFE

If humankind...lived according to a natural, inborn equilibrium, without following wherever their passions led, it is undeniable that diseases would no longer take the ascendant, nor diversify with such intensity.

But man hath perversely continued to serve his lustful appetites, and he would not content himself with simple foods...his attention was engrossed, and he abandoned the temperance and moderation of a natural way of life. The result was the engendering of diseases both violent and diverse.

'Abdu'l-Bahá

HAPPINESS IS THE GREATEST HEALER

We should all visit the sick. When they are in sorrow and suffering, it is a real help and benefit to have a friend come. Happiness is a great healer to those who are ill...You must always have this thought of love and affection when you visit the ailing and afflicted.

'Abdu'l-Bahá

Joy gives us wings! In times of joy our strength is more vital, our intellect keener...But when sadness visits us our strength leaves us.

'Abdu'l-Bahá

THE IMPORTANCE OF NUTRITION

The Bab hath said that the people of Bahá must develop the science of medicine to such a high degree that they will heal illnesses by means of foods...

At whatever time highly-skilled physicians shall have developed the healing of illnesses by means of foods, and shall make provision for simple foods, and shall prohibit humankind from living as slaves to their lustful appetites, it is certain that the incidence of chronic and diversified illnesses will abate, and the general health of all mankind will be much improved. This is destined to come about. In the same way, in the character, the conduct and the manners of men, universal modifications will be made.

'Abdu'l-Bahá

It is therefore evident that it is possible to cure by foods, aliments, and fruits; but as today the science of medicine is imperfect, this fact is not yet fully grasped. When the science of medicine reaches perfection, treatment will be given by foods, aliments, fragrant fruits, and vegetables, and by various waters, hot and cold in temperature.

'Abdu'l-Bahá

THE EATING OF MEAT WILL GRADUALLY CEASE AS MANKIND DEVELOPS

As humanity progresses, meat will be used less and less, for the teeth of man are not carnivorous. For example, the lion is endowed with carnivorous teeth, which are intended for meat, and if meat be not found, the lion starves. The lion cannot graze; its teeth are of different shape. The digestive system of the lion is such that it cannot receive nourishment save through meat. The eagle has a crooked beak, the lower part shorter than the upper. It cannot pick up grain; it cannot graze; therefore, it is compelled to partake of meat. The domestic animals have herbivorous teeth formed to cut grass, which is their fodder. The human teeth, the molars, are formed to grind grain. The front teeth, the incisors, are for fruits, etc. It is, therefore, quite apparent according to the implements for eating that man's food is intended to be grain and not meat. When mankind is more fully developed, the eating of meat will gradually cease.

'Abdu'l-Bahá

SEEK COMPETENT MEDICAL ADVICE

According to the explicit decree of Bahá'u'lláh one must not turn aside from the advice of a competent doctor. It is imperative to consult one even if the patient himself be a well-known and eminent physician. In short, the point is that you should maintain your health by consulting a highly-skilled physician.

'Abdu'l-Bahá

It is incumbent upon everyone to seek medical treatment and to follow the doctor's instructions, for this is in compliance with the divine ordinance, but, in reality, He Who giveth healing is God.

'Abdu'l-Bahá

Do not neglect medical treatment when it is necessary, but leave it off when health has been restored. Treat disease through diet, by preference, refraining from the use of drugs; and if you find what is required in a single herb, do not resort to a compounded medicament...Abstain from drugs when the health is good, but administer them when necessary.

Bahá'u'lláh

When at the bedside of a patient, cheer and gladden his heart and enrapture his spirit through celestial power. Indeed, such a heavenly breath quickeneth every mouldering bone and reviveth the spirit of every sick and ailing one.

'Abdu'l-Bahá

TABLET TO A PHYSICIAN

In God must be our trust. There is no God but Him, the Healer, the Knower, the Helper...Nothing in earth or heaven is outside the grasp of God.

O physician! In treating the sick, first mention the name of Thy God, the Possessor of the Day of Judgement, and then use what God hath destined for the healing of His creatures. By My Life! The physician who has drunk from the Wine of My Love, his visit is healing, and his breath is mercy and hope. Cling to him for the welfare of the constitution. He is confirmed by God in his treatment.

This knowledge (of the healing art) is the most important of all the sciences, for it is the greatest means from God, the Life-giver to the dust, for preserving the bodies of all people, and He has put it in the forefront of all sciences and wisdoms. For this is the day when you must arise for My Victory.

Say: Thy name is my healing, O my God, and remembrance of Thee is my remedy. Nearness to Thee is my hope, and love for Thee is my companion. Thy mercy to me is my healing and my succour in both this world and the world to come. Thou verily, art the All-Bountiful, the All-Knowing, the All-Wise.

Bahá'u'lláh

36
MUSIC

A wondrous melody is wings for the spirit, and maketh the soul to tremble for joy.

'Abdu'l-Bahá

MUSIC IS A PRAISEWORTHY ART

The musician's art is among those arts worthy of the highest praise and it moveth the hearts of all...

'Abdu'l-Bahá

Music is regarded as a praiseworthy science at the Threshold of the Almighty, so that thou mayest chant verses at large gatherings and congregations in a most wondrous melody and raise such hymns of praise at the Mashriqu'l-Adhkár as to enrapture the Concourse of High. By virtue of this, consider how much the art of music is admired and praised. Try, if, thou canst, to use spiritual melodies, songs and tunes, and to bring the earthly music into harmony with the celestial melody. Then thou wilt notice what a great influence music hath and what heavenly joy and life it conferreth. Strike up such a melody and tune as to cause the nightingales of divine mysteries to be filled with joy and ecstasy.

'Abdu'l-Bahá

The art of music is divine and effective. It is the food of the soul and spirit. Through the power and charm of music the spirit of man is uplifted. It has wonderful sway and effect in the hearts of children, for their hearts are pure and melodies have great influence in them. The latent talents with which the hearts of these children are endowed will find expression through the medium of music. Therefore you must exert yourselves to make them proficient; teach them to sing with excellence and effect. It is incumbent upon each child to know something of music, for without knowledge of this art, the melodies of instrument and voice cannot be rightly enjoyed. Likewise it is necessary that the schools teach it in order that the souls and hearts of the pupils may become vivified and exhilarated and their lives brightened with enjoyment.

'Abdu'l-Bahá

Music is one of the important arts. It has great effect upon the human spirit. Musical melodies are a certain something which prove to be accidental upon etheric vibrations, for voice is nothing but the expression of vibrations, which, reaching the tympanum, affect the nerves of hearing. Musical melodies are, therefore, those peculiar effects produced by, or from, vibration. However, they have the keenest effect upon the spirit. In sooth, although music is a material affair, yet its tremendous effect is spiritual, and its greatest attachment is to the realm of the spirit.

'Abdu'l-Bahá

MUSIC IS FOOD FOR THE SPIRIT

It is natural for the heart and spirit to take pleasure and enjoyment in all things that show forth symmetry, harmony, and perfection. For instance: a beautiful house, a well designed garden, a symmetrical line, a graceful motion, a well written book, pleasing garments-in fact, all things that have in themselves grace or beauty are pleasing to the heart and spirit-therefore, it is most certain that a true voice causes deep pleasures.

What is music? It is a combination of harmonious sounds...Melodies are like water. The voice is like a goblet. The pure water in a pure glass is pleasing. Therefore, it is acceptable. But even though the water be pure, if it be in a goblet which is not so, this receptacle will make it unacceptable. Therefore, a faulty voice even though the music be good, is unpleasing.

In short: melodies, though they are material, are connected with the spiritual, therefore, they produce a great effect.

'Abdu'l-Bahá

We have made it lawful for you to listen to music and singing. Take heed, however, lest listening thereto should cause you to overstep the bounds of propriety and dignity...We, verily, have made music as a ladder for your souls, a means whereby they may be lifted up unto the realm on

Music

high; make it not, therefore, as wings to self and passion. Truly, We are loath to see you numbered with the foolish.

Bahá'u'lláh

This wonderful age has rent asunder the veils of superstition and has condemned the prejudice of the people of the East.

Among some of the nations of the Orient, music and harmony was not approved of, but the Manifested light, Bahá'u'lláh, in this glorious period has revealed in Holy Tablets that singing and music are the spiritual food of the hearts and souls. In this dispensation, music is one of the arts that is highly approved and is considered to be the cause of the exaltation of sad and desponding hearts.

'Abdu'l-Bahá

...although sound is but the vibration of the air which affect the tympanum of the ear, and vibrations of the air are but an accident among the accidents which depend upon the air, consider how much marvellous notes or a charming song influence the spirits! A wonderful song giveth wings to the spirit and filleth the hearts with exaltation.

'Abdu'l-Bahá

37
UNITY AND JUSTICE

PROMOTION OF THE SECURITY & TRANQUILLITY OF THE PEOPLES OF THE WORLD

O my friend! In all circumstances one should seize upon every means which will promote security and tranquillity among the peoples of the world...In this glorious Day whatever will purge you from corruption and will lead you towards peace and composure, is indeed the straight Path...

This humble servant is filled with wonder, inasmuch as all men are endowed with the capacity to see and hear, yet we find them deprived of the privilege of using these faculties. This servant hath been prompted to pen these lines by virtue of the tender love he cherisheth for thee. The winds of despair are, alas, blowing from every direction, and the strife that divideth the afflicteth the human race is daily increasing. The signs of impending convulsions and chaos can now be discerned, inasmuch as the prevailing order appeareth to be lamentably defective. I beseech God, exalted be His glory, that He may graciously awaken the peoples of the earth, may grant that the end of their conduct may be profitable unto them, and aid them to accomplish that which beseemeth their station.

Were man to appreciate the greatness of his station and the loftiness of his destiny he would manifest naught save goodly character, pure deeds, and a seemly and praiseworthy conduct. If the learned and wise men of goodwill were to impart guidance unto the people, the whole earth would be regarded as one country. Verily this is the undoubted truth. This servant appealeth to every diligent and enterprising soul to exert his utmost endeavour and arise to rehabilitate the conditions in all regions and to quicken the dead with the living waters of wisdom and utterance, by virtue of the love he cherisheth for God, the One, the Peerless, the Almighty, the Beneficent.

Bahá'u'lláh

Justice is, in this day, bewailing its plight, and Equity groaneth beneath the yoke of oppression. The thick clouds of tyranny have darkened the face of the earth, and enveloped its peoples. Through the movement of Our Pen of glory We have, at the bidding of the omnipotent Ordainer, breathed a new life into every human frame, and instilled into every word a fresh potency. All created things proclaim the evidences of this worldwide regeneration. This is the most great, the most joyful tidings imparted by the pen of this wronged One to mankind...

Every man of insight will, in this day, readily admit that the counsels which the Pen of this wronged One hath revealed constitute the supreme animating power for the advancement of the world and the exaltation of its peoples.

Bahá'u'lláh

We, verily, have come to unite and weld together all that dwell on earth...Lay fast hold on whatever will profit you, and profit the peoples of the world.

Bahá'u'lláh

THE PURPOSE OF JUSTICE IS THE APPEARANCE OF UNITY

The light of men is Justice. Quench it not with the contrary winds of oppression and tyranny. The purpose of Justice is the appearance of unity among men.

...O ye men of wisdom among nations! Shut your eyes to estrangement, then fix your gaze upon unity. Cleave tenaciously unto that which will lead to the well-being and tranquillity of all mankind. This span of earth is but one homeland and one habitation. It behoveth you to abandon vainglory which causeth alienation and to set your hearts on whatever will ensure harmony. In the estimation of the people of Bahá man's glory lieth in his knowledge, his upright conduct, his praiseworthy character, his wisdom, and not in his nationality or rank. O people of earth! Appreciate the value of this heavenly word. Indeed it may be likened upon a ship for the ocean of knowledge and a shining luminary for the real of perception.

Bahá'u'lláh

THE WELL-BEING OF MANKIND RESTS UPON UNITY

My object is none other than the betterment of the world and the tranquillity of its peoples. The well-being of mankind, its peace and security, are unattainable unless and until its unity is firmly established. This unity can never be achieved so long as the counsels which the Pen of the Most High hath revealed are suffered to pass unheeded.

Bahá'u'lláh

Justice and equity are twin Guardians that watch over men. From them are revealed such blessed and perspicuous words as are the cause of the well-being of the world and the protection of the nations.

Bahá'u'lláh

The best beloved of all things in My sight is Justice; turn not away therefrom if thou desirest Me, and neglect it not that I may confide in thee. By its aid thou shalt see with thine own eyes and not through the eyes of others, and shalt know of thine own knowledge and not through the knowledge of thy neighbour. Ponder this in thy heart; how it behooveth thee to be. Verily justice is My gift to thee and the sign of My loving kindness. Set it then before thine eyes.

Bahá'u'lláh

THE UNIVERSALITY OF HUMAN EXISTENCE

Humanity shares in common the intellectual and spiritual faculties of a created endowment. All are equally subject to the various exigencies of human life and are similarly occupied in acquiring the means of earthly subsistence. From the viewpoint of creation human beings stand upon the same footing in every respect, subject to the same requirements and seeking and enjoyment and comfort of earthly conditions. Therefore, the things humanity shares in common are numerous and manifest. This equal participation in the physical, intellectual and spiritual problems of human existence is a valid basis for the unification of mankind...

Bahá'u'lláh said that God has sent religion for the purpose of establishing fellowship among humankind and not to create strife and discord, for all religion is founded upon the love of humanity...But when we make the remedy the cause of the disease, it would be better to do without the remedy.

Other sources of human dissension are political, racial and patriotic prejudices. These have been removed by Bahá'u'lláh. He has said, and has guarded His statement by rational proofs from the Holy Book, that the world of humanity is one race, the surface of the earth one place of residence and that these imaginary racial barriers and political boundaries are without right or foundation. Man is degraded in becoming the captive of his own illusions and suppositions. The earth is one earth, and the same atmosphere surrounds it.

'Abdu'l-Bahá

JUSTICE WILL TRANSFORM THE EARTH

Behold the disturbances which, for many a long year, have afflicted the earth, and the perturbation that hath seized its peoples. It hath either been ravaged by war, or tormented by sudden and unforeseen calamities. Though the world is encompassed with misery and distress, yet no man hath paused to reflect what the cause or source of that may be. Whenever the True Counsellor uttered a word in admonishment, lo, they all denounced Him as a mover of mischief and rejected His claim. How bewildering, how confusing is such behavior! No two men can be found who may be said to be outwardly and inwardly united. The evidences of discord and malice are apparent everywhere, though all were made for harmony and union...O well-beloved ones! The tabernacle of unity hath been raised; regard ye not one another as strangers. Ye are the fruits of one tree, and the leaves of one branch. We cherish the hope that the light of justice may shine upon the world and sanctify it from tyranny. If the rulers and kings of the earth, the symbols of the power of God, exalted be His glory, arise and resolve to dedicate themselves to whatever will promote the highest interests of the whole of humanity, the reign of justice will assuredly be established amongst the children of men, and the effulgence of its light will envelop the whole earth...The structure of world stability and order hath been reared upon, and will continue to be sustained by, the twin pillars of reward and punishment...Take heed, O concourse of the rulers of the world! There is no force on earth that can equal in its conquering power the force of justice and wisdom...There can be no doubt whatever that if the day star of justice, which the clouds of tyranny have obscured, were to shed it light upon men, the face of the earth would be completely transformed.

Bahá'u'lláh

If the learned and worldly-wise men of this age were to allow mankind to inhale the fragrance of fellowship and love, every understanding heart would apprehend the meaning of true liberty, and discover the secret of undisturbed peace and absolute composure.

Bahá'u'lláh

No light can compare with the light of justice. The establishment of order in the world and the tranquillity of the nations depend upon it.

Bahá'u'lláh

THIS IS THE DAY OF UNION

O ye beloved of the Lord! This day is the day of union, the day of the ingathering of all mankind. 'Verily God loveth those who, as though they were a solid wall, do battle for His Cause in serried lines!' [Qur'án 61:4] Note that He saith 'in serried lines'-meaning crowded and pressed together, one locked to the next, each supporting his fellows. To do battle, as stated in the sacred verse, doth not, in this greatest of all dispensations, mean to go forth with sword and spear, with lance and piercing arrow-but rather weaponed with pure intent, with righteous motives, with counsels helpful and effective, with godly attributes, with deeds pleasing to the Almighty, with the qualities of heaven. It signifieth education for all mankind, guidance for all men, the spreading far and wide of the sweet savours of the spirit, the promulgation of God's proofs, the setting forth of arguments conclusive and divine, the doing of charitable deeds.

'Abdu'l-Bahá

THE IMPORTANCE OF UNITY AMONG THE BAHÁ'ÍS

Today the one overriding need is unity and harmony among the beloved of the Lord, for they should have among them but one heart and soul and should, so far as in them lieth, unitedly withstand the hostility of all the peoples of the world; they must bring to an end the benighted prejudices of all nations and religions and must make known to every member of the human race that all are the leaves of one branch, the fruit of one bough.

Until such time, however, as the friends establish perfect unity among themselves, how can they summon others to harmony and peace?

That soul which hath itself not come alive, Can it then hope another to revive?

Reflect ye as to other than human forms of life and be ye admonished thereby: those clouds that drift apart cannot produce the bounty of the rain, and are soon lost; a flock of sheep, once scattered, falleth prey to the wolf, and birds that fly alone will be caught fast in the claws of the hawk. What greater demonstration could there be that unity leadeth to flourishing life, while dissension and withdrawing from others, will lead only to misery; for these are the sure ways to bitter disappointment and ruin.

'Abdu'l-Bahá

FAIRNESS

The foundation of the Kingdom of God is laid upon justice, fairness, mercy, sympathy and kindness to every soul. Then strive ye with heart and soul to practice love and kindness to the world of humanity at large, except to those souls who are selfish and insincere. It is not advisable to show kindness to a person who is a tyrant, a traitor or a thief because kindness encourages him to become worse and does not awaken him. The more kindness you show to a liar the more he is apt to lie, for he thinks that you know not, while you do know, but extreme kindness keeps you from revealing your knowledge.

'Abdu'l-Bahá

UNITY WITH VARIETY

A critic may object, saying that peoples, races, tribes and communities of the world are of different and varied customs, habits, tastes, character, inclinations and ideas, that opinions and thoughts are contrary to one another, and how, therefore, is it possible for real unity to be revealed and perfect accord among human souls to exist?

In answer we say that differences are of two kinds. One is the cause of annihilation and is like the antipathy existing among warring nations and conflicting tribes who seek each other's destruction, uprooting one another's families, depriving one another of rest and comfort and unleashing carnage. The other kind which is a token of diversity is the essence of perfection and the cause of appearance of bestowals of the Most Glorious Lord.

Consider the flowers of a garden: thought differing in kind, colour, form and shape, yet, inasmuch as they are refreshed by the water of one spring, revived by the breath of one wind, invigorated by the rays of one sun, this diversity increaseth their charm, and addeth unto their beauty. Thus when that unifying force, the penetrating influence of the Word of God, taketh effect, the difference of customs, manners, habits, ideas, opinions and dispositions embellisheth the world of humanity. This diversity, this difference is like the naturally created dissimilarity and variety of the limbs and organs of the human body, for each one contributeth to the beauty, efficiency and perfection of the whole. When these different limbs and organs come under the influence of man's sovereign soul, and the soul's power pervadeth the limbs and members, veins and arteries of the body, then difference reinforceth harmony, diversity strengtheneth love, and multiplicity is the greatest factor for coordination.

How unpleasing to the eye if all the flowers and plants, the leaves and blossoms, the fruits, the branches and the trees of that garden were all of the same shape and colour! Diversity of hues, form and shape, enricheth and adorneth the garden, and heighteneth the effect thereof. In like manner, when divers shades of thought, temperament and character, are brought together under the power and influence of one central agency, the beauty and glory of human perfection will be revealed and made manifest. Naught but the celestial potency of the Word of God, which ruleth and transcendeth the realities of all things, is capable of harmonizing the divergent thoughts, sentiments, ideas, and convictions of the children of men. Verily, it is the penetrating power in all things, the mover of souls and the binder and regulator in the world of humanity.

'Abdu'l-Bahá

Our greatest efforts must be directed towards detachment from the things of the world; we must strive to become more spiritual, more luminous, to follow the counsel of the Divine Teaching, to serve the cause of unity and true equality, to be merciful, to reflect the love of the Highest on all men, so that the light of the Spirit shall be apparent in all our deeds, to the end that all humanity shall be united, the stormy sea thereof calmed, and all rough waves disappear from off the surface of life's ocean henceforth unruffled and peaceful.

'Abdu'l-Bahá

PROVINCIALISM AND PREJUDICE ARE CENSURED

The call of Bahá'u'lláh is primarily directed against all forms of provincialism, all insularities and prejudices...For legal standards, political and economic theories are solely designed to safeguard the interests of humanity as a whole, and not humanity to be crucified for the preservation of the integrity of any particular law or doctrine...

The principle of the Oneness of Mankind-the pivot round which all the teachings of Bahá'u'lláh revolve-is no mere outburst of ignorant emotionalism or an expression of vague and pious hope...Its implications are deeper, its claims greater than any which the Prophets of old were allowed to advance. Its message is applicable not only to the individual, but concerns itself primarily with the nature of those essential relationships that must bind all the states and nations as members of one human family...

It represents the consummation of human evolution...

Shoghi Effendi

Such exhortations to union and concord as are inscribed in the Books of the Prophets by the Pen of the Most High bear reference unto specific matters; not a union that would lead to disunity or a concord which would create discord. This is the station where measures are set unto everything, a station where every deserving soul shall be given his due. Well is it with them that appreciate the meaning and grasp the intent of these words, and woe betide the heedless. Unto this all the evidences of nature, in their very essences, bear ample testimony. Every discerning man of wisdom is well acquainted with that which We have mentioned, but not those who have strayed far from the living fountain of fairmindedness and are roving distraught in the wilderness of ignorance and blind fanaticism.

Bahá'u'lláh

38
PEACE

O peoples of the earth! Verily the resplendent Light of God hath appeared in your midst, invested with this unerring Book, that ye may be guided aright to the ways of peace and, by the leave of God, step out of the darkness into the light and onto this far-extended Path of Truth...

The Báb

We cherish the hope that through the earnest endeavours of such as are the exponents of the power of God-exalted be His glory-the weapons of war throughout the world may be converted into instruments of reconstruction and that strife and conflict may be removed from the midst of men.

Bahá'u'lláh

For the establishment of international peace the blood of twenty thousand Bahá'ís was spilled. Their homes were destroyed, their children made captives and their possessions pillaged, yet none of these people waxed cold or wavered in devotion. Even to this day the Bahá'ís are persecuted, and quite recently a number were killed, for wherever they are found they put forth the greatest efforts to establish the peace of the world. They not only promulgate principles; they are people of action.

'Abdu'l-Bahá

SPIRITUAL POWER AND POSITIVE THOUGHTS

The Most Great Peace cannot be assured through racial force and effort; it cannot be established by patriotic devotion and sacrifice; for nations differ widely and local patriotism has limitations. Furthermore, it is evident that political power and diplomatic ability are not conductive to universal agreement, for the interests of governments are varied and selfish; nor will international harmony and reconciliation be an outcome of human opinions concentrated upon it, for opinions are faulty and intrinsically diverse. Universal peace is an impossibility through human and material agencies; it must be through spiritual power.

'Abdu'l-Bahá

I wonder at the human savagery that still exists in the world! How is it possible for men to fight from morning until evening, killing each other, shedding the blood of their fellow-men: And for what object? To gain possession of a part of the earth!

...Land belongs not to one people, but to all people. This earth is not man's home, but his tomb. It is for their tombs these men are fighting. There is nothing so horrible in this world as the tomb, the abode of the decaying bodies of men...

However great the conqueror, however many countries he may reduce to slavery, he is unable to retain any part of these devastated lands but one tiny portion-his tomb!

When soldiers of the world draw their swords to kill, soldiers of God clasp each other's hands! So may all the savagery of man disappear by the Mercy of God, working through the pure in heart and the sincere of soul. Do not think the peace of the world an ideal impossible to attain!

Nothing is impossible to the Divine Benevolence of God.

If you desire with all your heart, friendship with every race on earth, your thought, spiritual and positive, will spread; it will become the desire of others, growing stronger and stronger, until it reaches the minds of all men.

'Abdu'l-Bahá

THE CAUSES OF WAR

The greatest cause of bereavement and disheartening in the world of humanity is ignorance based upon blind imitation. It is due to this that wars and battles prevail; from this cause hatred and animosity arise continually among mankind.

'Abdu'l-Bahá

Bigotry and dogmatic adherence to ancient beliefs have become the central fundamental source of animosity among men, the obstacle to human progress, the cause of warfare and strife, the destroyer of peace, composure and the welfare in the world. Consider conditions in the Balkans today: fathers, mothers, children in grief and lamentation, the foundations of life overturned, cities laid waste and fertile lands made desolate by the ravages of war. The conditions are the outcome of hostility and hatred between nations and people of religion who imitate and adhere to the forms and violate the spirit and reality of the divine teachings.

'Abdu'l-Bahá

God created one earth and one mankind to people it. Man has no other habitation, but man himself has come forth and proclaimed imaginary boundary lines and territorial restrictions, naming them Germany, France, Russia, etc. And torrents of precious blood are spilled in defense of these imaginary divisions of our one human habitation, under the delusion of a fancied and limited patriotism.

After all, a claim and title to territory or native land is but a claim and attachment to the dust of earth. We live upon this earth for a few days and then rest beneath it forever. So it is our graveyard eternally. Shall man fight for the tomb which devours him, for his eternal sepulcher? What ignorance could be greater than this? To fight over his grave, to kill another for his grave! What heedlessness! What a delusion!

'Abdu'l-Bahá

THE WORLD ON THE VERGE OF WAR

All the European nations are on edge[1912], a single flame will set on fire the whole of that continent. Implements of war and death are multiplied and increased to an inconceivable degree, and the burden of military maintenance is taxing the various countries beyond the point of endurance. Armies, and navies devour the substance and possessions of the people; the toiling poor, the innocent and helpless are forced by taxation to provide munitions and armaments for governments bent upon conquest of territory and defense against powerful rival nations. There is no greater or more woeful ordeal in the world of humanity today than impending war.

'Abdu'l-Bahá

THE SUMMONS FOR A WORLD ASSEMBLY OF NATIONS

The time must come when the imperative necessity for the holding of a vast, an all-embracing assemblage of men will be universally realized. The rulers and kings of the earth must needs attend it, and, participating in its deliberations, must consider such ways and means as will lay the foundations of the world's Great Peace amongst men. Such a peace demandeth that the Great Powers should resolve, for the sake of the tranquillity of the people of the earth, to be fully reconciled among themselves. Should any king take up arms against another, all should unitedly arise and prevent him. If this be done, the nations of the world will no longer require any armaments, except for the purpose of preserving the security of their realms and of maintaining internal order within their territories. This will ensure the peace and composure of every people, government and nation.

Bahá'u'lláh

THE DANGER OF ATOMIC WEAPONS PROPHESIED

Strange and astonishing things exist in the earth but they are hidden from the minds and the understanding of men. These things are capable of changing the whole atmosphere of the earth and their contamination would prove lethal.

Bahá'u'lláh

THE CALL TO DISARMAMENT

Compose your differences, and reduce your armaments, that the burden of your expenditures may be lightened, and that your minds and hearts may be tranquillized. Heal the dissensions that divide you, and ye will no longer be in need of any armaments expect what the protection of your cities and territories demandeth. Fear ye God, and take heed not to outstrip the bounds of moderation, and be numbered among the extravagant.

    We have learned that you are increasing your outlay every year, and are laying the burden thereof on your subjects. This, verily, is more than they can bear, and is a grievous injustice. Decide justly between men, and be ye the emblems of justice amongst them. This, if ye judge fairly, is the thing that behoveth you, and beseemeth your station.

Bahá'u'lláh

They must put away the weapons of war, and turn to the instruments of universal reconstruction...If they attain unto this all-surpassing blessing, the people of each nation will pursue, with tranquillity and contentment, their own occupations, and the groanings and lamentations of most men would be silenced.

Bahá'u'lláh

39
POLITICAL QUESTIONS

INVOLVEMENT IN SEDITIOUS MOVEMENTS IS PROHIBITED

The Bahá'ís must not engage in political movements which lead to sedition. They must interest themselves in movements which conduce to law and order. In Persia at the present time the Bahá'ís have no part in the revolutionary upheavals which have terminated in lawlessness and rebellion. Nevertheless, a Bahá'í may hold a political office and be interested in politics of the right type. Ministers, state officials and governor-generals in Persia are Bahá'ís, and there are many other Bahá'ís holding governmental positions; but nowhere throughout the world should the followers of Bahá'u'lláh be engaged in seditious movements. For example, if there should be an uprising here in America having for its purpose the establishment of a despotic government, the Bahá'ís should not be connected with it.

'Abdu'l-Bahá

POLITICAL NEUTRALITY ENJOINED

Except to speak well of them, make thou no mention of the earth's kings, and the worldly governments thereof. Rather, confine thine utterance to spreading the blissful tidings of the Kingdom of God, and demonstrating the influence of the Word of God, and the holiness of the Cause of God.

'Abdu'l-Bahá

Let them willingly subject themselves to every just king, and to every generous ruler be good citizens. Let them obey the government and not meddle in political affairs, but devote themselves to the betterment of character and behaviour, and fix their gaze upon the Light of the world.

'Abdu'l-Bahá

Let them refrain from associating themselves, whether by word or by deed, with the political pursuits of their respective nations, with the policies of their governments and the schemes and programs of parties and factions. In such controversies they should assign no blame, take no side, further no design, and identify themselves with no system prejudicial to the best interests of that worldwide Fellowship which it is their aim to guard and foster. Let them beware lest they allow themselves to become the tools of unscrupulous politicians, or to be entrapped by the treacherous devices of the plotters and the perfidious among their countrymen. Let them so shape their lives and regulate their conduct that no charge of secrecy, of fraud, of bribery or of intimidation may, however ill-founded, be brought against them. Let them rise above all particularism and partisanship, above the vain disputes, the petty calculations, the transient passions that agitate the face, and engage the attention, of a changing world. It is their duty to strive to distinguish, as clearly as they possible can, and if needed with the aid of their elected representatives, such posts and functions as are either diplomatic or political from those that are purely administrative in character, and which under no circumstances are affected by the changes and chances that political activities and party government, in every land, must necessarily involve. Let them affirm their unyielding determination to stand, firmly and unreservedly, for the way of Bahá'u'lláh, to avoid the entanglements and bickerings inseparable from the pursuits of the politician, and to become worthy agencies of that Divine Polity which incarnates God's immutable Purpose for all men.

It should be made unmistakably clear that such an attitude implies neither the slightest indifference to the cause and interests of their own country, nor involves any insubordination on their part to the authority of recognized and established governments. Nor does it constitute a repudiation of their sacred obligation to promote, in the most effective manner, the best interests of their government and people. It indicates the desire cherished by every true and loyal follower of Bahá'u'lláh to serve, in an unselfish, unostentatious and patriotic fashion, the highest interests of the country to which he belongs, and in a way that would entail no departure from the high standards of integrity and truthfulness associated with the teachings of his Faith.

As the number of the Bahá'í communities in various parts of the world multiplies and their power, as a social force, becomes increasingly apparent, they will no doubt find themselves increasingly subjected to the pressure which men of authority and influence, in the political domain, will exercise in the hope of obtaining the support they require for the advancement of their aims. These communities will, moreover, feel a growing need of the good-will and the assistance of their respective governments in their efforts to widen the scope, and to consolidate the foundations, of the institutions committed to their charge. Let them beware lest, in their eagerness to further the aims of their beloved Cause, they should be led unwittingly to bargain with their Faith, to compromise with their essential principles, or to sacrifice, in return for any material advantage which their institutions may derive, the integrity of their spiritual ideals. Let them proclaim that in whatever country they reside, and however advanced their institutions, or profound their desire to enforce the laws, and apply the principles, enunciated by Bahá'u'lláh, they will, unhesitatingly, subordinate the operation of such laws and the application of such principles to the requirements and legal enactments of their respective governments. Theirs is not the purpose, while endeavoring to conduct and perfect the administrative affairs of their Faith, to violate, under any circumstances, the provisions of their country's constitution, much less to allow the machinery of their administration to supersede the government of their respective countries.

It should also be borne in mind that the very extension of the activities in which we are engaged, and the variety of the communities which labor under divers forms of government, so essentially different in their standards, policies, and methods, make it absolutely essential for all those who are the declared members of any of these communities to avoid any action that might, by arousing the suspicion or exciting the antagonism of any one government, involve their brethren in fresh persecutions or complicate the nature of their task. How else, might I ask, should such a far-flung Faith which transcends political and social boundaries, which includes within its pale so great a variety of races and nations, which will have to rely increasingly, as it forges ahead, on the good-will and support of the diversified and contending governments of the earth-how else could such a Faith succeed in preserving its unity, in safeguarding its interests, and in ensuring the steady and peaceful development of its institutions?

Such an attitude, however, is not dictated by considerations of selfish expediency, but is actuated, first and foremost, by the broad principle that the followers of Bahá'u'lláh will, under no circumstances, suffer themselves to be involved, whether as individuals or in their collective capacities, in matters that would entail the slightest departure from the fundamental verities and ideals of their Faith. Neither the charges which the uninformed and the malicious may be led to bring against them, nor the allurements of honors and rewards, will ever induce them to surrender their trust or to deviate from their path. Let their words proclaim, and their conduct testify, that they who follow Bahá'u'lláh, in whatever land they reside, are actuated by no selfish ambition, that they neither thirst for power, nor mind any wave of unpopularity, of distrust or criticism, which a strict adherence to their standards might provoke.

Difficult and delicate though be our task, the sustaining power of Bahá'u'lláh and of His Divine guidance will assuredly assist us if we follow steadfastly in His way, and strive to uphold the integrity of His laws. The light of His redeeming grace, which no earthly power can obscure, will if we persevere, illuminate our path, as we steer our course amid the snares and pitfalls of a troubled age, and will enable us to discharge our duties in a manner that would redound to the glory and the honor of His blessed Name.

Shoghi Effendi

40
BAHA'I CONSULTATION

CONSULTATION AND COMPASSION

The heaven of divine wisdom is illumined with the two luminaries of consultation and compassion and the canopy of world order is upraised upon the two pillars of reward and punishment.

Bahá'u'lláh

CONSULTATION SHOULD SERVE THE SEARCH AFTER TRUTH

In this cause consultation is of vital importance, but spiritual conference and not the mere voicing of personal views is intended. In France I was present at a session of the senate, but the experience was not impressive. Parliamentary procedure should have for its object the attainment of the light of truth upon questions presented and not furnish a battleground for opposition and self-opinion. Antagonism and contradiction are unfortunate and always destructive to truth. In the parliamentary meeting mentioned, altercation and useless quibbling were frequent; the result, mostly confusion and turmoil; even in one instance a physical encounter took place between two members. It was not consultation but comedy.

The purpose is to emphasize the statement that consultation must have for its object the investigation of truth. He who expresses an opinion should not voice it as correct and right but set it forth as a contribution to the consensus of opinion, for the light of reality becomes apparent when two opinions coincide. A spark is produced when flint and steel come together. Man should weigh his opinions with the utmost serenity, calmness and composure. Before expressing his own views he should carefully consider the views already advanced by others. If he finds that a previously expressed opinion is more true and worthy, he should accept it immediately and not willfully hold to an opinion of his own. By this excellent method he endeavors to arrive at unity and truth. Opposition and division are deplorable. It is better then to have the opinion of a wise, sagacious man; otherwise, contradiction and altercation in which varied and divergent views are presented, will make it necessary for a judicial body to render decision upon the question. Even a majority opinion or consensus may be incorrect. A thousand people may hold to one view and be mistaken, whereas one sagacious person may be right. Therefore, true consultation is spiritual conference in the attitude and atmosphere of love. Members must love each other in the spirit of fellowship in order that good results may be forthcoming. Love and fellowship are the foundation.

'Abdu'l-Bahá

THE SPARK OF TRUTH

...take counsel together in such wise that no occasion for ill-feeling or discord may arise. This can be attained when every member expresseth with absolute freedom his own opinion and setteth forth his argument. Should anyone oppose, he must on no account feel hurt for not until matters are fully discussed can the right way be revealed. The shining spark of truth cometh forth only after the clash of differing opinions. If after discussion, a decision be carried unanimously well and good; but if, the Lord forbid, differences of opinion should arise, a majority of voices must prevail.

'Abdu'l-Bahá

BAHÁ'Í CONSULTATION

The first condition is absolute love and harmony amongst the members of the assembly. They must be wholly free from estrangement and must manifest in themselves the Unity of God, for they are the waves of one sea, the drops of one river, the stars of one heaven, the rays of one sun, the trees of one orchard, the flowers of one garden. Should harmony of thought and absolute unity be non-existent, that gathering shall be dispersed and that assembly be brought to naught. The second condition: they must, when coming together, turn their faces to the Kingdom on high and ask aid from the Realm of Glory. They must then proceed with the utmost devotion, courtesy, dignity, care and moderation to express their views. They must in every matter search out the truth and not insist upon their own opinion, for stubbornness and persistence in one's views will lead ultimately to discord and wrangling and the truth will remain hidden. The honoured members must with all freedom express their own thoughts, and it is in no wise permissible for one to belittle the thought of another, nay, he must with moderation set forth the truth, and should differences of opinion arise a majority of voices must prevail, and all must obey and submit to the majority. It is again not permitted that any one of the honoured members object to or censure, whether in or out of the meeting, any decision arrived at previously, though that decision be not right, for such criticism would prevent any decision from being enforced. In short, whatsoever thing is arranged in harmony and with love and purity of motive, its result is light, and should the least trace of estrangement prevail the result shall be darkness.

'Abdu'l-Bahá

41
GOVERNMENT

THE OBLIGATION OF BAHÁ'ÍS

In every country where any of this people reside, they must behave towards the government of that country with loyalty, honesty and truthfulness. This is that which hath been revealed at the behest of Him Who is the Ordainer, the Ancient of Days.

Bahá'u'lláh

The only group of people which today submitteth peacefully and loyally to the laws and ordinances of government and dealeth honestly and frankly with the people, is none other than this wronged community.

'Abdu'l-Bahá

THE OBLIGATION OF EVERY CITIZEN

It is incumbent upon every man, in this Day, to hold fast unto whatsoever will promote the interests and exalt the station, of all nations and just governments.

Bahá'u'lláh

THE OBLIGATIONS OF ALL GOVERNMENTS

Governments should fully acquaint themselves with the conditions of those they govern, and confer upon them positions according to desert and merit. It is enjoined upon every ruler and sovereign to consider this matter with the utmost care that the traitor may not usurp the position of the faithful, nor the despoiler rule in the place of the trustworthy.

Bahá'u'lláh

Government

We call upon the manifestations of the power of God-the sovereigns and rulers on earth-to bestir themselves and do all in their power that haply they may banish discord from this world and illumine it with the light of concord.

Bahá'u'lláh

God hath committed into your hands the reins of the government of the people, that ye may rule with justice over them, safeguard the rights of the downtrodden, and punish the wrong-doers.

Bahá'u'lláh

Know ye that the poor are the trust of God in your midst. Watch that ye betray not His trust, that ye deal not unjustly with them and that ye walk not in the ways of the treacherous. Ye will most certainly be called upon to answer for His trust on the day when the Balance of Justice shall be set, the day when unto every one shall be rendered his due, when the doings of all men, be they rich or poor, shall be weighed...

If ye stay not the hand of the oppressor, if ye fail to safeguard the rights of the down-trodden, what right have ye then to vaunt yourselves among men? What is it of which ye can rightly boast? Is it on your food and your drink that ye pride yourselves, on the riches ye lay up in your treasures, on the diversity and the cost of the ornaments with which ye deck yourselves? If true glory were to consist in the possession of such perishable things, then the earth on which ye walk must needs vaunt itself over you, because it supplieth you, and bestoweth upon you, these very things, by the decree of the Almighty. In its bowels are contained, according to what God hath ordained, all that ye possess. From it, as a sign of His mercy, ye derive your riches. Behold then your state, the thing in which ye glory! Would that ye could perceive it!...

We see you increasing every year your expenditures, and laying the burden thereof on your subjects. This, verily, is wholly and grossly unjust. Fear the sighs and tears of this Wronged One, and lay not excessive burdens on your peoples. Do not rob them to rear palaces for yourselves; nay rather choose for them that which ye choose for yourselves. Thus We unfold to your eyes that which profiteth you, if ye but perceive. Your people are your treasures. Beware lest your rule violate the commandments of God, and ye deliver your wards to the hands of the robber. By them ye rule, by their means ye subsist, by their aid ye conquer. Yet, how disdainfully ye look upon them! How strange, how very strange!...

Bahá'u'lláh

THE SECRET OF STATESMANSHIP IS REVEALED

Take heed, O concourse of the rulers of the world! There is no force on earth that can equal in its conquering power the force of justice and wisdom. I, verily, affirm that there is not, and hath never been, a host more mighty than that of justice and wisdom...There can be no doubt whatever that if the daystar of justice, which the clouds of tyranny have obscured, were to shed its light upon men, the face of the earth would be completely transformed...

...The heaven of statesmanship is made luminous and resplendent by the brightness of the light of these blessed words which hath dawned from the dayspring of the Will of God: It behoveth every ruler to weigh his own being every day in the balance of equity and justice and then to judge between men and counsel them to do that which would direct their steps unto the path of wisdom and understanding. This is the cornerstone of statesmanship and the essence thereof. From these words every enlightened man of wisdom will readily perceive that which will foster such aims as the welfare, security and protection of mankind and the safety of human lives. Were men of insight to quaff their fill from the ocean of inner meanings which lie enshrined in these words and become acquainted therewith, they would bear witness to the sublimity and the excellence of this utterance. If this lowly one were to set forth that which he perceiveth, all would testify unto God's consummate wisdom. The secrets of statesmanship and that of which the people are in need lie enfolded within these words. This lowly servant earnestly entreateth the One true God-exalted be His glory-to illumine the eyes of the people of the world with the splendour of the light of wisdom that they, one and all, may recognize that which is indispensable in this day.

Bahá'u'lláh

LEGISLATORS SHOULD SERVE ALL HUMANITY

O ye elected representatives of the people of every Land! Take ye counsel together, and let your concern be only for that which profiteth mankind, and bettereth the condition thereof, if ye be of them that scan heedfully. Regard the world as the human body which, though at its creation whole and perfect, hath been afflicted, through various causes, with grave disorders and maladies. Not for one day did it gain ease, nay its sickness waxed more severe, and it fell under the treatment of ignorant physicians, who gave full rein to their personal desires, and have erred grievously. And if, at one time, through the care of an able physician, a member of that body was healed, the rest remained afflicted as before. Thus informeth you the All-Knowing, the All-Wise.

We behold it, in this day, at the mercy of rulers so drunk with pride that they cannot discern clearly their own best advantages, much less recognize a Revelation so bewildering and challenging as this. And whenever any one of them hath striven to improve its condition, his motive hath been his own gain, whether confessedly so or not; and the unworthiness of this motive hath limited his power to heal or cure.

That which the Lord hath ordained as the sovereign remedy and mightiest instrument for the healing of all the world is the union of all its peoples in one universal Cause, one common Faith. This can in no wise be achieved except through the power of a skilled, an all-powerful and inspired Physician. This, verily, is the truth, and all else naught but error.

Bahá'u'lláh

We have also heard that thou [Queen Victoria] hast entrusted the reins of counsel into the hands of the representatives of the people. Thou, indeed, hast done well, for thereby the foundations of the edifice of thine affairs will be strengthened, and the hearts of all that are beneath thy shadow, whether high or low, will be tranquillized. It behooveth them, however, to be trustworthy among His servants, and to regard themselves as the representatives of all that dwell on earth...Blessed is he that entereth the Assembly for the sake of God, and judgeth between men with pure justice. He, indeed, is of the blissful.

Bahá'u'lláh

ADVICE TO A KING

Beware, O King, that thou gather not around thee such ministers as follow the desires of a corrupt inclination, as have cast behind their backs that which hath been committed into their hands and manifestly betrayed their trust. Be bounteous to others as God hath been bounteous to thee, and abandon not the interests of thy people to the mercy of such ministers as these...Gather around thee those minister from whom thou canst perceive the fragrance of faith and of justice, and take thou counsel with them, and choose whatever is best in thy sight, and be of them that act generously...

Overstep not the bounds of moderation, and deal justly with them that serve thee. Bestow upon them according to their needs, and not to the extent that will enable them to lay up riches for themselves, to deck their persons, to embellish their homes, to acquire the things that are of no benefit unto them, and to be numbered with the extravagant. Deal with them with undeviating justice, so that none among them may either suffer want, or be pampered with luxuries. This is but manifest justice.

Allow not the abject to rule over and dominate them who are noble and worthy of honor, and suffer not the high-minded to be at the mercy of the contemptible and worthless, for this is what We observed upon Our arrival in the City (Constantinople), and to it We bear witness. We found among its inhabitants some who were possessed of an affluent fortune and lived in the midst of excessive riches, while others were in dire want and abject poverty. This ill beseemeth thy sovereignty, and is unworthy of thy rank...

Let My counsel be acceptable to thee, and strive thou to rule with equality among men, that God may exalt thy name and spread abroad the fame of thy justice in all the world. Beware lest thou aggrandize thy ministers at the expense of thy subjects. Fear the sighs of the poor and of the upright in heart who, at every break of day, bewail their plight, and be unto them a benignant sovereign. They, verily, are thy treasures on earth. It behoveth thee, therefore, to safeguard thy treasures from the assaults of them who wish to rob thee. Inquire into their affairs, and ascertain, every year, nay every month, their condition, and be not of them that are careless of their duty.

It behoveth every king to be as bountiful as the sun, which fostereth the growth of all beings, and giveth to each its due, whose benefits are not inherent in itself, but are ordained by Him Who is the Most Powerful, the Almighty. The King should be as generous, as liberal in his mercy as the clouds, the outpourings of whose bounty are showered upon every land, by the behest of Him Who is the Supreme Ordainer, the All-Knowing.

Have care not to entrust thine affairs of state entirely into another's hands. None can discharge thy functions better than thine own self. Thus do We make clear unto thee Our words of wisdom, and send down upon thee that which can enable thee to pass over from the left hand of oppression to the right hand of justice, and approach the resplendent ocean of His favors. Such is the path which the kings that were before thee have trodden, they that acted equitably towards their subjects, and walked in the ways of undeviating justice.

Thou art God's shadow on earth. Strive, therefore, to act in such a manner as befitteth so eminent, so august a station. If thou dost depart from following the things We have caused to descend upon thee and taught thee, thou wilt, assuredly, be derogating from that great and priceless honor. Return, then, and cleave wholly unto God, and cleanse thine heart from the world and all its vanities, and suffer not the love of any stranger to enter and dwell therein. Not until thou dost purify thine heart from every trace of such love can the brightness of the light of God shed its radiance upon it, for to none hath God given more than one heart. This, verily, hath been decreed and written down in His ancient Book. And as the human heart, as fashioned by God, is one and undivided, it behoveth thee to take heed that its affections be, also, one and undivided. Cleave thou, therefore, with the whole affection of thine heart, unto His love, and withdraw it from the love of any one besides Him, that He may aid thee to immerse thyself in the ocean of His unity, and enable thee to become a true upholder of His oneness. God is My witness. My sole purpose in revealing to thee these words is to sanctify thee to enter the realm of everlasting glory, that thou mayest, by the leave of God, be of them that abide and rule therein.

Bahá'u'lláh

ONE OF THE SIGNS OF THE MATURITY OF THE WORLD

One of the signs of the maturity of the world is that no one will accept to bear the weight of kingship. Kingship will remain with none willing to bear alone its weight. That day will be the day whereon wisdom will be manifested among mankind. Only in order to proclaim the Cause of God and spread abroad His Faith will anyone be willing to bear this grievous weight. Well is it with him who, for love of God and His Cause, and for the sake of God and for the purpose of proclaiming His Faith, will expose himself unto this great danger, and will accept this toil and trouble.

Bahá'u'lláh

Let none, however, mistake or unwittingly misrepresent the purpose of Bahá'u'lláh. Severe as has been His condemnation pronounced against those sovereigns who persecuted Him, and however strict the censure expressed collectively against those who failed signally in their clear duty to investigate the truth of His Faith and to restrain the hand of the wrong-doer, His teachings embody no principle that can, in any way, be construed as a repudiation, or even a disparagement, however veiled, of the institution of kingship.

Shoghi Effendi

A just king is the shadow of God on earth. All should seek shelter under the shadow of his justice, and rest in the shade of his favor. This is not a matter which is either specific or limited in its scope, that it might be restricted to one or another person, inasmuch as the shadow telleth of the One Who casteth it. God, glorified be His remembrance, hath called Himself the Lord of the worlds, for He hath nurtured and still nurtureth everyone. Glorified be, then, His grace that hath preceded all created things, and His mercy that hath surpassed the worlds.

Bahá'u'lláh

42
INTERNATIONAL AUXILIARY LANGUAGE

THE EARTH AS ONE COUNTRY

It behoveth the sovereigns of the world-may God assist them-or the ministers of the earth to take counsel together and to adopt one of the existing languages or a new one to be taught to children in schools throughout the world, and likewise one script. Thus the whole earth will come to be regarded as one country.

Bahá'u'lláh

The day is approaching when all the peoples of the world will have adopted one universal language and one common scrip. When this is achieved, to whatsoever city a man may journey, it shall be as if he were entering his own home. These things are obligatory and absolutely essential. It is incumbent upon every man of insight and understanding to strive to translate that which hath been written into reality and action.

Bahá'u'lláh

A KEY TO PROGRESS AND DEVELOPMENT

The heart is like a box, and language is the key. Only by using the key can we open the box and observe the gems it contains. Therefore, the question of an auxiliary international tongue has the utmost importance. Through this means international education and training become possible, the evidence and history of the past can be acquired. The spread of the known facts of the human world depends upon language...Therefore, the very first service to the world of man is to establish this auxiliary international means of communication. It will become the cause of the tranquillity of the human commonwealth.

Through it science and arts will be spread among the nations, and it will prove to be the means of the progress and development of all races. We must endeavor with all our powers to establish this international auxiliary language throughout the world.

'Abdu'l-Bahá

A STEP TOWARDS WORLD PEACE

One of the great steps towards universal peace would be the establishment of a universal language. Bahá'u'lláh commands that the servants of humanity should meet together, and either choose a language which now exists, or form a new one. This was revealed in the Kitáb-i-Aqdas forty years ago. It is there pointed out that the question of diversity of tongues is a very difficult one...

The races of mankind are not isolated as in former days. Now, in order to be in close relationship with all countries it is necessary to be able to speak their tongues.

A universal language would make intercourse possible with every nation. Thus it would be needful to know two languages only, the mother tongue and the universal speech. The latter would enable a man to communicate with any and every man in the world!

A third language would not be needed. To be able to talk with a member of any race and country without requiring an interpreter, how helpful and restful to all!

...Until such a language is in use, the world will continue to feel the vast need of this means of intercourse. Difference of speech is one of the most fruitful causes of dislike and distrust that exists between nations, which are kept apart by their inability to understand each other's language more than by any other reason.

If everybody could speak one language, how much more easy would it be to serve humanity!

'Abdu'l-Bahá

43
WORLD GOVERNMENT

The world's equilibrium hath been upset through the vibrating influence of this most great, this new World Order. Mankind's ordered life hath been revolutionized through the agency of this unique, this wondrous System-the like of which mortal eyes have never witnessed.

Bahá'u'lláh

CENTRALIZATION REJECTED

It is very evident that in the future there shall be no centralization in the countries of the world, be they constitutional in government, republican or democratic in form. The United States may be held up as the example of future government-that is to say, each province will be independent in itself, but there will be federal union protecting the interests of the various independent states. It may not be a republican or a democratic form. To cast aside centralization which promotes despotism is the exigency of the time. This will be productive of international peace. Another fact of equal importance in bringing about international peace is woman's suffrage...

'Abdu'l-Bahá

Let there be no misgivings as to the animating purpose of the world-wide Law of Bahá'u'lláh. Far from aiming at the subversion of the existing foundations of society, it seeks to broaden its basis, to remould its institutions in a manner consonant with the needs of an ever-changing world. It can conflict with no legitimate allegiances, nor can it undermine essential loyalties. Its purpose is neither to stifle the flame of a sane and intelligent patriotism in men's hearts, nor to abolish the system of national autonomy so essential if the evils of excessive centralization are to be avoided. It does not ignore, nor does it attempt to suppress, the diversity of ethnical origins, of climate, of history, of language and tradition, of thought and habit, that differentiate the peoples and nations of the world. It calls for a wider loyalty, for a larger aspiration than any that has animated the human race. It insists upon the subordination of national impulses and interests to the imperative claims of a unified world. It repudiates excessive centralization on one hand, and disclaims all attempts at uniformity on the other. Its watchword is unity in diversity...

Shoghi Effendi

'ABDU'L-BAHÁ ADDRESSES AN OFFICIAL OF THE UNITED STATES

You can best serve your country if you strive, in your capacity as a citizen of the world, to assist in the eventual application of the principle of federalism, underlying the government of your own country, to the relationships now existing between the peoples and nations of the world.

'Abdu'l-Bahá

THE CONSCIOUSNESS OF WORLD CITIZENSHIP

The Revelation of Bahá'u'lláh, whose supreme mission is none other but the achievement of this organic and spiritual unity of the whole body of nations, should, if we be faithful to its implications, be regarded as signalizing through its advent the coming of age of the entire human race. It should be viewed not merely as yet another spiritual revival in the ever-changing fortunes of mankind, not only as a further stage in a chain of progressive Revelations, nor even as the culmination of one of a series of recurrent prophetic cycles, but rather as marking the last and highest stage in the stupendous evolution of man's collective life on this planet. The emergence of a world community, the consciousness of world citizenship, the foundation of a world civilization and culture-all of which must synchronize with the initial stages in the unfoldment of the Golden Age of the Bahá'í Era-should, by their very nature, be regarded, as far as this planetary life is concerned, as the furthermost limits in the organization of human society, though man, as an individual, will, nay must indeed as a result of such a consummation, continue indefinitely to progress and develop.

Shoghi Effendi

THE ESTABLISHMENT OF A WORLD COMMONWEALTH

It is incumbent upon the Sovereigns of the world...to convene an all-inclusive assembly, which either they themselves or their ministers will attend, and to enforce whatever measures are required to establish unity and concord amongst men. They must put away the weapons of war, and turn to the instruments of universal reconstruction. Should one king rise up against another, all the other kings must arise to deter him. Arms and armaments will, then, be no more needed beyond that which is necessary to insure the internal security of their respective countries. If they attain unto this all-surpassing blessing, the people of each nation will pursue, with tranquillity and contentment, their own occupations, and the groaning and lamentations of most men would be silenced.

Bahá'u'lláh

The unity of the human race, as envisaged by Bahá'u'lláh, implies the establishment of a world commonwealth in which all nations, races, creeds and classes are closely and permanently united, and in which the autonomy of its state members and the personal freedom and initiative of the individuals that compose them are definitely and completely safeguarded. This commonwealth must, as far as we can visualize it, consists of a world legislature, whose members will, as the trustees of the whole of mankind, ultimately control the entire resources of all the component nations, and will enact such laws as shall be required to regulate the life, satisfy the needs and adjust the relationships of all races and peoples. A world executive, backed by an international Force, will carry out the decisions arrived at, and apply the laws enacted by, this world legislature, and will safeguard the organic unity of the whole commonwealth. A world tribunal will adjudicate and deliver its compulsory and final verdict in all and any disputes that may arise between the various elements constituting this universal system.

Shoghi Effendi

THE INFRASTRUCTURE OF A WORLD CIVILIZATION

A mechanism of world intercommunication will be devised, embracing the whole planet, freed from national hindrance and restrictions, and functioning with marvellous swiftness and perfect regularity. A world metropolis will act as the nerve centre of a world civilization, the focus towards which the unifying forces of life will converge and from which its energizing influences will radiate. A world language will either be invented or chosen from among the existing languages and will be taught in the schools of all the federated nations as an auxiliary to their mother tongue. A world script, a world literature, a uniform and universal system of currency, of weights and measures, will simplify and facilitate intercourse and understanding among the nations and races of mankind. In such a world society science and religion, the two most potent forces in human life, will be reconciled, will co-operate, and will harmoniously develop. The press will, under such a system, while giving full scope to the expression of the diversified views and convictions of mankind, cease to be mischievously manipulated by vested interests, whether private or public, and will be liberated from the influence of contending governments and peoples. The economic resources of the world will be organized, its sources of raw materials will be tapped and fully utilized, its markets will be co-ordinated and developed, and the distribution of its products will be equitably regulated.

Shoghi Effendi

FUTURE SOCIAL DEVELOPMENT

National rivalries, hatreds, and intrigues will cease, and racial animosity and prejudice will be replaced by racial amity, understanding and co-operation. The causes of religious strife will be permanently removed, economic barriers and restrictions will be completely abolished, and the inordinate distinction between classes will be obliterated. Destitution on the one hand, and gross accumulation of ownership on the other, will disappear. The enormous energy dissipated and wasted on war, whether economic or political, will be consecrated to such ends as will extend the range of human inventions and technical development, to the increase of the productivity of mankind, to the extermination of disease, to the extension of scientific research, to the raising of the standards of physical health, to the sharpening and refinement of the human brain, to the exploitation of the unused and unsuspected resources of the planet, to the prolongation of human life, and to the furtherance of any other agency that can stimulate the intellectual, the moral, and spiritual life of the entire human race....

WORLD UNITY THE HALL-MARK OF A MATURE WORLD

Unification of the whole of mankind is the hall-mark of the stage which human society in now approaching. Unity of family, of tribe, of city-state, and nation have been successively attempted and fully established. World unity is the goal toward which a harassed humanity is striving. Nation-building has come to an end. The anarchy inherent in state sovereignty is moving towards a climax. A world, growing to maturity, must abandon this fetish, recognize the oneness and wholeness of human relationships, and establish once and for all the machinery that can best incarnate this fundamental principle of its life.

Shoghi Effendi

44
CIVILIZATION

SIGNS OF IMPENDING CHAOS

Whatsoever passeth beyond the limits of moderation will cease to exert a beneficial influence. Consider for instance such things as liberty, civilization and the like. However much men of understanding may favorably regard them, they will, if carried to excess, exercise a pernicious influence upon men...Please God, the peoples of the world may be led, as the result of the high endeavors exerted by their rulers and the wise and learned amongst men, to recognize their best interests...The winds of despair are, alas, blowing from every direction, and the strife that divideth and afflicteth the human race is daily increasing. The signs of impending convulsions and chaos can now be discerned, inasmuch as the prevailing order appeareth to be lamentably defective. I beseech God, exalted be His glory, that He may graciously awaken the peoples of the earth, may grant that the end of their conduct may be profitable unto them, and aid them to accomplish that which beseemeth their station.

Bahá'u'lláh

Soon will the present-day order be rolled up, and a new one spread out in its stead. Verily, thy Lord speaketh the truth, and is the Knower of things unseen.

Bahá'u'lláh

A new life is, in this age, stirring within all the peoples of the earth; and yet none hath discovered its cause or perceived its motive. Consider the peoples of the West. Witness how, in their pursuit of that which is vain and trivial, they have sacrificed, and are still sacrificing, countless lives for the sake of its establishment and promotion. The peoples of Persia, on the other hand, though the repository of a perspicuous and luminous

Revelation, the glory of whose loftiness and renown hath encompassed the whole earth, are dispirited and sunk in deep lethargy.

Bahá'u'lláh

JUSTICE AND MODERATION

Whoso cleaveth to justice, can, under no circumstances, transgress the limits of moderation. He discerneth the truth in all things, through the guidance of Him Who is the All-Seeing. The civilization, so often vaunted by the learned exponents of arts and sciences, will, if allowed to overleap the bounds of moderation, bring great evil upon men. Thus warneth you He Who is the All-Knowing. If carried to excess, civilization will prove as prolific a source of evil as it had been of goodness when kept within the restraints of moderation.

Bahá'u'lláh

COMPASSION

All men have been created to carry forward an ever-advancing civilization. The Almighty beareth Me witness: To act like the beasts of the field is unworthy of man. Those virtues that befit his dignity are forbearance, mercy, compassion and loving kindness towards all the peoples and kindreds of the earth.

Bahá'u'lláh

COOPERATION

Consequently, when thou traversest the regions of the world, thou shalt conclude that all progress is the result of association and cooperation, while ruin is the outcome of animosity and hatred. Notwithstanding this, the world of humanity doth not take warning, nor doth it awake from the slumber of heedlessness. Man is still causing differences, quarrels and strife in order to marshal the cohorts of war and, with his legions, rush into the field of bloodshed and slaughter.

'Abdu'l-Bahá

LIBERTY MUST BE BALANCED WITH DIGNITY AND MODERATION

Consider the pettiness of men's minds. They ask for that which injureth them, and cast away the thing that profiteth them. They are, indeed, of those that are far astray. We find some men desiring liberty, and priding themselves therein...

Liberty must, in the end, lead to sedition, whose flames none can quench. Thus warneth you He Who is the Reckoner, the All-Knowing. Know ye that the embodiment of liberty and its symbol is the animal. That which beseemeth man is submission unto such restraints as will protect him from his own ignorance, and guard him against the harm of the mischief-maker. Liberty causeth man to overstep the bounds of propriety, and to infringe on the dignity of his station. It debaseth him to the level of extreme depravity and wickedness...

Were men to observe that which We have sent down unto them from the Heaven of Revelation, they would, of a certainty, attain unto perfect liberty. Happy is the man that hath apprehended the Purpose of God in whatever He hath revealed from the Heaven of His Will, that pervadeth all created things.

Bahá'u'lláh

THE PROCESS OF GROWTH & ADAPTATION

Similarly, there are periods and stages in the life of the aggregate world of humanity, which at one time was passing through its degree of childhood, at another its time of youth but now has entered its long presaged period of maturity, the evidences of which are everywhere visible and apparent. Therefore, the requirements and conditions of former periods have changed and merged into exigencies which distinctly characterize the present age of the world of mankind. That which was applicable to human needs during the early history of the race could neither meet nor satisfy the demands of this day and period of newness and consummation. Humanity has emerged from its former degrees of limitation and preliminary training. Man must now become imbued with new virtues and powers, new moralities, new capacities. New bounties, bestowals and perfections are awaiting and already descending upon him. The gifts and graces of the period of youth, although timely and sufficient during the adolescence of the world of mankind, are now incapable of meeting the requirements of its maturity. The playthings of childhood and infancy no longer satisfy or interest the adult mind.

From every standpoint the world of humanity is undergoing a reformation. The laws of former governments and civilizations are in process of revision; scientific ideas and theories are developing and advancing to meet a new range of phenomena; invention and discovery are penetrating hitherto unknown fields, revealing new wonders and hidden secrets of the material universe; industries have vastly wider scope and production; everywhere the world of mankind is in the throes of evolutionary activity indicating the passing of the old conditions and advent of the new age of reformation. Old trees yield no fruitage; old ideas and methods are obsolete and worthless now. Old standards of ethics, moral codes and methods of living in the past will not suffice for the present age of advancement and progress.

'Abdu'l-Bahá

KNOWLEDGE SHOULD BE USED TO POSITIVE ENDS

God's greatest gift to man is that of intellect, or understanding...

God gave this power to man that it might be used for the advancement of civilization, for the good of humanity, to increase love and concord and peace...

I hope that you will use your understanding to promote the unity and tranquillity of mankind, to give enlightenment and civilization to the people, to produce love in all around you, and to bring about universal peace.

Study the sciences, acquire more and more knowledge. Assuredly one may learn to the end of one's life! Use your knowledge always for the benefit of others; so may war cease on the face of this beautiful earth, and a glorious edifice of peace and concord be raised. Strive that your high ideals may be realized in the Kingdom of God on earth, as they will be in Heaven.

'Abdu'l-Bahá

The principles of the Teachings of Bahá'u'lláh should be carefully studied, one by one, until they are realized and understood by mind and heart-so will you become strong followers of the light, truly spiritual, heavenly soldiers of God, acquiring and spreading the true civilization...in the whole world.

'Abdu'l-Bahá

THE LIMITS OF MATERIAL CIVILIZATION

Until the heavenly civilization is founded, no result will be forthcoming from material civilization, even as you observe.

'Abdu'l-Bahá

The heavenly Jerusalem is none other than divine civilization, and it is now ready. It is to be and shall be organized, and the oneness of humankind will be a visible fact. Humanity will then be brought together as one. The various religions will be united, and different races will be known as one kind. The Orient and Occident will be conjoined, and the banner of international peace will be unfurled. The world shall at last find peace, and the equalities and rights of men shall be established. The capacity of humankind will be tested, and a degree shall be attained where equality is a reality.

All the peoples of the world will enjoy like interests, and the poor shall possess a portion of the comforts of life. Just as the rich are surrounded by their luxuries in palaces, the poor will have at least their comfortable and pleasant places of abode; and just as the wealthy enjoy a variety of food, the needy shall have their necessities and no longer live in poverty...

Consider: What is this material civilization of the day giving forth? Has it not produced the instruments of warfare and destruction? In olden times the weapon of war was the sword; today it is the smokeless gun. Warships a century ago were sailing vessels; now we have dreadnoughts. Instruments and means of human destruction have enormously multiplied in this era of material civilization. But if material civilization shall become organized in conjunction with divine civilization, if the man of moral integrity and intellectual acumen shall unite for human betterment and uplift with the man of spiritual capacity, the happiness and progress of the human race will be assured. All the nations of the world will then be closely related and companionable, and the religions will merge into one, for the divine reality within them all is one reality...

For centuries and cycles humanity has been engaged in war and conflict. At one time the pretext for war has been religion, at another time patriotism, racial prejudice, national politics, territorial conquest or commercial expansion; in brief, humanity has never been at peace during the period of known history...Ferocity has characterized men even more than animals. The lion cannot graze; its teeth are fitted only for food of flesh. This is also true of other wild animals. Ferocity is natural to them as their means of subsistence; but human ferocity proceeds from selfishness, greed and oppression. It springs from no natural necessity. Man needlessly kills a thousand fellow creatures, becomes a hero and is glorified through centuries of posterity. A great city is destroyed in one day by a commanding general. How ignorant, how inconsistent is humankind!...If a man steals one dollar, he is called a thief and put into prison; if he rapes and pillages an innocent country by military invasion, he is crowned a hero...Material civilization has advanced unmistakably, but because it is not associated with divine civilization, evil and wickedness abound. In ancient times if two nations were at war twelve months, not over twenty thousand men would be killed; now the instruments of death have become so multiplied and perfected that one hundred thousand can be destroyed in a day...The cause is the absence of divine civilization.

'Abdu'l-Bahá

SPIRITUAL CIVILIZATION IS THE ULTIMATE AIM

...until material achievements, physical accomplishments and human virtues are reinforced by spiritual perfections, luminous qualities and characteristics of mercy, no fruit or result shall issue therefrom, nor will the happiness of the world of humanity, which is the ultimate aim, be attained. For although, on the one hand, material achievements and the development of the physical world produce prosperity, which exquisitely manifests its intended aims, on the other hand dangers, severe calamities and violent afflictions are imminent.

Consequently, when thou lookest at the orderly pattern of kingdoms, cities and villages, with the attractiveness of their adornments, the freshness of their natural resources, the refinement of their means of travel, the extent of knowledge available about the world of nature, the great inventions, the colossal enterprises, the noble discoveries and scientific researches, thou wouldst conclude that civilization conduceth to the happiness and the progress of the human world. Yet shouldst thou turn thine eye to the discovery of destructive and infernal machines, to the development of forces of demolition and the invention of fiery implements, which uproot the tree of life, it would become evident and manifest unto thee that civilization is conjoined with barbarism. Progress and barbarism go hand in hand, unless material civilization be confirmed by Divine Guidance, by the revelations of the All-Merciful and by godly virtues, and be reinforced by spiritual conduct, by the ideals of the Kingdom and by the outpourings of the Realm of Might.

Consider now, that the most advanced and civilized countries of the world have been turned into arsenals of explosives, that the continents of the globe have been transformed into huge camps and battlefields, that the peoples of the world have formed themselves into armed nations, and that the governments of the world are vying with each other as to who will first step into the field of carnage and bloodshed, thus subjecting mankind to the utmost degree of affliction.

Therefore, this civilization and material progress should be combined with the Most Great Guidance so that this nether world may become the scene of the appearance of the bestowals of the Kingdom, and physical achievements may be conjoined with the effulgences of the Merciful. This in order that the beauty and perfection of the world of man may be unveiled and be manifested before all in the utmost grace and splendour. Thus everlasting glory and happiness shall be revealed...

...in the contingent world, the human species hath undergone progressive physical changes and, by a slow process, hath scaled the ladder of civilization, realizing in itself the wonders, excellencies and gifts of humanity in their most glorious form, until it gained the capacity to express the splendours of spiritual perfections and divine ideals and became capable of hearkening to the call of God.

'Abdu'l-Bahá

THE GREAT AGE TO COME

The ages of its infancy and childhood are past, never again to return, while the Great Age, the consummation of all ages, which must signalize the coming of age of the entire human race, is yet to come. The convulsions of this transitional and most turbulent period in the annals of humanity are the essential prerequisites, and herald the inevitable approach, of that Age of Ages, "the time of the end," in which the folly and tumult of strife that has, since the dawn of history, blackened the annals of mankind, will have been finally transmuted into the wisdom and the tranquillity of an undisturbed, a universal, and lasting peace, in which the discord and separation of the children of men will have given way to the world-wide reconciliation, and the complete unification of the divers elements that constitute human society.

This will indeed be the fitting climax of that process of integration which, starting with the family, the smallest unit in the scale of human organization, must, after having called successively into being the tribe, the city-state and the nation, continue to operate until it culminates in the unification of the whole world, the final object and the crowning glory of human evolution of this planet. It is this stage which humanity, willingly or unwillingly, is resistlessly approaching.

Shoghi Effendi

45
THE BÁB

AN EXCERPT FROM THE NARRATIVE OF THE WIFE OF THE BÁB

So, with both astonishment and trepidation, I went up the steps at the northern side of the courtyard. There I saw Him standing in that chamber, His hands raised heavenwards, intoning a prayer in a most melodious voice, with tears streaming down His face. And His face was luminous; rays of light radiated from it. He looked so majestic and resplendent that fear seized me, and I stood transfixed where I was, trembling uncontrollably. I could neither enter the room nor retrace my steps. My will-power was gone, and I was on the point of screaming, when He made a gesture with His blessed hands, telling me to go back. This movement of His hands gave me back my courage, and I returned to my room and my bed...Sleep was impossible that night, and then came the dawn, so foreboding, and I heard the muezzin's call to prayer.

...He was quietly drinking His tea. He raised His face to me, and received me with great kindness and affection, bidding me be seated...His kindness restored my courage, and when He asked me what it was that troubled me, I boldly replied that it was the change in Him which weighed heavily on my mind. "You are no longer", I told Him, "the same person I knew in our childhood. We grew up together, and we have been married for two years, living in this house, and now I see a different person before me. You have been transformed." I further remarked that this had made me anxious and uneasy. He smiled and said that although He had not wished to be seen by me in the condition of the previous night, God had ordained otherwise. "It was the will of God", He said, "that you should have seen Me in the way you did last night, so that no shadow of doubt should ever cross your mind, and you should come to know with absolute certitude that I am that Manifestation of God

Whose advent has been expected for a thousand years. This light radiates from My heart and from My Being." As soon as I heard Him speak these words I believed in Him. I prostrated myself before Him and my heart became calm and assured. From that moment I lived only to serve Him, evanescent and self-effacing before Him, no thought of self ever intruding.

Khadíjih Bagum, The Wife of the Báb

THE NARRATIVE OF MULLÁ HUSAYN THE FIRST INDEPENDENT SEEKER TO RECOGNIZE THE STATION OF THE BÁB

I sat enraptured by the magic of His voice and the sweeping force of His revelation..."This night," He declared, "this very hour will, in the days to come, be celebrated as one of the greatest and most significant of all festivals" [Two hours and eleven minutes after sunset May 23, 1844]

...I sat spellbound by His utterance, oblivious of time and of those who awaited me. Suddenly the call of the muadhdin, summoning the faithful to their morning prayer, awakened me from the state of ecstasy into which I seemed to have fallen. All the delights, all the ineffable glories, which the Almighty has recounted in His Book as the priceless possessions of the people of Paradise-these I seemed to be experiencing that night...

Sleep had departed from me that night. I was enthralled by the music of that voice which rose and fell as He chanted; now swelling forth as He revealed verses...again acquiring ethereal, subtle harmonies as He uttered the prayers He was revealing...

This Revelation, so suddenly and impetuously thrust upon me, came as a thunderbolt which, for a time, seemed to have benumbed my faculties. I was blinded by its dazzling splendour and overwhelmed by its crushing force. Excitement, joy, awe, and wonder stirred the depths of my soul. Predominant among these emotions was a sense of gladness and strength which seemed to have transfigured me. How feeble and impotent, how dejected and timid, I had felt previously! Then I could neither write nor walk, so tremulous were my hands and feet. Now, however, the knowledge of His Revelation had galvanised my being. I felt possessed of such courage and power that were the world, all its peoples and its potentates, to rise against me, I would, alone and undaunted, withstand their onslaught. The universe seemed but a handful of dust in my grasp. I seemed to be the Voice of Gabriel personified, calling unto all mankind: "Awake, for, lo! the morning Light has broken. Arise, for His Cause is made manifest. The portals of His grace is open wide; enter therein, O peoples of the world! For He who is your promised One is come!"

Mullá Husayn

THE BÁB ON HIS STATION

O concourse of light! By the righteousness of God, We speak not according to selfish desire, nor hath a single letter of this Book been revealed save by the leave of God, the Sovereign Truth...entertain no doubts regarding His Cause, for verily, the Mystery of this Gate is shrouded in the mystic utterances of His Writ and hath been written beyond the impenetrable veil of concealment by the hand of God, the Lord of the visible and the invisible.

Indeed God hath created everywhere around this Gate oceans of divine elixir, tinged crimson with the essence of existence and vitalized through the animating power of the desired fruit; and for them God hath provided Arks of ruby, tender, crimson-coloured, wherein none shall sail but the people of Bahá, by the leave of God, the Most Exalted; and verily He is the All-Glorious, the All-Wise.

The Báb

Verily I am none other but the servant of God and His Word, and none but the first one to bow down in supplication before God, the Most Exalted; and indeed God witnesseth all things.

The Báb

I am the 'Gate of God' and I give you to drink, by the leave of God, the sovereign Truth, of the crystal-pure waters of His Revelation which are gushing out from the incorruptible Fountain situate upon the Holy Mount. And those who earnestly strive after the One True God, let them then strive to attain this Gate...

These verses, clear and conclusive, are a token of the mercy of thy Lord and a source of guidance for all mankind. They are a light unto those who believe in them...

The Báb

O peoples of the earth! Give ear to God's holy Voice proclaimed by this Arabian Youth Whom the Almighty hath graciously chosen for His Own

Self. He is indeed none other than the True One, Whom God hath entrusted with this mission from the midst of the Burning Bush...Unravel what Thou pleasest from the secrets of the All-Glorious, for the ocean is surging high at the behest of the incomparable Lord.

The Báb

THE BÁB ON HIS REVELATION

Verily the equivalent of that which God revealed unto Muhammad during twenty-three years, hath been revealed unto Me within the space of two days and two nights. However, as ordained by God, no distinction is to be drawn between the two...

My Revelation is indeed far more bewildering than that of Muhammad, the Apostle of God, if thou dost but pause to reflect upon the days of God. Behold, how strange that a person brought up amongst the people of Persia should be empowered by God to proclaim such irrefutable utterances as to silence every man of learning, and be enabled to spontaneously reveal verses far more rapidly than anyone could possible set down in writing.

The Báb

Do not say, 'How can He speak of God while in truth His age is no more than twenty-five?' Give ye ear unto Me. I swear by the Lord of the heavens and of the earth; I am verily a servant of God. I have been made the Bearer of irrefutable proofs from the presence of Him Who is the long-expected Remnant of God. Here is My Book before your eyes, as indeed inscribed in the presence of God...God indeed made Me blessed, wheresoever I may be, and hath enjoined upon Me to observe prayer and fortitude so long as I shall live on earth amongst you.

The Báb

Indeed, if any living creature were to pause to meditate he would undoubtedly realize that these verses are not the work of man, but are solely to be ascribed unto God, the One, the Peerless, Who causeth them to flow forth from the tongue of whomsoever He willeth, and hath not revealed nor will He reveal them save through the Focal Point of God's Primal Will. He it is, through Whose dispensations divine Messengers are raised up and heavenly Books are sent down. Had human beings been able to accomplish this deed surely someone would have brought forth at least one verse during the period of twelve hundred and seventy years which hath elapsed since the revelation of the Qur'án until that of the Bayán.

The Báb

There is no doubt that the Almighty hath sent down these verses unto Him [the Báb], even as He sent down unto the Apostle of God. Indeed no less than a hundred thousand verses similar to these have already been disseminated among the people, not to mention His Epistles, His Prayers or His learned and philosophical treatises...He reciteth verses at a speed consonant with the capacity of His amanuensis to set them down. Thus, it may well be considered that if from the inception of this Revelation until now He had been left unhindered, how vast then would have been the volume of writings disseminated from His pen.

The Báb

And if anyone should reflect on the appearance of this Tree [the Báb], he will undoubtedly testify to the loftiness of the Cause of God. For if one from whose life only twenty-four years have passed, and who is devoid of those sciences wherein all are learned, now reciteth verses after such fashion without thought or hesitation, writes a thousand verses of prayer in the course of five hours without pause of the pen, and produceth commentaries and learned treaties on such lofty themes as the true understanding of God and of the oneness of His Being, in a manner which doctors and philosophers confess surpasseth their power of understanding, then there is no doubt that all that hath been manifested is divinely inspired. Notwithstanding their life-long diligent study, what pains do these divines take when writing a single line in Arabic! Yet after such efforts the result is but words which are unworthy of mention. All these things are for a proof unto the people; otherwise the religion of God is too mighty and glorious for anyone to comprehend through aught but itself; rather by it all else is understood.

The Báb

THE BÁB EXHORTS HIS DISCIPLES TO PREPARE FOR THE ADVENT OF THE PROMISED ONE: BAHÁ'U'LLÁH

O My beloved friends! You are the bearers of the name of God in this Day. You have been chosen as the repositories of His mystery. It behoves each one of you to manifest the attributes of God, and to exemplify by your deeds and words the signs of His righteousness, His power and glory. The very members of your body must bear witness to the loftiness of your purpose, the integrity of your life, the reality of your faith, and the exalted character of your devotion...Ponder the words of Jesus addressed to His disciples, as He sent them forth to propagate the Cause of God. In words such as there, He bade them arise and fulfil their mission: "Ye are even as the fire which in the darkness of the night has been kindled upon the mountain-top. Let your light shine before the eyes of men. Such must be the purity of your character and the degree of your renunciation, that the people of the earth may through you recognise and be drawn closer to the heavenly Father who is the Source of purity and grace. For none has seen the Father who is in heaven. You who are His spiritual children must by your deeds exemplify His virtues, and witness to His glory. You are the salt of the earth, but if the salt have lost its savour, wherewith shall it be salted? Such must be the degree of your detachment, that into whatever city you enter to proclaim and teach the Cause of God, you should in no wise expect either meat or reward from its people. Nay, when you depart out of that city, you should shake the dust from off your feet. As you have entered it pure and undefiled, so must you depart from that city. For verily I say, the heavenly Father is ever with you and keeps watch over you. If you be faithful to Him, He will assuredly deliver into your hands all the treasures of the earth, and will exalt you above all the rulers and kings of the world." O My Letters! Verily I say, immensely exalted is this Day above the days of the Apostles of old. Nay, immeasurable is the difference! You are the partakers of the mystic chalice of His Revelation...Purge your hearts of worldly desires, and let angelic virtues be your adorning. Strive that by your deeds you may bear witness to the truth of these words of God...The days when idle worship was deemed sufficient are ended. The time is come when naught but the purest motive, supported by deeds of stainless purity, can ascend to the throne of the Most High and be acceptable unto Him...You have been called to this station; you will attain to it, only if you arise to trample beneath your feet every earthly desire...Beseech the Lord your God to grant that no earthly entanglements, no worldly affections, no ephemeral pursuits, may tarnish the purity, or embitter the sweetness, of that grace which flows through you. I am preparing you for the advent of a mighty Day. Exert your utmost endeavour that, in the world to come, I, who am now instructing you, may, before the mercy-seat of God, rejoice in your deeds and glory in your achievements. The secret of the Day that is to come is now concealed. It can neither be divulged nor estimated. The newly born babe of that Day excels the wisest and most venerable men of this time, and the lowliest and most unlearned of that period shall surpass in understanding the most erudite and accomplished divines of this age. Scatter throughout the length and breadth of this land, and, with steadfast feet and sanctified hearts, prepare the way for His coming. Heed not your weaknesses and frailty; fix your gaze upon the invincible power of the Lord, your God, the Almighty. Has He not, in past days, caused Abraham, in spite of His seeming helplessness, to triumph over the forces of Nimrod? Has He not enabled Moses, whose staff was His only companion, to vanquish Pharaoh and his hosts? Has He not established the ascendancy of Jesus, poor and lowly as He was in the eyes of men, over the combined forces of the Jewish people? Has He not subjected the barbarous and militant tribes of Arabia to the holy and transforming discipline of Muhammad, His Prophet? Arise in His name, put your trust wholly in Him, and be assured of ultimate victory.

The Báb

THE BÁB ON HIS LIFE

Thou art aware, O My God, that since the day Thou didst call Me into being [October 20, 1819] out of the water of Thy love till I reached fifteen years of age I lived in the land which witnessed My birth [Shíráz]. Then Thou didst enable Me to go to the seaport [Búshihr] where for five years I was engaged in trading with the goodly gifts of Thy realm and was occupied in that with which Thou hast favoured Me through the wondrous essence of Thy loving-kindness. I proceeded therefrom to the Holy Land [Karbilá] where I sojourned for one year. Then I returned to the place of My birth. There I experienced the revelation of Thy sublime bestowals and the evidences of Thy boundless grace. I yield Thee praise for all Thy goodly gifts and I render Thee thanksgiving for all Thy bounties. Then at the age of twenty-five I proceeded to thy sacred House [Mecca], and by the time I returned to the place where I was born, a year had elapsed. There I tarried patiently in the path of Thy love and beheld the evidences of Thy manifold bounties and of thy loving-kindness until Thou didst ordain for Me to set out in Thy direction and to migrate to Thy presence. Thus I departed therefrom by Thy leave, spending six months in the land of Sád [Iṣfahán] and seven months in the First Mountain [prison fortress of Mákú], where Thou didst rain down upon Me that which befitteth the sublimity of Thy gracious gifts and favours. Now, in

My thirtieth year, Thou beholdest Me, O My God, in this Grievous Mountain [the prison fortress of Chihríq] where I have dwelt for one whole year.

The Báb

From the first day that I cautioned thee [the Shah] not to wax proud before God until the present time, four years have elapsed, and during this space naught have I witnessed, either from thee or from thy soldiers, except dire oppression and disdainful arrogance.. Methinks thou dost imagine that I wish to gain some paltry substance from this earthly life. Nay, by the righteousness of My Lord! In the estimation of them that have fixed their eyes upon the merciful Lord, the riches of the world and its trappings are worth as much as the eye of a dead body, nay even less. Far from His glory be what they associate with Him!... I seek patience only in God. Verily He is the best protector and the best helper. No refuge do I seek save God. Verily He is the guardian and the best supporter...

The Báb

BAHÁ'U'LLÁH ADDRESSES THOSE RESPONSIBLE FOR THE MARTYRDOM OF THE BÁB

How many those who, every year, and every month, have because of you been put to death! How manifold the injustices ye have perpetrated...How numerous the babes and sucklings who were made orphans, and the fathers who lost their sons, because of your cruelty, O ye unjust doers! How oft hath a sister pined away and mourned over her brother, and how oft hath a wife lamented after her husband and sole sustainer!

Your iniquity waxed greater and greater until ye slew Him Who had never taken His eyes away from the face of God, the Most Exalted, the Most Great. Would that ye had put Him to death after the man are wont to put one another to death! Ye slew Him, however, in such circumstances as no man hath ever witnessed. The heavens wept sore over Him, and the souls of them who are nigh unto God cried out for His affliction...

Bahá'u'lláh

BAHÁ'U'LLÁH AFFIRMS THE TRUTH OF THE BÁB'S MISSION

Another proof and evidence of the truth of this Revelation, which amongst all other proofs shineth as the sun, is the constancy of the eternal Beauty in proclaiming the Faith of God. Though young and tender of age, and though the Cause He revealed was contrary to the desire of all the peoples of earth, both high and low, rich and poor, exalted and abased, king and subject, yet He arose and steadfastly proclaimed it. All have known and heard this. He was afraid of no one; He was regardless of consequences. Could such a thing be made manifest except through the power of a divine Revelation, and the potency of God's invincible Will? By the righteousness of God! Were any one to entertain so great a Revelation in his heart, the thought of such a declaration would alone confound him! Were the hearts of all men to be crowded into his heart, he would still hesitate to venture upon so awful an enterprise. He could achieve it only by the permission of God, only if the channel of his heart were to be linked with the Source of divine grace, and his soul be assured of the unfailing sustenance of the Almighty. To what, We wonder, do they ascribe so great a daring? Do they accuse Him of folly as they accused the Prophets of old? Or do they maintain that His motive was none other than leadership and the acquisition of earthly riches?

Gracious God! In His Book...He prophesied His own martyrdom. In it is this passage: "O thou Remnant of God! I have sacrificed myself wholly for Thee; I have accepted curses for Thy sake; and have yearned for naught but martyrdom in the path of Thy love. Sufficient Witness unto me is God, the Exalted, the Protector, the Ancient of Days!"

...Could the Revealer of such utterance be regarded as walking any way but the way of God, and as having yearned for aught else except His good-pleasure?...

And among the evidences of the truth of His manifestation were the ascendancy, the transcendent power, and supremacy which He, the Revealer of being and Manifestation of the Adored, hath, unaided and alone, revealed throughout the world. No sooner had that eternal Beauty revealed Himself in Shiráz, in the year sixty, and rent asunder the veil of concealment, than the signs of ascendancy, the might, the sovereignty, and power, emanating from the Essence of Essences and Sea of Seas, were manifest in every land. So much so, that from every city there appeared the sign, the evidences, the tokens, the testimonies of that divine Luminary. How many were those pure and kindly hearts which faithfully reflected the light of that eternal Sun, and how manifold the emanations of knowledge from that Ocean of divine wisdom which encompassed all beings! In every city, all the divines and dignitaries rose to hinder and repress them, and girded up the loins of malice, of envy, and tyranny for their suppression. How great the number of those holy souls, those essences of justice, who, accused of tyranny, were put to death! And how many embodiments of purity, who showed forth naught but true knowledge and stainless deeds, suffered an agonizing death! Notwithstanding all this, each of these holy beings, up to his last moment, breathed the Name of God, and soared in the realm of submission and resignation. Such was the potency and transmuting influence which He exercised over them, that they ceased to cherish any desire but His will, and wedded their soul to His remembrance.

Bahá'u'lláh

THE EXAMPLE OF THE BÁB

Let us take for our example the great and sacred Tree of the exalted Báb...Like Him let us bare our breasts to the shafts of agony, like Him make our hearts to be targets for the spears decreed by God. Let us, like candles, burn away; as moths, let us scorch our wings; as the field larks, vent our plaintive cries; as the nightingales, burst forth in lamentations.

Even as the clouds let us shed down tears, and as the lightening flashes let us laugh at our coursings through east and west. By day, by night, let us think but of spreading the sweet savours of God. Let us not keep on forever with our fancies and illusions, with our analysing and interpreting and circulating of complex dubieties. Let us put aside all thoughts of self; let us close our eyes to all on earth, let us neither make known our sufferings nor complain of our wrongs. Rather let us become oblivious of our own selves and drinking down the wine of heavenly grace, let us cry out our joy, and lose ourselves in the beauty of the All-Glorious.

'Abdu'l-Bahá

BAHÁ'U'LLÁH ON THE FAILURE OF MUSLIMS TO RECOGNIZE THE APPEARANCE OF THE BÁB

Twelve hundred and eighty years have passed since the dawn of the Muhammadan Dispensation, and with every break of day, these blind and ignoble people have recited the Qur'án, and yet have failed to grasp one letter of that Book! Again and again they read those verses which clearly testify to the reality of these holy themes, and bear witness to the truth of the Manifestations of eternal Glory, and still apprehend not their purpose. They have even failed to realize, all this time, that, in every age, and reading of the scriptures of the holy books is for no other purpose except to enable the reader to apprehend their meaning and unravel their innermost mysteries. Otherwise reading, without understanding, is of no abiding profit unto man.

Bahá'u'lláh

46
BAHÁ'U'LLÁH

Well is it with him who fixeth his gaze upon the Order of Bahá'u'lláh and rendereth thanks unto his Lord!

The Báb

Bahá'u'lláh hath become manifest to educate all the peoples of the world. He is the Universal Educator, whether of the rich or the poor, whether of black or white, or of peoples from east or west, or north or south.

'Abdu'l-Bahá

EYE-WITNESS ACCOUNT OF THE FIRST BELIEVER TO RECOGNIZE THE STATION OF BAHÁ'U'LLÁH

...I beheld His blessed Person rise and walk towards me. When He reached me He said: 'You, too, are awake.' Whereupon He began to chant and pace back and forth. How shall I ever describe that voice and the verses it intoned, and His gait, as He strode before me! Methinks, with every step He took and every word He uttered thousands of oceans of light surged before my face, and thousands of worlds of incomparable splendor were unveiled to my eyes, and thousands of suns blazed their light upon me!

Mirzá Aqa Ján

THE PEN-PORTRAIT OF BAHÁ'U'LLÁH BY A WESTERN NON-BAHÁ'Í SCHOLAR

... my conductor paused for a moment while I removed my shoes. Then, with a quick movement of the hand, he withdrew, and, as I passed, replaced the curtain; and I found myself in a large apartment, along the upper end of which ran a low divan, while on the side opposite to the door were placed two or three chairs. Though I dimly suspected whither I was going and whom I was to behold (for no distinct intimation had been given to me), a second or two elapsed ere, with a throb of wonder and awe, I became definitely conscious that the room was not untenanted. In the corner where the divan met the wall sat a wondrous and venerable figure ... The face of him on whom I gazed I can never forget, though I cannot describe it. Those piercing eyes seemed to read one's very soul; power and authority sat on that ample brow, while the deep lines on the forehead and face implied an age which the jet-black hair and beard flowing down in indistinguishable luxuriance almost to the waist seemed to belie. No need to ask in whose presence I stood, as I bowed myself before one who is the object of a devotion and love which kings might envy and emperors sigh for in vain!

A mild dignified voice bade me be seated, and then continued: - 'Praise be to God that thou hast attained!... Thou hast come to see a prisoner and an exile... We desire but the good of the world and the happiness of the nations; yet they deem us a stirrer up of strife and sedition worthy of bondage and banishment...That all nations should become one in faith and all men as brothers; that the bonds of affection and unity between the sons of men should be strengthened; that diversity of religion should cease, and differences of race be annulled- what harm is there in this?...Yet so it shall be; these fruitless strifes, these ruinous wars shall pass away, and the 'Most Great Peace' shall come...Do not you in Europe need this also? Is not this that which Christ foretold?...Yet do we see your kings and rulers lavishing their treasures more freely on means for the destruction of the human race than on that which would conduce to the happiness of mankind...These strifes and this bloodshed and discord must cease, and all men be as one kindred and one family...Let not a man glory in this, that he loves his country; let him rather glory in this, that he loves his kind...'

Such, so far as I can recall them, were the words which, besides many others, I heard from Behá. Let those who read them consider well with themselves whether such doctrines merit death and bonds, and whether the world is more likely to gain or lose by their diffusion.

Professor Edward G. Browne, Cambridge

'ABDU'L-BAHÁ RECOUNTS THE LIFE OF BAHÁ'U'LLÁH

Tonight I wish to tell you something of the history of the Bahá'í Revelation.

The Blessed Perfection, Bahá'u'lláh, belonged to the nobility of Persia. From earliest childhood He was distinguished among His relatives and friends. They said, "This child has extraordinary power." In wisdom, intelligence and as a source of new knowledge, He was advanced beyond His age and superior to His surroundings. All who knew Him were astonished at His precocity. It was usual for them to say, "Such a child will not live," for it is commonly believed that precocious children do not reach maturity. During the period of youth the Blessed Perfection did not enter school. He was not willing to be taught. This fact is well established among the Persians of Tihrán. Nevertheless, He was capable of solving the difficult problems of all who came to Him. In whatever meeting, scientific assembly or theological discussion He was found, He became the authority of explanation upon intricate and abstruse questions presented.

Until His father passed away, Bahá'u'lláh did not seek position or political station notwithstanding His connection with the government. This occasioned surprise and comment. It was frequently said, "How is it that a young man of such keen intelligence and subtle perception does not seek lucrative appointments? As a matter of fact, every position is open to him." This is an historical statement fully attested by the people of Persia.

He was most generous, giving abundantly to the poor. None who came to Him were turned away. The doors of His house were open to all. He always had many guests. This unbounded generosity was conductive to greater astonishment from the fact that He sought neither position nor prominence. In commenting upon this His friends said He would become impoverished, for His expenses were many and His wealth becoming more and more limited.

"Why is he not thinking of his own affairs?" they inquired of each other; but some who were wise declared, "This personage is connected with another world; he has something sublime within him that is not evident now; the day is coming when it will be manifested." In truth, the Blessed Perfection was a refuge for every weak one, a shelter for every fearing one, kind to every indigent one, lenient and loving to all creatures.

He became well-known in regard to these qualities before the Báb appeared. Then Bahá'u'lláh declared the Báb's mission to be true and promulgated His teachings. The Báb announced that the greater Manifestation would take place after Him and called the Promised One "Him Whom God shall make manifest," saying that nine years later the reality of His own mission would become apparent. In His writings He stated that in the ninth year this expected One would be known; in the ninth year they would attain to all glory and felicity; in the ninth year they would advance rapidly. Between Bahá'u'lláh and the Báb there was communication privately. The Báb wrote a letter containing three hundred and sixty derivatives of the root Bahá. The Báb was martyred in Tabríz; and Bahá'u'lláh, exiled into Iráq in 1852, announced Himself in Baghdád. For the Persian government had decided that as long as He remained in Persia the peace of the country would be disturbed; therefore, He was exiled in the expectation that Persia would become quiet. His banishment, however, produced the opposite effect. New tumult arose, and the mention of His greatness and influence spread everywhere throughout the country. The proclamation of His manifestation and mission was made in Baghdád. He called His friends together there and spoke to them of God.

At one point He left the city and went alone into the mountains of Kurdistán, where He made His abode in caves and grottoes. A part of this time He lived in the city of Sulaymáníyyih. Two years passed during which neither His friends nor family knew just where He was.

Although Bahá'u'lláh was solitary, secluded and unknown in His retirement, the report spread throughout Kurdistán that this was a most remarkable and learned Personage, gifted with a wonderful power of attraction. In a short time Kurdistán was magnetized with His love. During this period Bahá'u'lláh lived in poverty. His garments were those of the poor and needy. His food was that of the indigent and lowly. An atmosphere of majesty haloed Him as the sun at midday. Everywhere He was greatly revered and beloved.

After two years He returned to Baghdád. Friends He had known in Sulaymáníyyih came to visit Him. They found Him in His accustomed environment of ease and affluence and were astonished at the appointments of One Who had lived in seclusion under such frugal conditions in Kurdistán.

The Persian government believed the banishment of the Blessed Perfection from Persia would be the extermination of His Cause in that country. These rulers now realized that it spread more rapidly. His

Bahá'u'lláh

prestige increased; His teachings became more widely circulated. The chiefs of Persia then used their influence to have Bahá'u'lláh exiled from Baghdád. He was summoned to Constantinople by the Turkish authorities. While in Constantinople He ignored every restriction, especially the hostility of ministers of state and clergy. The official representatives of Persia again brought their influence to bear upon the Turkish authorities and succeeded in having Bahá'u'lláh banished from Constantinople to Adrianople, the object being to keep Him as far away as possible from Persia and render His communication with that country more difficult. Nevertheless, the Cause still spread and strengthened.

Finally, they consulted together and said, "We have banished Bahá'u'lláh from place to place, but each time he is exiled his cause is more widely extended, his proclamation increases in power, and day by day his lamp is becoming brighter. This is due to the fact that we have exiled him to large cities and populous centers. Therefore, we will send him to a penal colony as a prisoner so that all may know he is the associate of murderers, robbers and criminals; in a short time he and his followers will perish." The Sultán of Turkey then banished Him to the prison of 'Akká in Syria [now Israel].

When Bahá'u'lláh arrived in 'Akká, through the power of God He was able to hoist His banner. His light at first had been a star; now it became a mighty sun, and the illumination of His Cause expanded from the East to the West. Inside prison walls He wrote Epistles to all the kings and rulers of nations, summoning them to arbitration and universal peace. Some of the kings received His words with disdain and contempt. One of these was the Sultán of the Ottoman kingdom. Napoleon III of France did not reply. A second Epistle was addressed to him. It stated, "I have written you an Epistle before this, summoning you to the Cause of God, but you are of the heedless. You have proclaimed that you were the defender of the oppressed; now it hath become evident that you are not. Nor are you kind to your own suffering and oppressed people. Your actions are contrary to your own interests, and your kingly pride must fall. Because of your arrogance God shortly will destroy your sovereignty. France will flee away from you, and you will be overwhelmed by a great conquest. There will be lamentation and mourning, women bemoaning the loss of their sons." This arraignment of Napoleon III was published and spread.

Read it and consider: one prisoner, single and solitary, without assistant or defender, a foreigner and stranger imprisoned in the fortress of 'Akká, writing such letters to the Emperor of France and Sultán of

Turkey. Reflect upon this: how Bahá'u'lláh upraised the standard of His Cause in prison. Refer to history. It is without parallel. No such thing has happened before that time nor since-a prisoner and an exile advancing His Cause and spreading His teachings broadcast so that eventually He became powerful enough to conquer the very king who banished Him.

His Cause spread more and more. The Blessed Perfection was a prisoner twenty-five years. During all this time He was subjected to the indignities and revilement of the people. He was persecuted, mocked and put in chains. In Persia His properties were pillaged and His possessions confiscated. First, there was banishment from Persia to Baghdád, then to Constantinople, then to Adrianople, finally from Rumelia to the prison fortress of 'Akká.

During His lifetime He was intensely active. His energy was unlimited. Scarcely one night passed in restful sleep. He bore these ordeals, suffered these calamities and difficulties in order that a manifestation of selflessness and service might become apparent in the world of humanity; that the Most Great Peace should become a reality; that human souls might appear as the angels of heaven; that heavenly miracles would be wrought among men; that human faith should be strengthened and perfected; that the precious, priceless bestowal of God- the human mind-might be developed to its fullest capacity in the temple of the body; and that man might become the reflection and likeness of God, even as it hath been revealed in the Bible, "Let us make man in our image."

Briefly, the Blessed Perfection bore all these ordeals and calamities in order that our hearts might become enkindled and radiant, our spirits be glorified, our faults become virtues, our ignorance be transformed into knowledge; in order that we might attain the real fruits of humanity and acquire heavenly graces; in order that, although pilgrims upon earth, we should travel the road of the heavenly Kingdom, and, although needy and poor, we might receive the treasures of eternal life. For this has He borne these difficulties and sorrows.

Trust all to God. The lights of God are resplendent. The blessed Epistles are spreading. The blessed teachings are promulgated throughout the East and West. Soon you will see that the heavenly Words have established the oneness of the world of humanity. The banner of the Most Great Peace has been unfurled, and the great community is appearing.

'Abdu'l-Bahá

'ABDU'L-BAHÁ RECOUNTS BAHÁ'U'LLÁH'S SUFFERING

No torment was there left that His sacred form was subjected to, no suffering that did not descend upon Him. How many a night, when He was chained, did He go sleepless because of the weight of His iron collar; how many a day the burning pain of the stocks and fetters gave Him no moment's peace. From Níyávarán to Tihrán they made Him run-He, that embodied spirit, He Who had been accustomed to repose against cushions of ornamented silk-chained, shoeless, His head bared; and down under the earth, in the thick darkness of that narrow dungeon, they shut Him up with murderers, rebels and thieves. Ever and again they assailed Him with a new torment, and all were certain that from one moment to the next He would suffer a martyr's death. After some time they banished Him from His native land, and sent Him to countries alien and far away. During many a year in 'Iráq, no moment passed but the arrow of a new anguish struck His holy heart; with every breath a sword came down upon that sacred body, and He could hope for no moment of security and rest. From every side His enemies mounted their attack with unrelenting hate; and singly and alone He withstood them all. After all these tribulations, these body blows, they flung Him out of 'Iráq in the continent of Asia, to the continent of Europe, and in that place of bitter exile, of wretched hardships...My pen is powerless to tell it all; but ye have surely been informed of it. Then, after twenty-four years in this, the Most Great Prison, in agony and sore affliction, His days drew to a close.

To sum it up, the Ancient Beauty was ever, during His sojourn in this transitory world, either a captive bound with chains, or living under a sword, or subjected to extreme suffering and torment, or held in the Most Great Prison. Because of His physical weakness, brought on by His afflictions, His blessed body was worn away to a breath; it was light as a cobweb from long grieving. And His reason for shouldering this heavy load and enduring all this anguish, which was even as an ocean that hurleth its waves to high heaven-His reason for putting on the heavy iron chains and for becoming the very embodiment of utter resignation and meekness, was to lead every soul on earth to concord, to fellow-feeling, to oneness; to make known amongst all peoples the sign of the singleness of God, so that at last the primal oneness deposited at the heart of all created things would bear its destined fruit...

Let us turn our eyes away from empty fantasies of this world's divergent forms, and serve instead this pre-eminent purpose, this grand design.

'Abdu'l-Bahá

BAHÁ'U'LLÁH RECALLS HIS SUFFERINGS

The tribulations that have touched Us, the destitution from which We suffer, the various troubles with which We are encompassed, shall all pass away, as shall pass away the pleasures in which they delight and the affluence they enjoy. This is the truth which no man on earth can reject. The days in which We have been compelled to dwell in the dust will soon be ended, as will the days in which they occupied the seats of honor. God shall, assuredly, judge with truth between Us and them, and He, verily, is the best of judges.

We render thanks unto God for whatsoever hath befallen Us, and We patiently endure the things He hath ordained in the past or will ordain in the future. In Him have I placed My trust; and into His hands have I committed My Cause.

Bahá'u'lláh

Recall thou to mind My sorrows, My cares and anxieties, My woes and trials, the state of My captivity, the tears that I have shed, the bitterness of Mine anguish, and now My imprisonment in this far-off land...Be thou grateful to God, that We have refused to divulge unto thee the secrets of those unsearchable decrees that have been sent down unto Us from the heaven of the Will of thy Lord, the Most Powerful, the Almighty.

...Every morning I arose from My bed, I discovered the hosts of countless afflictions massed behind My door; and every night when I lay down, lo! My heart was torn with agony at what it had suffered from the fiendish cruelty of its foes. With every piece of bread the Ancient Beauty breaketh is coupled the assault of a fresh affliction, and with every drop He drinketh is mixed the bitterness of the most woeful of trials. He is preceded in every step He taketh by an army of unforeseen calamities, while in His rear follow legions of agonizing sorrows.

Such is My plight, wert thou to ponder it in thine heart. Let not, however, thy soul grieve over that which God hath rained down upon Us. Merge thy will in His pleasure, for We have, at no time, desired anything whatsoever except His Will, and have welcomed each one of His irrevocable decrees. Let thine heart be patient, and be thou not dismayed. Follow not in the way of them that are sorely agitated.

Bahá'u'lláh

But for the tribulations that have touched Me in the path of God, life would have held no sweetness for Me, and My existence would have profited Me nothing. For them who are endued with discernment, and whose eyes are fixed upon the Sublime Vision, it is no secret that I have been, most of the days of My life, even as a slave, sitting under a sword hanging on a thread, knowing not whether it would fall soon or late upon him. And yet, notwithstanding all this We render thanks unto God, the Lord of the worlds.

Bahá'u'lláh

BAHÁ'U'LLÁH RELATES HIS WITHDRAWAL TO THE WILDERNESS

What more shall We say? The universe, were it to gaze with the eye of justice, would be incapable of bearing the weight of this utterance! In the early days of Our arrival in this land, when We discerned the signs of impending events, We decided, ere they happened, to retire. We betook Ourselves to the wilderness, and there, separated and alone, led for two years a life of complete solitude. From Our eyes there rained tears of anguish, and in Our bleeding heart there surged an ocean of agonizing pain. Many a night We had no food for sustenance, and many a day Our body found no rest. By Him Who hath My being between His hands! Notwithstanding these showers of afflictions and unceasing calamities, Our soul was wrapt in blissful joy, and Our whole being evinced an ineffable gladness. For in Our solitude We were unaware of the harm or benefit, the health or ailment, of any soul. Alone, We communed with Our spirit, oblivious of the world and all that is therein. We knew not, however, that the mesh of divine destiny exceedeth the vastest of mortal conceptions, and the dart of His decree transcendeth the boldest of human designs. None can escape the snares He setteth, and no soul can find release except through submission to His will. By the righteousness of God! Our withdrawal contemplated no return, and Our separation hoped for no reunion. The one object of Our retirement was to avoid becoming a subject of discord among the faithful, a source of disturbance unto Our companions, the means of injury to any soul, or the cause of sorrow to any heart. Beyond these, We cherished no other intention, and apart from them, We had no end in view. And yet, each person schemed after his own desire, and pursued his own idle fancy, until the hour when, from the Mystic Source, there came the summons bidding Us return whence We came. Surrendering Our will to His, We submitted to His injunction.

Bahá'u'lláh

HIS PURPOSE

The Ancient Beauty hath consented to be bound with chains that mankind may be released from its bondage, and hath accepted to be made a prisoner within this most mighty Stronghold that the whole world may attain unto true liberty. He hath drained to its dregs the cup of sorrow, that all the peoples of the earth may attain unto abiding joy, and be filled with gladness. This is of the mercy of your Lord, the Compassionate, the Most Merciful. We have accepted to be abased, O believers in the Unity of God, that ye may be exalted, and have suffered manifold afflictions, that ye might prosper and flourish. He Who hath come to build anew the whole world, behold, how they that have joined partners with God have forced Him to dwell within the most desolate of cities!

Bahá'u'lláh

Were anyone to ponder in his heart that which hath, in this Revelation, streamed forth from the Pen of Glory, he would be assured that whatever this Wronged One hath affirmed He hath had no intention of establishing any position or distinction for Himself. The purpose hath rather been to attract the souls, through the sublimity of His words, unto the summit of transcendent glory and to endow them with the capacity of perceiving that which will purge and purify the peoples of the world from the strife and dissension which religious differences provoke. Unto this bear witness My heart, My Pen, My inner and My outer Being. God grant that all men may turn unto the treasuries latent within their own beings.

Bahá'u'lláh

This Wronged One hath, at all times, summoned the peoples of the world unto that which will exalt them, and draw them nigh unto God. From the Most Sublime Horizon there hath shone forth that which leaveth no room unto any one for vacillation, repudiation or denial.

Bahá'u'lláh

The eyes of this Wronged One are turned towards naught save trustworthiness, truthfulness, purity, and all that profiteth men.

Bahá'u'lláh

HIS REVELATION

Oh, would that the world could believe Me! Were all the things that lie enshrined within the heart of Bahá, and which the Lord, His God, the Lord of all names, hath taught Him, to be unveiled to mankind, every man on earth would be dumbfounded.

How great the multitude of truths which the garment of words can never contain! How vast the number of such verities as no expression can adequately describe, whose significance can never be unfolded, and to which not even the remotest allusions can be made! How manifold are the truths which must remain unuttered until the appointed time is come!

Bahá'u'lláh

My holy, My divinely ordained Revelation may be likened unto an ocean in whose depths are concealed innumerable pearls of great price, of surpassing luster. It is the duty of every seeker to bestir himself and strive to attain the shores of this ocean, so that he may, in proportion to the eagerness of his search and the efforts he hath exerted, partake of such benefits as have been pre-ordained in God's irrevocable and hidden Tablets. If no one be willing to direct his steps towards its shores, if every one should fail to arise and find Him, can such failure be said to have robbed this ocean of its power or to have lessened, to any degree, its treasure?...This most great, this fathomless and surging Ocean is near, astonishingly near, unto you. Behold it is closer to you than your life-vein! Swift as the twinkling of an eye ye can, if ye but wish it, reach and partake of this imperishable favor, this God-given grace, this incorruptible gift, this most potent and unspeakably glorious bounty.

Bahá'u'lláh

Well nigh a hundred volumes of luminous verses and perspicuous words have already been sent down from the heaven of the will of Him Who is the Revealer of signs, and are available unto all. It is for thee to direct thyself towards the Ultimate Goal, and the Supreme End, and the Most Sublime Pinnacle, that thou mayest hear and behold what hath been revealed by God, the Lord of the worlds.

Bahá'u'lláh

Wert thou to perceive, be it less than a needle's eye, the breaths of Mine utterance, thou wouldst abandon the world and all that is therein, and wouldst set thy face towards the lights of the countenance of the Desired One. Briefly, in the sayings of Him Who is the Spirit [Jesus] unnumbered significances lie concealed. Unto many things did He refer, but as He found none possessed of a hearing ear or a seeing eye He chose to conceal most of these things. Even as He saith: "But ye cannot bear them now." That Dawning-Place of Revelation saith that on that Day He Who is the Promised One will reveal the things which are to come.

Bahá'u'lláh

HIS IMPRISONMENT

We were consigned for four months to a place foul beyond comparison. As to the dungeon in which this Wronged One and others similarly wronged were confined, a dark and narrow pit were preferable. Upon Our arrival We were first conducted along a pitch-black corridor, from whence We descended three steep flights of stairs to the place of confinement assigned to Us. The dungeon was wrapped in thick darkness, and Our fellow-prisoners numbered nearly a hundred and fifty souls: thieves, assassins and highwaymen. Though crowded, it had no other outlet than the passage by which We entered. No pen can depict that place, nor any tongue describe its loathsome smell... God alone knoweth what befell Us in that most foul-smelling and gloomy place!

Bahá'u'lláh

My imprisonment doeth Me no harm, neither the tribulations I suffer, nor the things that have befallen Me at the hands of My oppressors. That which harmeth Me is the conduct of those who, though they bear My name, yet commit that which maketh My heart and My pen to lament. They that spread disorder in the land, lay hands on the property of others, and enter a house without leave of its owner, We, verily, are clear of them, unless they repent and return unto God, the Ever-Forgiving, the Most Merciful.

Bahá'u'lláh

BAHÁ'U'LLÁH ON THE END OF HIS EARTHLY EXISTENCE

Be not dismayed, O peoples of the world, when the day-star of My beauty is set, and the heaven of My tabernacle is concealed from your eyes. Arise to further My Cause, and to exalt My Word amongst men. We are with you at all times, and shall strengthen you through the power of truth. We are truly almighty. Whoso hath recognized Me will arise and serve Me with such determination that the powers of earth and heaven shall be unable to defeat his purpose.

Bahá'u'lláh

Let not your hearts be perturbed, O people, when the glory of My Presence is withdrawn, and the ocean of My utterance is stilled. In My presence amongst you there is a wisdom, and in My absence there is yet another, inscrutable to all but God, the Incomparable, the All-Knowing. Verily, We behold you from Our realm of glory, and shall aid whosoever will arise for the triumph of Our Cause with the hosts of the Concourse on high and a company of Our favored angels.

Bahá'u'lláh

47
MIRACLES

BAHÁ'U'LLÁH ENTREATS HIS FOLLOWERS NOT TO DEGRADE HIS STATION BY RELATING MIRACLES

We entreat Our loved ones not to besmirch the hem of Our raiment with the dust of falsehood, neither to allow references to what they have regarded as miracles and prodigies to debase Our rank and station, or to mar the purity and sanctity of Our name.

Bahá'u'lláh

MIRACLES ARE NOT A SOUND BASIS FOR BELIEF

I do not wish to mention the miracles of Bahá'u'lláh, for it may perhaps be said that these are traditions, liable both to truth and to error, like the accounts of the miracles of Christ in the Gospel, which come to us from the apostles and not from any one else, and are denied by the Jews. Though if I wish to mention the supernatural acts of Bahá'u'lláh, they are numerous; they are acknowledged in the Orient, and even by some strangers to the Cause. But these narratives are not decisive proofs and evidences to all; the hearer might perhaps say that this account may not be in accordance with what occurred...

Briefly, my meaning is that many wonderful things were done by Bahá'u'lláh, but we do not recount them; as they do not constitute proofs and evidences for all the peoples of the earth; and they are not decisive proofs even for those who see them, they may think that they are merely enchantments.

Also, most of the miracles of the Prophets which are mentioned have an inner significance...Our purpose is not to deny such miracles; our only meaning is that they do not constitute decisive proofs, and that they have an inner significance.

'Abdu'l-Bahá

THE TRUE GREATNESS OF A PROPHET IS NOT DUE TO MIRACLES

What, then, is the mission of the divine Prophets? Their mission is the education and advancement of the world of humanity. They are the real Teachers and Educators, the universal Instructors of mankind. If we wish to discover whether any one of these great Souls or Messengers was in reality a Prophet of God, we must investigate the facts surrounding His life and history, and the first point of our investigation will be the education He bestowed upon mankind. If He has been an Educator, if He has really trained a nation or people, causing it to rise from the lowest depths of ignorance to the highest station of knowledge, then we are sure that He was a Prophet. This is a plain and clear method of procedure, proof that is irrefutable. We do not need to seek after other proofs. We do not need to mention miracles, saying that out of rock water gushed forth, for such miracles and statements may be denied and refused by those who hear them. The deeds of Moses are conclusive evidences of His Prophethood. If a man be fair, unbiased and willing to investigate reality, he will undoubtedly testify to the fact that Moses was, verily, a man of God and a great Personage.

'Abdu'l-Bahá

But in the day of the Manifestation the people with insight see that all the conditions of the Manifestation are miracles, for they are superior to all others, and this alone is an absolute miracle. Recollect that Christ, solitary and alone, without a helper or protector, without armies and legions, and under the greatest oppression, uplifted the standard of God before all the people of the world, and withstood them, and finally conquered all, although outwardly he was crucified. Now this is a veritable miracle which can never be denied. There is no need of any other proof of the truth of Christ.

The outward miracles have no importance for the people of Reality. If a blind man receive sight, for example, he will finally again become sightless, for he will die, and be deprived of all his senses and powers. Therefore causing the blind man to see is comparatively of little importance, for this faculty of sight will at last disappear. If the body of a dead person be resuscitated, of what use is it since the body will die again? But it is important to give perception and eternal life, that is, the spiritual and divine life. For this physical life is not immortal, and its existence is equivalent to non-existence. So it is that Christ said to one of his disciples: 'Let the dead bury their dead'; for 'That which is born of the flesh is flesh, and that which is born of the spirit is spirit.'

...The meaning is not that the Manifestations are unable to perform miracles, for they have all power. But for them inner sight, spiritual healing, and eternal life are the valuable and important things.

'Abdu'l-Bahá

48
THE STATION OF BAHÁ'U'LLÁH

This is the day of Bahá'u'lláh, the age of the Blessed Perfection, the cycle of the Greatest Name. If you do not smile now, for what time will you await and what greater happiness could you expect?

'Abdu'l-Bahá

That which is conducive to the regeneration of the world and the salvation of the peoples and kindreds of the earth hath been sent down from the heaven of the utterance of Him Who is the Desire of the world. Give ye a hearing ear to the counsels of the Pen of Glory. Better is this for you than all that is on the earth. Unto this beareth witness My glorious and wondrous Book.

Bahá'u'lláh

We have laid bare the divine mysteries and in most explicit language foretold future events, that neither the doubts of the faithless, nor the denials of the froward, nor the whisperings of the heedless may keep back the seekers of truth from the Source of the light of the One true God.

Bahá'u'lláh

So powerful is the light of unity that it can illuminate the whole earth...Exert yourselves that ye may attain this transcendent and most sublime station, the station that can insure the protection and security of all mankind...At one time We spoke in the language of the lawgiver; at another in that of the truth-seeker and the mystic, and yet Our supreme purpose and highest wish hath always been to disclose the glory and sublimity of this station. God, verily, is a sufficient witness!

Bahá'u'lláh

MAN AND MANIFESTATION

Know verily that whenever this Youth turneth His eyes towards His own self, he findeth it the most insignificant of all creation. When He contemplates, however, the bright effulgences He hath been empowered to manifest, lo, that self is transfigured before Him into a sovereign Potency permeating the essence of all things visible and invisible. Glory be to Him Who, through the power of truth, hath sent down the Manifestation of His own Self and entrusted Him with His message unto all mankind.

Bahá'u'lláh

SUBSERVIENT TO GOD

Certain ones among you have said: "He it is Who hath laid claim to be God." By God! This is a gross calumny. I am but a servant of God Who hath believed in Him and in His signs, and in His Prophets and in His angels. My tongue, and My heart, and My inner and My outer being testify that there is no God but Him, that all others have been created by His behest, and been fashioned through the operation of His Will. There is none other God but Him, the Creator, the Raiser from the dead, the Quickener, the Slayer. I am He that telleth abroad the favors with which God hath, through His bounty, favored Me. If this be My transgression, then I am truly the first of the transgressors. I and My kindred are at your mercy. Do ye as ye please, and be not of them that hesitate, that I might return to God my Lord...This, indeed, is My dearest wish, My most ardent desire. Of My state God is, verily, sufficiently informed, observant.

Bahá'u'lláh

This station is the station in which one dieth to himself and liveth in God. Divinity, whenever I mention it, indicateth My complete and absolute self-effacement. This is the station in which I have no control over mine own weal or woe nor over my life nor over my resurrection.

Bahá'u'lláh

Know verily that the veil hiding Our countenance hath not been completely lifted. We have revealed Our Self to a degree corresponding to the capacity of the people of Our age. Should the Ancient Beauty be unveiled in the fullness of His glory mortal eyes would be blinded by the dazzling intensity of His revelation.

Bahá'u'lláh

This Servant, this Wronged One, is abashed to claim for Himself any existence whatever, how much more those exalted grades of being! Every man of discernment, while walking upon the earth, feeleth indeed abashed, inasmuch as he is fully aware that the thing which is the source of his prosperity, his wealth, his might, his exaltation, his advancement and power is, as ordained by God, the very earth which is trodden beneath the feet of all men. There can be no doubt that whoever is cognizant of this truth, is cleansed and sanctified from all pride, arrogance, and vainglory.

Bahá'u'lláh

NOT A MATTER OF CHOICE

How foolish are those who murmur against the premature birth of His light...It is neither within your power nor mine to set the time at which it should be made manifest. God's inscrutable Wisdom hath fixed its hour beforehand...Had it been in my power, I would have, under no circumstances, consented to distinguish myself amongst men, for the Name I bear utterly disdaineth to associate itself with this generation whose tongues are sullied and whose hearts are false. And whenever I chose to hold my peace and be still, lo, the voice of the Holy Ghost, standing on my right hand, aroused me, and the Supreme Spirit appeared before my face, and Gabriel overshadowed me, and the Spirit of Glory stirred within my bosom, bidding me arise and break my silence...

Bahá'u'lláh

I have never aspired after worldly leadership. My sole purpose hath been to hand down unto men that which I was bidden to deliver by God, the Gracious, the Incomparable, that it may detach them from all that pertaineth to this world, and cause them to attain such heights as neither the ungodly can conceive, nor the froward imagine.

Bahá'u'lláh

TRUST IN GOD

Know ye that I am afraid of none except God. In none but Him have I placed My trust; to none will I cleave but Him, and wish for naught except the thing He hath wished for Me. This, indeed, is My heart's desire, did ye but know it. I have offered up My soul and My body as a sacrifice for God, the Lord of all worlds. Whoso hath known God shall know none but Him, and he that feareth God shall be afraid of no one except Him, though the powers of the whole earth rise up and be arrayed against him. I speak naught except at His bidding, and follow not, through the power of God and His might, except His truth. He verily, shall recompense the truthful.

Bahá'u'lláh

BAHÁ'U'LLÁH REFLECTS ON HIS MISSION

I was but a man like others...when lo, the breezes of the All-Glorious were wafted over Me, and taught Me the knowledge of all that hath been. This thing is not from Me, but from One Who is Almighty and All-Knowing. And He bade Me lift up My voice between earth and heaven, and for this there befell Me what hath caused the tears of every man of understanding to flow. The learning current amongst men I studied not; their schools I entered not. Ask of the city wherein I dwelt, that thou mayest be well assured that I am not of them who speak falsely. This is but a leaf which the winds of the will of thy Lord, the Almighty, the All-Praised, have stirred. Can it be still when the tempestuous winds are blowing? ...They move it as they list. The evanescent is as nothing before Him Who is the Ever-Abiding. His all-compelling summons hath reached Me, and caused Me to speak His praise amidst all people. I was indeed as one dead when His behest was uttered. The hand of the will of thy Lord, the Compassionate, the Merciful, transformed Me.

Bahá'u'lláh

Ever since the day Thou didst create me at Thy bidding, O my God, and didst arouse me through the gentle winds of Thy tender mercies, I have summoned all mankind unto the shores of the ocean of Thy oneness and the heaven of Thine all-glorious unity. I have sought, all my days, not to guard myself from the mischief of the rebellious among Thy creatures, but rather to exalt Thy name amidst Thy people. I have, thereby, suffered what none of Thy creatures hath suffered.

How many the days, O my God, which I spent in utter loneliness with the transgressors amongst Thy servants, and how many the nights, O my Best-Beloved, during which I lay a captive in the hands of the wayward amidst Thy creatures! In the midst of my troubles and tribulations I have continued to celebrate Thy praise before all who are in Thy heaven and on Thy earth, and have not ceased to extol Thy wondrous glory in the kingdoms of Thy Revelation and of Thy creation, though all that I have been capable of showing forth hath fallen short of the greatness and the majesty of Thy oneness, and is unworthy of Thine exaltation and of Thine omnipotence...

...O my God...the gentle winds of Thy grace and Thy loving-kindness passed over me, and wakened me through the power of Thy sovereignty and Thy gifts, and bade me arise before Thy servants, and speak forth Thy praise, and glorify Thy word. Thereupon most of Thy people reviled me...Thou hast Thyself announced this Revelation unto them in the Scrolls of Thy commandment and the Tablets of Thy decree, and hast covenanted with them concerning this youth in every word sent down by Thee unto Thy creatures and Thy people.

...Every time I hold my peace, and cease to extol Thy wondrous virtues, Thy Spirit impelleth me to cry out before all who are in Thy heaven and on Thy earth; and every time I am still, the breaths wafted from the right hand of Thy will and purpose pass over me, and stir me up, and I find myself to be as a leaf which lieth at the mercy of the winds of Thy decree, and is carried away whithersoever Thou dost permit or command it. Every man of insight who considereth what hath been revealed by me, will be persuaded that Thy Cause is not in my hands, but in Thy hands, and will recognize that the reins of power are held not held in my grasp but in Thy grasp, and are subject to Thy sovereign might. And yet, Thou seest O my God, how the inhabitants of Thy realm have arrayed themselves against me, and inflict upon me every moment of my life what causeth the realities of Thy chosen ones and trusted ones to tremble...

...I swear by Thy might, O my Beloved! Every morning I waken to find that I am made a target for the darts of their envy, and every night, when I lie down to rest, I discover that I have fallen a victim to the spears of their hate. Though Thou hast made known unto me the secrets of their hearts, and hast set me above them, I have refused to uncover their deeds, and have dealt patiently with them, mindful of the time which Thou has fixed...

I am the one, O my God, who, through the love I bear to Thee, hath been able to dispense with all who are in heaven and on earth. Armed with this Love, I am afraid of no one, though all the peoples of the world unite to hurt me.

Bahá'u'lláh

49
'ABDU'L-BAHÁ THE MOST GREAT BRANCH

A PEN-PORTRAIT OF 'ABDU'L-BAHÁ BY PROFESSOR E.G. BROWNE

Seldom have I seen one whose appearance impressed me more. A tall strongly-built man holding himself straight as an arrow, with white turban and raiment, long black locks reaching almost to the shoulder, broad powerful forehead indicating a strong intellect combined with an unswerving will, eyes keen as a hawk's, and strongly-marked but pleasing features-such was my first impression of 'Abbás Effendí, 'the master' as he par excellence is called by the Bábís. Subsequent conversation with him served only to heighten the respect with which his appearance had from the first inspired me. One more eloquent of speech, more ready of argument, more apt of illustration, more intimately acquainted with the sacred books of the Jews, the Christians, and the Muhammadans, could, I should think, scarcely by found even amongst the eloquent, ready, and subtle race to which he belongs. These qualities, combined with a bearing at once majestic and genial, made me cease to wonder at the influence and esteem which he enjoyed even beyond the circle of his father's followers. About the greatness of this man and his power no one who had seen him could entertain a doubt.

A CHRISTIAN MINISTER'S IMPRESSION OF 'ABDU'L-BAHÁ

He made Truth and Love so beautiful and royal that the heart perforce did reverence. He showed me by His voice, manner, bearing, smile, how I should be, knowing that out of the pure soil of being the good fruit of deeds and words would surely spring.

There was a strange, awe-inspiring mingling of humility and majesty, relaxation and power in His slightest word or gesture which made me long to understand its source. What made Him so different, so immeasurably superior to any other man I had ever met?

...It was my inestimable privilege to watch and talk with...the Son of Bahá'u'lláh, the Center of His Covenant, the perfect exemplar of His Word and Life...

Here I saw a man who, outwardly, like myself, lived in the world of confusion, yet, inwardly, beyond the possibility of doubt, lived and worked in that higher and real world. All His concepts, all His motives, all His actions, derived their springs from that "World of Light.".

Howard Colby Ives, Unitarian minister

PHOEBE HEARST RECALLS 'ABDU'L-BAHÁ

...I must say He is the Most Wonderful Being I have ever met or ever expect to meet in this world. Tho He does not seek to impress one at all, strength, power, purity, love and holiness are radiated from His majestic, yet humble, personality, and the spiritual atmosphere which surrounds Him and most powerfully affects all those who are blest by being near Him, is indescribable...

LADY BLOMFIELD DESCRIBES 'ABDU'L-BAHÁ

...His hair and short beard were of that snowy whiteness which had once been black; His eyes were large, blue-grey with long black lashes and well-marked eyebrows; His face was a beautiful oval with warm, ivory-coloured skin, a straight, finely-modelled nose, and firm, kind mouth. These are merely outside details by which an attempt is made to convey an idea of His arresting personality.

His figure was of such perfect symmetry, and so full of dignity and grace, that the first impression was that of considerable height. He seemed an incarnation of loving understanding, of compassion and power, of wisdom and authority, of strength, and of a buoyant youthfulness, which somehow defied the burden of His years...

'ABDU'L-BAHÁ DEFINES HIS OWN STATION

My name is 'Abdu'l-Bahá [Servant of Bahá'u'lláh]. My qualification is 'Abdu'l-Bahá. My reality is 'Abdu'l-Bahá. My praise is 'Abdu'l-Bahá. Thraldom to the Blessed Perfection is my glorious and refulgent diadem, and servitude to all the human race my perpetual religion...No name, no title, no mention, no commendation have I, nor will ever have, except 'Abdu'l-Bahá. This is my longing. This is my greatest yearning. This is my eternal life. This is my everlasting glory.

'Abdu'l-Bahá

I am the servant of Bahá'u'lláh, the Founder; and in this I glory. No honor do I consider greater than this, and it is my hope that I may be confirmed in servitude to Bahá'u'lláh. This is my station.

'Abdu'l-Bahá

SHOGHI EFFENDI CLARIFIES THE STATION OF 'ABDU'L-BAHÁ

... 'Abdu'l-Bahá is not a Manifestation of God... He gets His light, His inspiration and sustenance direct from the Fountain-head of the Bahá'í Revelation... He reflects even as a clear and perfect Mirror the rays of Bahá'u'lláh's glory, and does not inherently possess that indefinable yet all-pervading reality the exclusive possession of which is the hallmark of Prophethood... His words are not equal in rank, though they possess an equal validity with the utterances of Bahá'u'lláh...

Shoghi Effendi

That 'Abdu'l-Bahá is not a Manifestation of God, that, though the successor of His Father, He does not occupy a cognate station, that no one else except the Báb and Bahá'u'lláh can ever lay claim to such a station before the expiration of a full thousand years-are verities which lie embedded in the specific utterances of both the Founder of our Faith and the Interpreter of His teachings...

...we should not by any means infer that 'Abdu'l-Bahá is merely one of the servants of the Blessed Beauty, or at best one whose function is to be confined to that of an authorized interpreter of His Father's teachings. Far be from me to entertain such a notion or to wish to instill such sentiments...

He is, and should for all time be regarded, first and foremost, as the Center and Pivot of Bahá'u'lláh's peerless and all-enfolding Covenant, His most exalted handiwork, the stainless Mirror of His light, the perfect Exemplar of His teachings, the unerring Interpreter of His Word, the embodiment of every Bahá'í ideal, the incarnation of every Bahá'í virtue, the Most Mighty Branch sprung from the Ancient Root...

Shoghi Effendi

BAHÁ'U'LLÁH NAMES 'ABDU'L-BAHÁ AS THE CENTRE OF THE COVENANT

When the ocean of My presence hath ebbed and the Book of My Revelation is ended, turn your faces toward Him Whom God hath purposed, Who hath branched from this Ancient Root. The object of this sacred verse is none other except the Most Mighty Branch ['Abdu'l-Bahá].

Bahá'u'lláh

They who deprive themselves of the shadow of the Branch, are lost in the wilderness of error...

Bahá'u'lláh

Blessed, doubly blessed, is the ground which His footsteps have trodden, the eye that hath been cheered by the beauty of His countenance, the ear that hath been honoured by hearkening to His call, the heart that hath tasted the sweetness of His love, the breast that hath dilated through His remembrance, the pen that hath voiced His praise, the scroll that hath borne the testimony of His writings.

Bahá'u'lláh

'ABDU'L-BAHÁ'S IMPRISONMENT

This prison is sweeter to me and more to be desired than a garden of flowers; to me, this bondage is better than the freedom to go my way, and I find this narrow place more spacious than wide and open plains. Do not grieve over me. And should my Lord decree that I be blessed with sweet martyrdom's cup, this would but mean receiving what I long for most.

Fear not if this Branch be severed from this material world and cast aside its leaves; nay, the leaves thereof shall flourish, for this Branch will grow after it is cut off from this world below, it shall reach the loftiest pinnacles of glory, and it shall bear such fruits as will perfume the world with their fragrance.

'Abdu'l-Bahá

I myself was in prison forty years-one year alone would have been impossible to bear-nobody survived that imprisonment more than a year! But, thank God, during all those forty years I was supremely happy! Every day, on waking, it was like hearing good tidings, and every night infinite joy was mine. Spirituality was my comfort, and turning to God was my greatest joy. If this had not been so, do you think it possible that I could have lived through those forty years in prison?

Thus, spirituality is the greatest of God's gifts, and 'Life Everlasting' means 'Turning to God.' May you, one and all, increase daily in spirituality, may you be strengthened in all goodness, may you be helped more and more by the Divine consolation, be made free by the Holy Spirit of God, and may the power of the Heavenly Kingdom live and work among you.

This is my earnest desire, and I pray to God to grant you this favour.

'Abdu'l-Bahá

BAHÁ'U'LLÁH ALLUDES TO THE POWER OF 'ABDU'L-BAHÁ

The force of the utterance of the Most Great Branch and His powers are not as yet fully revealed. In the future it will be seen how He, alone and unaided, shall raise the banner of the Most Great Name in the midmost heart of the world, with power and authority and Divine effulgence. It will be seen how He shall gather together the peoples of the earth under the tent of peace and concord.

Bahá'u'lláh

50
SHOGHI EFFENDI THE GUARDIAN

A RECOLLECTION OF SHOGHI EFFENDI

Shoghi Effendi's love of learning, his eagerness to know and understand, a refined artistic taste combined with a great ability to do things, the remarkable energy he possessed, all these, together with much common sense and such superior spiritual powers that all who came into contact with him were subjugated by his love, made it clear that the striking qualities so evident in his maternal Grandfather ['Abdu'l-Bahá] had appeared in him to the fullest extent...

He was of a gentle nature, his manners were cordial, remarkably loving and aristocratic, and his memory was extraordinary...With regard to his appearance, my first impression was one of wonder. His gentle, graceful figure was enhanced by the power and authority which emanated from him; his broad forehead, his fine hazel eyes filled with light...the striking purity and innocence and integrity which emanated from his whole being, all made a perfect vehicle for the tremendous forces of the spirit which were channelled through him.

Dr. Ugo Giachery

'ABDU'L-BAHÁ APPOINTS SHOGHI EFFENDI AS THE GUARDIAN

O my loving friends! After the passing away of this wronged one, it is incumbent upon...the loved ones of the Abhá Beauty to turn unto Shoghi Effendi-the youthful branch...as he is the sign of God, the chosen branch, the guardian of the Cause of God, he unto whom all ...His loved ones must turn...

The sacred and youthful branch, the guardian of the Cause of God as well as the Universal House of Justice, to be universally elected and

established, are both under the care and protection of the Abhá
beauty...Whatsoever they decide is of God. It is incumbent upon the
House of Justice, upon all...to show their obedience, submissiveness, and
subordination unto the guardian of the Cause of God...

'Abdu'l-Bahá

SHOGHI EFFENDI ELABORATES THE FUNCTION OF THE GUARDIAN

Dearly-beloved friends! Exalted as is the position and vital as is the function of the institution of the Guardianship in the Administrative Order of Bahá'u'lláh, and staggering as must be the weight of responsibility which it carries, its importance must, whatever be the language of the Will, be in no wise over-emphasized. The Guardian of the Faith must no under any circumstances, and whatever his merits or his achievements, be exalted to the rank that will make him a co-sharer with 'Abdu'l-Bahá in the unique position which the Center of the Covenant occupies-much less to the station exclusively ordained for the Manifestation of God. So grave a departure from the established tenets of our Faith is nothing short of open blasphemy. As I have already stated, in the course of my references to 'Abdu'l-Bahá's station, however great the gulf that separates Him from the Author of a Divine Revelation it can never measure with the distance that stands between Him Who is the Center of Bahá'u'lláh's Covenant and the Guardians who are its chosen ministers. There is a far, far greater distance separating the Guardian from the Center of the Covenant than there is between the Center of the Covenant and its Author.

No Guardian of the Faith, I feel it my solemn duty to place on record, can ever claim to be the perfect exemplar of the teachings of Bahá'u'lláh or the stainless mirror that reflects His light. Though overshadowed by the unfailing, the unerring protection of Bahá'u'lláh and of the Báb, and however much he may share with 'Abdu'l-Bahá the right and obligation to interpret the Bahá'í teachings, he remains essentially human and cannot, if he wishes to remain faithful to his trust, arrogate to himself, under any pretense whatsoever, the rights, the privileges and prerogatives which Bahá'u'lláh has chosen to confer upon His Son. In the light of this truth to pray to the Guardian of the Faith, to address him as lord and master, to designate him as his holiness, to seek his benediction, to celebrate his birthday, or to commemorate any event associated with his life would be tantamount to a departure from those established truths that are enshrined with our beloved Faith. The fact that the Guardian has been specifically endowed with such power as he may need to reveal the purport and disclose the implications of the utterances of Bahá'u'lláh and of 'Abdu'l-Bahá does not necessarily confer upon him a station co-equal with those Whose words he is called upon to interpret. He can exercise that right and discharge this obligation and yet remain infinitely inferior to both of them in rank and different in nature.

51
THE COVENANT

THE POWER OF THE COVENANT

So firm and mighty is this Covenant that from the beginning of time until the present day no religious Dispensation hath produced its like. Whatsoever is latent in the innermost of this holy cycle shall gradually appear and be made manifest, for now is but the beginning of its growth and the dayspring of the revelation of its signs. Fear not, fear not if this Branch be severed from this material world and cast aside its leaves; nay, the leaves thereof shall flourish, for this Branch will grow after it is cut off from this world below, it shall reach the loftiest pinnacles of glory, and it shall bear such fruits as will perfume the world with their fragrance.

'Abdu'l-Bahá

If it is considered with insight, it will be seen that all the forces of the universe, in the last analysis serve the Covenant. In the future it shall be made evident and manifest.

'Abdu'l-Bahá

Today, every wise, vigilant and foresighted person is awakened, and to him are unveiled the mysteries of the future which show that nothing save the power of the Covenant is able to stir and move the heart of humanity, just as the New and Old Testaments propounded throughout all regions the Cause of Christ and were the pulsating power in the body of the human world. A tree that hath a root shall bear fruit, while the tree that hath none, no matter how high and hardy it may be, will eventually wither, perish and become but a log fit for the fire.

The Covenant of God is like unto a vast and fathomless ocean. A billow shall rise and surge therefrom and shall cast ashore all accumulated foam.

'Abdu'l-Bahá

FIRMNESS IN THE COVENANT

May the brightness of His glory shining above the horizon of bounty rest upon you, O people of Bahá, upon every one who standeth firm and steadfast and upon those that are well grounded in the Faith and are endued with true understanding.

Bahá'u'lláh

There shineth nothing else in Mine heart except the unfading light of the Morn of Divine guidance, and out of My mouth proceedeth naught but the essence of truth, which the Lord your God hath revealed. Follow not, therefore, your earthly desires, and violate not the Covenant of God, nor break your pledge to Him. With firm determination, with the whole affection of your heart, and with the full force of your words, turn ye unto Him, and walk not in the ways of the foolish.

Bahá'u'lláh

THE UNIQUENESS OF THE COVENANT

As to the most great characteristic of the revelation of Bahá'u'lláh, a specific teaching not given by any of the Prophets of the past: It is the ordination and appointment of the Center of the Covenant ['Abdu'l-Bahá]. By this appointment and provision He has safeguarded and protected the religion of God against differences and schisms, making it impossible for anyone to create a new sect or faction of belief. To ensure unity and agreement He has entered into a Covenant with all the people of the world, including the interpreter and explainer of His teachings, so that no one may interpret or explain the religion of God according to his own view or opinion and thus create a sect founded upon his individual understanding of the divine Words. The Book of the Covenant or Testament of Bahá'u'lláh is the means of preventing such a possibility, for whosoever shall speak from the authority of himself alone shall be degraded. Be ye informed and cognizant of this. Beware lest anyone shall secretly question or deny this to you. There are some people of self-will and desire who do not communicate their intentions to you in clear language. They envelop their meanings in secret statements and insinuations... Be ye aware of this! Be awakened and enlightened! For Christ has said that no one hides the lamp under a bushel. The purport of my admonition is that certain people will endeavor to influence you in the direction of their own personal views and opinions. Therefore, be upon your guard in order that none may assail the oneness and integrity of Bahá'u'lláh's Cause. Praise be to God! Bahá'u'lláh left nothing unsaid. He explained everything. He left no room for anything further to be said. Yet there are some who for the sake of personal interest and prestige will attempt to sow the seeds of sedition and disloyalty among you. To protect and safeguard the religion of God from this and all other attack, the Center of the Covenant has been named and appointed by Bahá'u'lláh...

My purpose is to explain to you that it is your duty to guard the religion of God so that none shall be able to assail it outwardly or inwardly. If you find harmful teachings are being set forth by some individual, no matter who that individual be, even though he should be my own son, know, verily that I am completely severed from him. If anyone speaks against the Covenant, even though he should be my son, know that I am opposed to him. Those who speak falsehoods, who covet worldly things and seek to accumulate the riches of this earth are not of me. But when you find a person living up to the teachings of Bahá'u'lláh, following the precepts of the Hidden Words, know that he belongs to Bahá'u'lláh; and, verily, I proclaim that he is of me. If, on the other hand, you see anyone whose deeds and conduct are contrary to and not in conformity with the good pleasure of the Blessed Perfection and against the spirit of the Hidden Words, let that be your standard and criterion of judgement against him, for know that I am altogether severed from him no matter who he may be. This is the truth.

...I pray that God may confirm you in order that you may live according to the teachings of Bahá'u'lláh.

'Abdu'l-Bahá

Bahá'u'lláh has written a Covenant and Testament with His own pen, declaring that the One Whom He has appointed the Center of the Covenant shall be turned to and obeyed by all. Therefore, thank God that Bahá'u'lláh has made the pathway straight. He has clearly explained all things and opened every door for advancing souls. There is no reason for hesitation by anyone. The purpose of the Covenant was simply to ward off disunion and differences...

'Abdu'l-Bahá

THE ADMINISTRATIVE ORDER

It should be noted in this connection that this Administrative Order is fundamentally different from anything that any Prophet has previously established, inasmuch as Bahá'u'lláh has Himself revealed its principles, established its institutions, appointed the person to interpret His Word and conferred the necessary authority on the body designed to supplement and apply His legislative ordinances. Therein lies the secret of its strength, its fundamental distinction, and the guarantee against disintegration and schism. Nowhere in the sacred scriptures of any of the world's religious systems...do we find any provisions establishing a covenant or providing for an administrative order that can compare in scope and authority with those that lie at the very basis of the Bahá'í Dispensation.

Shoghi Effendi

THE STRUCTURE OF THE ADMINISTRATIVE ORDER

The Administrative Order of the Faith of Bahá'u'lláh must in no wise be regarded as purely democratic in character inasmuch as the basic assumption which requires all democracies to depend fundamentally upon getting their mandate from the people is altogether lacking in this Dispensation. In the conduct of the administrative affairs of the Faith, in the enactment of the legislation necessary to supplement the laws of the Kitáb-i-Aqdas, the members of the Universal House of Justice, it should be borne in mind, are not, as Bahá'u'lláh's utterances clearly imply, responsible to those whom they represent, nor are they allowed to be governed by the feelings, the general opinion, and even the convictions of the mass of the faithful, or of those who directly elect them. They are to follow, in a prayerful attitude, the dictates and promptings of their conscience. They may, indeed they must, acquaint themselves with the conditions prevailing among the community, must weigh dispassionately in their minds the merits of any case presented for their consideration, but must reserve for themselves the right of an unfettered decision. "God will verily inspire them with whatsoever He willeth," is Bahá'u'lláh's incontrovertible assurance. They, and not the body of those who either directly or indirectly elect them, have thus been made the recipients of the divine guidance which is at once the life-blood and ultimate safeguard of this Revelation. Moreover, he who symbolizes the hereditary principle in this Dispensation [the Guardian] has been made the interpreter of the words of its Author, and ceases consequently, by virtue of the actual authority vested in him, to be the figurehead invariably associated with the prevailing systems of constitutional monarchies.

Nor can the Bahá'í Administrative Order be dismissed as a hard and rigid system of unmitigated autocracy or as an idle imitation of any form of absolutistic ecclesiastical government, whether it be the Papacy, the Imamate or any other similar institution, for the obvious reason that upon the international elected representative of the followers of Bahá'u'lláh has been conferred the exclusive right of legislating on matters not expressly revealed in the Bahá'í Writings. Neither the Guardian of the Faith nor any institution apart from the International House of Justice can ever usurp this vital and essential power or encroach upon that sacred right. The abolition of professional priesthood with its accompanying sacraments of baptism, of communion and of confession of sins, the laws requiring the election by universal suffrage of all local, national, and international Houses of Justice, the total absence of episcopal authority with its attendant privileges, corruptions and bureaucratic tendencies, are further evidences of the non-autocratic character of the Bahá'í Administrative Order and of its inclination to democratic methods in the administration of its affairs.

Nor is this Order identified with the name of Bahá'u'lláh to be confused with any system of purely aristocratic government in view of the fact that it upholds, on the one hand, the hereditary principle and entrusts the Guardian of the Faith with the obligation of interpreting its teachings, and provides, on the other, for the free and direct election from among the mass of the faithful of the body that constitutes its highest legislative organ.

Whereas this Administrative Order cannot be said to have been modeled after any of these recognized systems of government, it nevertheless embodies, reconciles and assimilates within its framework such wholesome elements as are to be found in each one of them. The hereditary authority which the Guardian is called upon to exercise, the vital and essential functions which the Universal House of Justice discharges, the specific provisions requiring its democratic election by the representatives of the faithful-these combine to demonstrate the truth that this divinely revealed Order, which can never be identified with any of the standard type of government referred to by Aristotle in his works, embodies and blends with the spiritual verities on which it is based the beneficent elements which are to be found in each one of them. The admitted evils inherent in each of these systems being rigidly and permanently excluded, this unique Order, however long it may endure and however extensive its ramifications, cannot ever degenerate into any form of depotism, of oligarchy, or of demagogy which must sooner or later corrupt the machinery of all man-made and essentially defective political institutions.

Shoghi Effendi

THE FOUNDATION OF THE ADMINISTRATIVE ORDER

Let no one, while this System is still in its infancy, misconceive its character, belittle its significance or misrepresent its purpose. The bedrock on which this Administrative Order is founded is God's immutable Purpose for mankind in this day. The Source from which it derives its inspiration is no one less than Bahá'u'lláh Himself. Its shield and defender are the embattled hosts of the Abhá Kingdom. Its seed is the blood of no less than twenty thousand martyrs who have offered up their lives that it may be born and flourish. The axis round which its institutions revolve are the authentic provisions of the Will and Testament of 'Abdu'l-Bahá. Its guiding principles are the truths which He Who is the unerring Interpreter of the teachings of our Faith has so clearly enunciated in His public addresses throughout the West. The laws that govern its operation and limit its functions are those which have been expressly ordained in the Kitáb-i-Aqdas. The seat round which its spiritual, its humanitarian and administrative activities will cluster are the Mashriqu'l-Adhkár [House of Worship] and its Dependencies. The pillars that sustain its authority and buttress its structure are the twin institution of the Guardianship and of the Universal House of Justice. The central, the underlying aim which animates it is the establishment of the New World Order as adumbrated by Bahá'u'lláh. The methods it employs, the standard it inculcates, incline it to neither East nor West, neither Jew nor Gentile, neither rich nor poor, neither white nor colored. Its watchword is the unification of the human race; its standard the "Most Great Peace"; its consummation the advent of that golden millennium—the Day when the kingdoms of this world shall have become the Kingdom of God Himself, the Kingdom of Bahá'u'lláh.

Shoghi Effendi

HOUSE OF JUSTICE

The Lord hath ordained that in every city a House of Justice be established wherein shall gather counsellors to the number of Bahá, and should it exceed this number it doth not matter. They should consider themselves as entering the Court of the presence of God, the Exalted, the Most High, and as beholding Him Who is the Unseen. It behoveth them to be the trusted ones of the Merciful among men and to regard themselves as the guardians appointed of God for all that dwell on earth. It is incumbent upon them to take counsel together and to have regard for the interests of the servants of God, for His sake, even as they regard their own interests, and to choose that which is meet and seemly. Thus hath the Lord your God commanded you. Beware lest ye put away that which is clearly revealed in His Tablet. Fear God, O ye that perceive.

Bahá'u'lláh

O people of God! That which traineth the world is Justice, for it is upheld by two pillars, reward and punishment. These two pillars are the sources of life to the world. Inasmuch as for each day there is a new problem and for every problem an expedient solution, such affairs should be referred to the Ministers of the House of Justice that they may act according to the needs and requirements of the time. They that, for the sake of God, arise to serve His Cause, are the recipients of divine inspiration from the unseen Kingdom. It is incumbent upon all to be obedient unto them. All matters of State should be referred to the House of Justice, but acts of worship must be observed according to that which God hath revealed in His Book.

Bahá'u'lláh

It is incumbent upon the Trustees of the House of Justice to take counsel together regarding those things which have not outwardly been revealed in the Book, and to enforce that which is agreeable to them. God will verily inspire them with whatsoever He willeth, and He, verily, is the Provider, the Omniscient.

...We exhort the men of the House of Justice and command them to ensure the protection and safeguarding of men, women and children. It is incumbent upon them to have the utmost regard for the interests of the people at all times and under all conditions. Blessed is the ruler who succoureth the captive, and the rich one who careth for the poor, and the just one who secureth from the wrong doer the rights of the downtrodden, and happy the trustee who observeth that which the Ordainer, the Ancient of Days hath prescribed unto him.

Bahá'u'lláh

We have decreed that a third part of all fines shall go to the Seat of Justice, and We admonish its men to observe pure justice, that they may expend what is thus accumulated for such purposes as have been enjoined upon them by Him Who is the All-Knowing, the All-Wise. O ye Men of Justice! Be ye, in the realm of God, shepherds unto His sheep and guard them from the ravening wolves that have appeared in disguise, even as ye would guard your own sons. Thus exhorteth you the Counsellor, the Faithful.

Bahá'u'lláh

...essential sinlessness belongs especially to the Universal Manifestations, and the acquired sinlessness is granted to every holy soul. For instance, the Universal House of Justice, if it be established under the necessary conditions-with members elected from all the people-that House of Justice will be under the protection and the guardianship of God. If that House of Justice shall decide unanimously, or by a majority, upon any question not mentioned in the Book [Kitab-i-Aqdas], that decision and command will be guarded from mistake. Now the members of the House of Justice have not, individually, essential sinlessness; but the body of the House of Justice is under the protection of God: this is called conferred infallibility.

'Abdu'l-Bahá

Inasmuch as the House of Justice hath power to enact laws that are not expressly recorded in the Book and bear upon daily transactions, so also it hath power to repeal the same...This it can do because these laws form no part of the divine explicit text.

Shoghi Effendi

THE GUARDIAN

The sacred and youthful Branch, the Guardian of the Cause of God, as well as the Universal House of Justice to be universally elected and established, are both under the care and protection of the Abhá Beauty, under the shelter and unerring guidance of the Exalted One...Whatsoever they decide is of God.

'Abdu'l-Bahá

From these statements it is made indubitably clear and evident that the Guardian of the Faith has been made the Interpreter of the Word and that the Universal House of Justice has been invested with the function of legislating on matters not expressly revealed in the teachings. The interpretation of the Guardian, functioning within his own sphere, is as authoritative and binding as the enactments of the International House of Justice, whose exclusive right and prerogative is to pronounce upon and deliver the final judgement on such laws and ordinances as Bahá'u'lláh has not expressly revealed. Neither can, nor will ever, infringe upon the sacred and prescribed domain of the other. Neither will seek to curtail the specific and undoubted authority with which both have been divinely invested.

Shoghi Effendi

52
LAWS & COMMANDMENTS

HAPPINESS AND PROTECTION

We school you with the rod of wisdom and laws, like unto the father who educateth his son, and this for naught but the protection of your own selves and the elevation of your stations. By My life, were ye to discover what We have desired for you in revealing Our holy laws, ye would offer up your very souls for this sacred, this mighty, and most exalted Faith.

Bahá'u'lláh

They whom God hath endued with insight will readily recognize that the precepts laid down by God constitute the highest means for the maintenance of order in the world and the security of its people...

O ye peoples of the world! Know assuredly that My commandments are the lamps of My loving providence among My servants, and the keys of My mercy for My creatures...

Think not that We have revealed unto you a mere code of laws. Nay, rather, We have unsealed the choice Wine with the fingers of might and power. To this beareth witness that which the Pen of Revelation hath revealed. Meditate upon this, O men of insight!

Bahá'u'lláh

Were men to discover the motivating purpose of God's Revelation, they would assuredly cast away their fears, and, with hearts filled with gratitude, rejoice with exceeding gladness.

Bahá'u'lláh

OBEDIENCE TO THE LAW

The ordinances of God have been sent down from the heaven of His most august Revelation. All must diligently observe them. Man's supreme distinction, his real advancement, his final victory, have always depended, and will continue to depend, upon them. Whoso keepeth the commandments of God shall attain everlasting felicity.

Bahá'u'lláh

There is no paradise, in the estimation of the believers in the Divine Unity, more exalted than to obey God's commandments, and there is no fire in the eyes of those who have known God and His signs, fiercer than to transgress His laws and to oppress another soul, even to the extent of a mustard seed...God will, in truth, judge all men, and we all verily plead for His grace.

The Báb

Reduce not the ordinances of God to fanciful imaginations of your own; rather observe all the things which God hath created at His behest with the eye of the spirit, even as ye see things with the eyes of your bodies.

The Báb

O people of Bahá! Each one of the ordinances We have revealed is a mighty stronghold for the preservation of the world of being. Verily, this Wronged One desireth naught but your security and elevation.

Bahá'u'lláh

Wert thou to speed through the immensity of space and traverse the expanse of heaven, yet thou wouldst find no rest save in submission to Our command and humbleness before Our Face.

Bahá'u'lláh

LAWS MUST REFLECT THE EXIGENCIES OF THE TIMES

Moses lived in the wilderness of Sinai where crime necessitated direct punishment. There were no penitentiaries or penalties of imprisonment. Therefore, according to the exigency of the time and place it was a law of God that an eye should be given for an eye and a tooth for a tooth. It would not be practicable to enforce this law at the present time-for instance, to blind a man who accidentally blinded you. In the Torah there are many commands concerning the punishment of a murderer. It would not be allowable or possible to carry out these ordinances today. Human conditions and exigencies are such that even the question of capital punishment-the one penalty which most nations have continued to enforce for murder...is now under discussion by wise men who are debating its advisability. In fact, laws for the ordinary conditions of life are only valid temporarily. The exigencies of the time of Moses justified cutting off a man's hand for theft, but such a penalty is not allowable now. Time changes conditions, and laws change to suit conditions. We must remember that these changing laws are not the essentials; they are the accidentals of religion. The essential ordinances established by a Manifestation of God are spiritual; they concern moralities, the ethical development of man and faith in God. They are ideal and necessarily permanent-expressions of the one foundation and not amenable to change or transformation.

'Abdu'l-Bahá

THE BOOK OF LAWS THE MOST HOLY BOOK

While in prison We have revealed a Book which We have entitled 'The Most Holy Book'. We have enacted laws therein and adorned it with the commandments of thy Lord, Who exerciseth authority over all that are in the heavens and on the earth. Say: Take hold of it, O people, and observe that which hath been sent down in it of the wondrous precepts of your Lord, the Forgiving, the Bountiful. It will truly prosper you both in this world and in the next and will purge you of whatsoever ill beseemeth you.

Bahá'u'lláh

We announce unto everyone the joyful tidings concerning that which We have revealed in Our Most Holy Book - a Book from above whose horizon the day-star of My commandments shineth upon every observer and every observed one. Hold ye fast unto it and fulfil that which is revealed therein. Indeed better is this for you than whatsoever hath been created in the world, did ye but know it. Beware lest the transitory things of human life withhold you from turning unto God, the True One. Ponder ye in your hearts the world and its conflicts and changes, so that ye may discern its merit and the station of those who have set their hearts upon it and have turned away from that which hath been sent down in Our Preserved Tablet.

Bahá'u'lláh

'ABDU'L-BAHÁ APPOINTED AS THE CENTRE OF THE COVENANT AND AUTHORIZED INTERPRETER

When the ocean of My presence hath ebbed and the Book of My Revelation is ended, turn your faces toward Him Whom God hath purposed, Who hath branched from this Ancient Root.

Bahá'u'lláh

O people of the World! When the Mystic Dove will have winged its flight from its Sanctuary of Praise and sought its far-off goal, its hidden habitation, refer ye whatsoever ye understand not in the Book to Him Who hath branched from this mighty Stock.

Bahá'u'lláh

BACKBITING FORBIDDEN

The seeker should, also, regard backbiting as grievous error, and keep himself aloof from its dominion, inasmuch as backbiting quencheth the light of the heart, and extinguisheth the life of the soul.

Bahá'u'lláh

If any soul speak ill of an absent one, the only result will clearly be this: he will dampen the zeal of the friends and tend to make them indifferent. For backbiting is divisive, it is the leading cause among the friends of a disposition to withdraw. If any individual should speak ill of one who is absent, it is incumbent on his hearers, in a spiritual and friendly manner, to stop him, and say in effect: would this detraction serve any useful purpose? Would it please the Blessed Beauty, contribute to the lasting honour of the friends, promote the holy Faith, support the Covenant, or be of any possible benefit to any soul? No, never! On the contrary, it would make the dust to settle so thickly on the heart that the ears would hear no more, and the eyes would no longer behold the light of truth.

If, however, a person setteth about speaking well of another, opening his lips to praise another, he will touch an answering chord in his hearers and they will be stirred up by the breathings of God. Their hearts and souls will rejoice to know that, God be thanked, here is a soul in the Faith who is a focus of human perfections, a very embodiment of the bounties of the Lord, one whose tongue is eloquent, and whose face shineth, in whatever gathering he may be, one who hath victory upon his brow, and who is a being sustained by the sweet savours of God.

'Abdu'l-Bahá

MARRIAGE

God hath prescribed matrimony unto you...Whoso contenteth himself with a single partner from among the maidservants of God, both he and she shall live in tranquillity...Enter into wedlock, O people, that ye may bring forth one who will make mention of Me amid My servants...

It hath been laid down in the Bayán that marriage is dependent upon the consent of both parties. Desiring to establish love, unity and harmony amidst Our servants, We have conditioned it, once the couple's wish is known, upon the permission of their parents, lest enmity and rancour should arise amongst them. And in this We have yet other purposes. Thus hath Our commandment been ordained.

Bahá'u'lláh

THE FAST

O people of the World! We have enjoined upon you fasting during a brief period, and at its close have designated for you Naw-Rúz as a feast. Thus hath the Day-Star of Utterance shone forth above the horizon of the Book as decreed by Him Who is the Lord of the beginning and the end. Let the days in excess of the months be placed before the month of fasting. We have ordained that these, amid all nights and days, shall be the manifestations of the letter Há, and thus they have not been bounded by the limits of the year and its months. It behoveth the people of Bahá, throughout these days, to provide good cheer for themselves, their kindred and, beyond them, the poor and needy, and with joy and exultation to hail and glorify their Lord, to sing His praise and magnify His Name; and when they end-these days of giving that precede the season of restraint-let them enter upon the Fast. Thus hath it been ordained by Him Who is the Lord of all mankind. The traveller, the ailing, those who are with child or giving suck, are not bound by the Fast; they have been exempted by God as a token of His grace. He, verily, is the Almighty, the Most Generous.

These are the ordinances of God that have been set down in the Books and Tablets by His Most Exalted Pen. Hold ye fast unto His statutes and commandments, and be not of those who, following their idle fancies and vain imaginings, have clung to the standards fixed by their own selves, and cast behind their backs the standards laid down by God. Abstain from food and drink from sunrise to sundown, and beware lest desire deprive you of this grace that is appointed in the Book.

Bahá'u'lláh

Fasting is a symbol. Fasting signifies abstinence from lust...But mere abstention from food has no effect on the spirit. It is only a symbol, a reminder. Otherwise it is of no importance.

'Abdu'l-Bahá

NINETEEN DAY FEAST

Verily, it is enjoined upon you to offer a feast, once in every month, though only water be served; for God hath purposed to bind hearts together, albeit through both earthly and heavenly means.

Bahá'u'lláh

As to the Nineteen Day Feast, it rejoiceth mind and heart. If this feast be held in the proper fashion, the friends will, once in nineteen days, find themselves spiritually restored, and endued with a power that is not of this world.

'Abdu'l-Bahá

THE RIGHT OF GOD

Good God! is it possible that, seeing one of his fellow-creatures starving, destitute of everything, a man can rest and live comfortably in his luxurious mansions? He who meets another in the greatest misery, can he enjoy his fortune? That is why, in the Religion of God, it is prescribed and established that wealthy men each year give over a certain part of their fortune for the maintenance of the poor and unfortunate. That is the foundation of Religion of God, and the most essential of the Commandments.

As now man is not forced nor obliged by the Government, if by the natural tendency of his good heart, with the greatest spirituality, he goes to this expense for the poor, this will be a thing very much praised, approved and pleasing.

'Abdu'l-Bahá

The Right of God is an obligation upon everyone. This commandment hath been revealed and set down in the Book by the Pen of Glory.

However, it is not permissible to solicit or demand it. If one is privileged to pay the Huqúq, and doeth so in a spirit of joy and radiance, such an act is acceptable, and not otherwise.

Bahá'u'lláh

The payment of the Right of God is conditional upon one's financial ability. If a person is unable to meet his obligation, God will verily excuse him. He is the All-Forgiving, the All-Generous.

Bahá'u'lláh

Reference to this matter is in no wise permissible...Ye may relinquish the whole world but must not allow the detraction of even one jot or tittle from the dignity of the Cause of God...Let him who wisheth observe it, and let him who wisheth ignore it. Verily, thy Lord is the Self-Sufficing, the All-Praised. Indeed, independence of all things is as a door of guidance unto His faithful servants. Well is it with them that have severed themselves from the world and have arisen to serve His Cause. Verily, they are numbered with the people of Bahá at the court of His resplendent Beauty.

Bahá'u'lláh

SLAVERY FORBIDDEN

It is forbidden you to trade in slaves, be they men or women. It is not for him who is himself a servant to buy another of God's servants, and this hath been prohibited in His Holy Tablet. Thus, by His mercy, hath the commandment been recorded by the Pen of justice. Let no man exalt himself above another; all are but bondslaves before the Lord, and all exemplify the truth that there is none other God but Him. He, verily, is the All-Wise, Whose wisdom encompasseth all things.

Bahá'u'lláh

THE CONCEPT OF "UNCLEANNESS" IS FORMALLY ABOLISHED

God hath, likewise, as a bounty from His presence, abolished the concept of "uncleanness", whereby divers things and peoples have been held to be impure. He, of a certainty, is the Ever-Forgiving, the Most Generous. Verily, all created things were immersed in the sea of purification when, on that first day of Ridván, We shed upon the whole of creation the splendours of Our most excellent Names and Our most exalted

Attributes. This, verily, is a token of My loving providence, which hath encompassed all the world. Consort ye then with the followers of all religions, and proclaim ye the Cause of your Lord, the Most Compassionate; this is the very crown of deeds, if ye be of them who understand.

Bahá'u'lláh

CLEANLINESS ENJOINED

God hath enjoined upon you to observe the utmost cleanliness, to the extent of washing what is soiled with dust, let alone with hardened dirt and similar defilement...Make use of rose-water, and of pure perfume; this, indeed, is that which God hath loved from the beginning that hath no beginning, in order that there may be diffused from you what your Lord, the Incomparable, the All-Wise, desireth.

Bahá'u'lláh

It hath been enjoined upon you to pare your nails...Immerse yourselves in clean water; it is not permissible to bathe yourselves in water that hath already been used...If the bather, instead of entering the water, wash himself by pouring it upon his body, it shall be better for him and shall absolve him of the need for bodily immersion. The Lord, verily, hath willed, as a bounty from His presence, to make life easier for you that ye may be of those who are truly thankful.

Bahá'u'lláh

APPAREL AND APPEARANCE

The Lord hath relieved you, as a bounty on His part, of the restrictions that formerly applied to clothing and to the trim of the beard. He, verily, is the Ordainer, the Omniscient. Let there be naught in your demeanour of which sound and upright minds would disapprove, and make not yourselves the playthings of the ignorant. Well is it with him who hath adorned himself with the vesture of seemly conduct and a praiseworthy character. He is assuredly reckoned with those who aid their Lord through distinctive and outstanding deeds.

Bahá'u'lláh

The choice of clothing and the cut of the beard and its dressing are left to the discretion of men. But beware, O people, lest ye make yourselves the playthings of the ignorant.

Bahá'u'lláh

THE STATURE OF THE CAUSE

This is not a Cause which may be made a plaything for your idle fancies, nor is it a field for the foolish and faint of heart. By God, this is the arena of insight and detachment, of vision and upliftment, where none may spur on their chargers save the valiant horsemen of the Merciful, who have severed all attachment to the world of being. These, truly, are they that render God victorious on earth, and are the dawning-places of His sovereign might amidst mankind.

Bahá'u'lláh

Immerse yourselves in the ocean of My words, that ye may unravel its secrets, and discover all the pearls of wisdom that lie hid in its depths. Take heed that ye do not vacillate in your determination to embrace the truth of this Cause-a Cause through which the potentialities of the might of God have been revealed, and His sovereignty established. With faces beaming with joy, hasten ye unto Him. This is the changeless Faith of God, eternal in the past, eternal in the future. Let him that seeketh, attain it; and as to him that hath refused to seek it-verily, God is Self-Sufficient, above any need of His creatures.

Bahá'u'lláh

PRESERVING THE SANCTITY OF THE SACRED WRITINGS

To none is it permitted to mutter sacred verses before the public gaze as he walketh in the street or marketplace; nay rather, if he wish to magnify the Lord, it behoveth him to do so in such places as have been erected for this purpose, or in his own home. This is more in keeping with sincerity and godliness. Thus hath the sun of Our commandment shone forth above the horizon of Our utterance. Blessed, then, be those who do Our bidding.

Bahá'u'lláh

Whoso interpreteth what hath been sent down from the heaven of Revelation, and altereth its evident meaning, he, verily, is of them that have perverted the Sublime Word of God, and is of the lost ones in the Lucid Book.

Bahá'u'lláh

CONCERNING HEALTH CARE

Resort ye, in times of sickness, to competent physicians; We have not set aside the use of material means, rather have We confirmed it through this Pen, which God hath made to be the Dawning-place of His shining and glorious Cause.

Bahá'u'lláh

BEGGING FORBIDDEN

It is unlawful to beg, and it is forbidden to give to him who beggeth. All have been enjoined to earn a living, and as for those who are incapable of doing so, it is incumbent on the Deputies of God and on the wealthy to make adequate provision for them. Keep ye the statutes and commandments of God; nay, guard them as ye would your very eyes, and be not of those who suffer grievous loss.

Bahá'u'lláh

CONTENTION PROHIBITED

Ye have been forbidden in the Book of God to engage in contention and conflict, to strike another, or to commit similar acts whereby hearts and souls may be saddened...Wish not for others what ye wish not for yourselves; fear God, and be not of the prideful. Ye are all created out of water, and unto dust shall ye return. Reflect upon the end that awaiteth you, and walk not in the ways of the oppressor. Give ear unto the verses of God which He Who is the sacred Lote-Tree reciteth unto you. They are assuredly the infallible balance, established by God, the Lord of this world and the next. Through them the soul of man is caused to wing its flight towards the Dayspring of Revelation, and the heart of every true believer is suffused with light. Such are the laws which God hath enjoined upon you, such His commandments prescribed unto you in His Holy Tablet; obey them with joy and gladness, for this is best for you, did ye but know.

Bahá'u'lláh

RESPONDING TO ANGER

Should anyone wax angry with you, respond to him with gentleness; and should anyone upbraid you, forbear to upbraid him in return, but leave him to himself and put your trust in God, the omnipotent Avenger, the Lord of might and justice.

Bahá'u'lláh

PROPER TREATMENT OF ANIMALS

Burden not an animal with more than it can bear. We, truly, have prohibited such treatment through a most binding interdiction in the Book. Be ye the embodiments of justice and fairness amidst all creation.

Bahá'u'lláh

ESCHEWING VICES

Gambling and the use of opium have been forbidden unto you. Eschew them both, O people, and be not of those who transgress. Beware of using any substance that induceth sluggishness and torpor in the human temple and inflicteth harm upon the body. We, verily, desire for you naught save what shall profit you, and to this bear witness all created things, had ye but ears to hear.

Bahá'u'lláh

But there are other forbidden things which do not cause immediate harm, and the injurious effects of which are only gradually produced: such acts are also repugnant to the Lord, and blameworthy in His sight, and repellent. The absolute unlawfulness of these, however, hath not been expressly set forth in the Text, but their avoidance is necessary to purity, cleanliness, the preservation of health, and freedom from addiction.

Among these latter is smoking tobacco, which is dirty, smelly, offensive-an evil habit and one the harmfulness of which gradually becometh apparent to all. Every qualified physician hath ruled- and this hath also been proven by tests-that one of the components of tobacco is a deadly poison, and that the smoker is vulnerable to many and various diseases. This is why smoking hath been plainly set forth as repugnant from the standpoint of hygiene.

The Báb, at the outset of His mission, explicitly prohibited tobacco, and the friends one and all abandoned its use. But since those were times when dissimulation was permitted, and every individual who abstained from smoking was exposed to harassment, abuse and even death-the friends, in order not to advertise their beliefs, would smoke. Later on, the Book of Aqdas was revealed, and since smoking tobacco was not specifically forbidden there, the believers did not give it up. The Blessed Beauty, however, always expressed repugnance for it, and although, in the early days, there were reasons why He would smoke a little tobacco, in time He completely renounced it, and those sanctified souls who followed Him in all things also abandoned its use.

My meaning is that in the sight of God, smoking tobacco is deprecated, abhorrent, filthy in the extreme; and, albeit by degrees, highly injurious to health. It is also a waste of money and time, and maketh the user a prey to a noxious addiction. To those who stand firm in the Covenant, this habit is therefore censured both by reason and experience, and renouncing it will bring relief and peace of mind to all men. Furthermore, this will make it possible to have a fresh mouth and unstained fingers, and hair that is free of a foul and repellent smell. On receipt of this missive, the friends will surely, by whatever means and even over a period of time, forsake this pernicious habit. Such is my hope.

'Abdu'l-Bahá

As to opium, it is foul and accursed. God protect us from the punishment He inflicteth on the user. According to the explicit Text of the Most Holy Book, it is forbidden, and its use is utterly condemned. Reason showeth that smoking opium is a kind of insanity, and experience attesteth that the user is completely cut off from the human kingdom. May God protect all against the perpetration of an act so hideous as this, an act which layeth in ruins the very foundations of what it is to be human, and which causeth the user to be dispossessed for ever and ever. For opium fasteneth on the soul, so that the user's conscience dieth, his mind is blotted away, his perceptions are eroded. It turneth the living into the dead. It quencheth the natural heat. No greater harm can be conceived than that which opium inflicteth. Fortunate are they who never even speak the name of it; then think how wretched is the user.

O ye lovers of God! In this, the cycle of Almighty God, violence and force, constraint and oppression, are one and all condemned. It is, however, mandatory that the use of opium be prevented by any means whatsoever, that perchance the human race may be delivered from this most powerful of plagues...

O ye, God's loved ones! Experience hath shown how greatly the renouncing of smoking, of intoxicating drink, and of opium, conduceth to health and vigour, to the expansion and keenness of the mind and to bodily strength. There is today a people [the Sikhs] who strictly avoid tobacco, intoxicating liquor and opium. This people is far and away superior to others, for strength and physical courage, for health, beauty and comeliness...

Make ye then a mighty effort, that the purity and sanctity which, above all else, are cherished by 'Abdu'l-Bahá, shall distinguish the people of Bahá; that in every kind of excellence the people of God shall surpass all other human beings; that both outwardly and inwardly they shall prove superior to the rest; that for purity, immaculacy, refinement, and the preservation of health, they shall be leaders in the vanguard of those who know. And that by their freedom from enslavement, their knowledge, their self-control, they shall be fist among the pure, the free and the wise.

'Abdu'l-Bahá

A DESCRIPTION OF THE KITÁB-I-AQDAS THE BOOK OF LAWS

Unique and stupendous as was this Proclamation, it proved to be but a prelude to a still mightier revelation of the creative power of its Author, and to what may well rank as the most signal act of His ministry-the promulgation of the Kitáb-i-Aqdas. Alluded to in the Kitáb-i-Iqán, the principal repository of that Law which the Prophet Isaiah described as the "new heaven" and the "new earth", as "the Tabernacle of God", as the "Holy City", as the "Bride", the "New Jerusalem coming down from God", this "Most Holy Book", whose provisions must remain inviolate for no less than a thousand years, and whose system will embrace the entire planet, may well be regarded as the brightest emanation of the mind of Bahá'u'lláh, as the Mother Book of His Dispensation, and the Charter of His New World Order.

Revealed soon after Bahá'u'lláh had been transferred to the house of 'Udi Khammár (circa 1873), at a time when He was still encompassed by the tribulations that had afflicted Him, through the acts committed by His enemies and the professed adherents of His Faith, this Book, this treasury enshrining the priceless gems of His Revelation, stands out, by virtue of the principles it inculcates, the administrative institutions it ordains and the function with which it invests the appointed Successor of its Author, unique and incomparable among the world's sacred Scriptures. For, unlike the Old Testament and the Holy Books which preceded it, in which the actual precepts uttered by the Prophet Himself are non-existent; unlike the Gospels, in which the few sayings attributed to Jesus

Christ afford no clear guidance regarding the future administration of the affairs of His Faith; unlike even the Qur'án which, though explicit in the laws and ordinances formulated by the Apostle of God, is silent on the all-important subject of the succession, the Kitáb-i-Aqdas, revealed from first to last by the Author of the Dispensation Himself, not only preserves for posterity the basic laws and ordinances on which the fabric of His future World Order must rest, but ordains, in addition to the function of interpretation which it confers upon His Successor, the necessary institutions through which the integrity and unity of His Faith can alone be safeguarded.

In this Charter of the future world civilization its Author-at once the Judge, the Lawgiver, the Unifier and Redeemer of mankind-announces to the kings of the earth the promulgation of the "Most Great Law"; pronounces them to be His vassals; proclaims Himself the "King of Kings"; disclaims any intention of laying hands on their kingdoms; reserves for Himself the right to "seize and possess the hearts of men"; warns the world's ecclesiastical leaders not to weigh the "Book of God" with such standards as are current amongst them; and affirms that the Book itself is the "Unerring Balance" established amongst men. In it He formally ordains the institution of the "House of Justice", defines its functions, fixes its revenues, and designates its members as the "Men of Justice", the "Deputies of God", the "Trustees of the All-Merciful"; alludes to the future Centre of His Covenant, and invests Him with the right of interpreting His holy Writ; anticipates by implication the institution of Guardianship; bears witness to the revolutionizing effect of His World Order; enunciates the doctrine of the "Most Great Infallibility" of the Manifestation of God; asserts this infallibility to be the inherent and exclusive right of the Prophet; and rules out the possibility of the appearance of another Manifestation ere the lapse of at least one thousand years.

In this Book He, moreover, prescribes the obligatory prayers; designates the time and period of fasting; prohibits congregational prayer except for the dead; fixes the Qiblih; institutes the Huqúqu'lláh (Right of God); formulates the law of inheritance; ordains the institution of the Mashriqu'l-Adhkár; establishes the Nineteen Day Feast, the Bahá'í festivals and the Intercalary Days; abolishes the institution of priesthood; prohibits slavery, asceticism, mendicancy, monasticism, penance, the use of pulpits and the kissing of hands; prescribes monogamy; condemns cruelty to animals, idleness and sloth, backbiting and calumny; censures divorce; interdicts gambling, the use of opium, wine and other intoxicating drinks, specifies the punishments for murder, arson, adultery and theft; stresses the importance of marriage and lays down its essential conditions; imposes the obligation of engaging in some trade or profession, exalting such occupation to the rank of worship; emphasizes the necessity of providing the means for the education of children; lays upon every person the duty of writing a testament and of strict obedience to one's government.

Apart form these provisions Bahá'u'lláh exhorts His followers to consort, with amity and concord and without discrimination, with the adherents of all religions; warns them to guard against fanaticism, sedition, pride, dispute and contention; inculcates upon them immaculate cleanliness, strict truthfulness, spotless chastity, trustworthiness, hospitality, fidelity, courtesy, forbearance, justice and fairness; counsels them to be "even as the fingers of one hand and the limbs of one body"; calls upon them to arise and serve His Cause; assures them of His undoubted aid. He, furthermore, dwells upon the instability of human affairs; declares that true liberty consists in man's submission to His commandments; cautions them not to be indulgent in carrying out His statutes; prescribes the twin inseparable duties of recognizing the "Dayspring of God's Revelation" and of observing all the ordinances revealed by Him, neither of which, He affirms, is acceptable without the other.

The significant summons issued to the Presidents of the Republics of the American continent to seize their opportunity in the Day of God and to champion the cause of justice; the injunction to the members of parliaments throughout the world, urging the adoption of an universal script and language; His warnings to William I, the conqueror of Napoleon III; the reproof He administers to Francis Joseph, the Emperor of Austria; His reference to "the lamentations of Berlin" in His apostrophe to "the banks of the Rhine"; His condemnation of "the throne of tyranny" established in Constantinople, and His prediction of the extinction of its "outward splendour" and of the tribulations destined to overtake its inhabitants; the words of cheer and comfort He addresses to His native city, assuring her that God had chosen her to be "the source of the joy of all mankind"; His prophecy that "the voice of the heroes of Khurásán" will be raised in glorification of their Lord; His assertion that men "endued with mighty valour" will be raised up in Kirmán who will make mention of Him; and finally, His magnanimous assurance to a perfidious brother who had afflicted Him with such anguish, that an "ever-forgiving, all-bounteous" God would forgive him his iniquities were he only to repent-all these further enrich the contents of a Book designated by its Author as "the source of true felicity", as the "Unerring Balance", as the "Straight Path" and as the "quickener of mankind.".

Shoghi Effendi

In such a manner hath the Kitáb-i-Aqdas been revealed that it attracteth and embraceth all the divinely appointed Dispensations. Blessed those who peruse it! Blessed those who apprehend it! Blessed those who meditate upon it! Blessed those who ponder its meaning! So vast is its range that it hath encompassed all men ere their recognition of it. Erelong will its sovereign power, its pervasive influence and greatness of its might be manifested on earth.

Bahá'u'lláh

53
THE CURRENT AGE

THE GREATNESS OF THIS DAY

God, the Eternal Truth, beareth Me witness. The Celestial Youth hath, in this Day, raised above the heads of men the glorious Chalice of Immortality, and is standing expectant upon His seat, wondering what eye will recognize His glory, and what arm will, unhesitatingly, be stretched forth to seize the Cup from His snow-white Hand and drain it. Only a few have as yet quaffed from this peerless, this soft-flowing grace of the Ancient King. These occupy the loftiest mansions of Paradise, and are firmly established upon the seats of authority. By the righteousness of God! Neither the mirrors of His glory, nor the revealers of His names, nor any created thing, that hath been or will ever be, can ever excel them, if ye be of them that comprehend this truth.

...The excellence of this Day is immensely exalted above the comprehension of men, however extensive their knowledge, however profound their understanding. How much more must it transcend the imaginations of them that have strayed from its light...Shouldst thou rend asunder the grievous veil that blindeth thy vision, thou wouldst behold such a bounty as naught, from the beginning that hath no beginning till the end that hath no end, can either resemble or equal. What language should He Who is the Mouthpiece of God choose to speak, so that they who are shut out as by a veil from Him can recognize His glory?

Bahá'u'lláh

Should the greatness of this Day be revealed in its fullness, every man would forsake a myriad lives in his longing to partake, though it be for one moment, of its great glory-how much more this world and its corruptible treasures!

Bahá'u'lláh

Invested though each day may be with its pre-ordained share of God's wondrous grace, the Days immediately associated with the Manifestation of God possess a unique distinction and occupy a station which no mind can ever comprehend. Such is the virtue infused into them that, if the hearts of all that dwell in the heavens and the earth were, in those days of everlasting delight, to be brought face to face with that Day Star of unfading glory and attuned to His Will, each would find itself exalted above all earthly things, radiant with His light, and sanctified through His grace. All hail to this grace which no blessing, however great, can excel, and all honor to such a loving-kindness the like of which the eye of creation hath not seen!

Bahá'u'lláh

A GLORIOUS CENTURY

The thoughts of man shall take such upward flight that former accomplishments shall appear as the play of children, for the ideas and beliefs of the past and the prejudices regarding race and religion have ever lowered and been destructive to human evolution. I am most hopeful that in this century these lofty thoughts shall be conducive to human welfare. Let this century be the sun of previous centuries, the effulgences of which shall last forever, so that in times to come they shall glorify the twentieth century, saying the twentieth century was the century of lights, the twentieth century was the century of life, the twentieth century was the century of international peace, the twentieth century was the century of divine bestowals, and the twentieth century has left traces which shall last forever.

'Abdu'l-Bahá

Sciences have advanced; industries have progressed; justice is awakening. This is the century of motion, divine stimulus and accomplishment, the century of human solidarity and altruistic service, the century of universal peace and the reality of divine Kingdom.

'Abdu'l-Bahá

In the estimation of historians this radiant century is equivalent to one hundred centuries of the past. If comparison be made with the sum total of all former human achievements, it will be found that the discoveries, scientific advancement and material civilization of this present century have equaled, yea far exceeded the progress and outcome of one hundred former centuries...

The Current Age

All conditions and requisites of the past unfitted and inadequate for the present time are undergoing radical reform. It is evident, therefore, that counterfeit and spurious religious teachings, antiquated forms of belief and ancestral imitations which are at variance with the foundations of divine reality must also pass away and be reformed. They must be abandoned and new conditions be recognized. The morals of humanity must undergo change. New remedies and solution for human problems must be adopted. Human intellects themselves must change and be subject to the universal reformation. Just as the thoughts and hypotheses of past ages are fruitless today, likewise dogmas and codes of human invention are obsolete and barren of product in religion. Therefore, it is our duty in this radiant century to investigate the essentials of divine religion, seek the realities underlying the oneness of the world of humanity and discover the source of fellowship and agreement which will unite mankind in the heavenly bond of love. This unity is the radiance of eternity, the divine spirituality, the effulgence of God and the bounty of the Kingdom... For if we remain fettered and restricted by human inventions and dogmas, day by day the world of mankind will be degraded, day by day warfare and strife will increase...

'Abdu'l-Bahá

Truly, this can be called the miracle of centuries, for it is replete with manifestations of the miraculous. The time has come when all mankind shall be united, when all races shall be loyal to one fatherland, all religions become one religion, and racial and religious bias pass away. It is a day in which the oneness of humankind shall uplift its standard and international peace, like the true morning, flood the world with its light.

'Abdu'l-Bahá

This is the century of science, inventions, discoveries and universal laws. This is the century of the revelation of the mysteries of God...Therefore, you must render thanks and glorification to God that you were born in this age. Furthermore, you have listened to the call of Bahá'u'lláh...You must live in the utmost happiness...He has destined eternal bounty for you; He has bestowed everlasting glory upon you. Therefore, these glad tidings should cause you to soar in the atmosphere of joy forever and ever. Render continual thanks unto God so that the confirmations of God may encircle you all.

'Abdu'l-Bahá

Verily, the century of radiance has dawned, minds are advancing, perceptions are broadening, realizations of human possibilities are becoming universal, susceptibilities are developing, the discovery of realities is progressing. Therefore, it is necessary that we should cast aside all the prejudices of ignorance, discard superannuated beliefs in traditions of past ages and raise aloft the banner of international agreement. Let us cooperate in love and through spiritual reciprocity enjoy eternal happiness and peace.

'Abdu'l-Bahá

In every century a particular and central theme is, in accordance with the requirements of that century, confirmed by God. In this illumined age that which is confirmed is the oneness of the world of humanity. Every soul who serveth this oneness will undoubtedly be assisted and confirmed.

'Abdu'l-Bahá

This is the first age, and the early beginnings of the dispensation of the Most Great Light, wherefore, within this century, virtues must be acquired, goodly qualities must be perfected with this span of time. In these very days the Abhá Paradise must pitch its pavilions on the plains of the world...And out of pure hearts, and through heavenly bounties, all the perfections, qualities and attributes of the divine must now be made manifest.

'Abdu'l-Bahá

These days are very precious; grasp the present opportunity and ignite a candle that shall never be extinguished, and which shall pour out its light eternally illuminating the world of mankind!

'Abdu'l-Bahá

A WORLD IN TRAVAIL

The world is in travail, and its agitation waxeth day by day. Its face is turned towards waywardness and unbelief. Such shall be its plight, that to disclose it now would not be meet and seemly. Its perversity will long continue. And when the appointed hour is come, there shall suddenly appear that which shall cause the limbs of mankind to quake. Then, and only then, will the Divine Standard be unfurled, and the Nightingale of Paradise warble its melody.

Bahá'u'lláh

The day is approaching when We will have rolled up the world and all that is therein, and spread out a new order in its stead. He, verily, is powerful over all things.

Bahá'u'lláh

FORCES SHAPING HUMANITY

As we view the world around us, we are compelled to observe the manifold evidences of that universal fermentation which, in every continent of the globe and in every department of human life, be it religious, social, economic or political, is purging and reshaping humanity in anticipation of the Day when the wholeness of the human race will have been recognized and its unity established. A twofold process, however, can be distinguished, each tending, in its own way and with an accelerated momentum, to bring to a climax the forces that are transforming the face of our planet. The first is essentially an integrating process, while the second is fundamentally disruptive. The former, as it steadily evolves, unfolds a System which may well serve as a pattern for the world polity towards which a strangely-disordered world is continually advancing; while the latter, as its disintegrating influence deepens, tends to tear down, with increasing violence, the antiquated barriers that seek to block humanity's progress towards its destined goal. The constructive process stands associated with the nascent Faith of Bahá'u'lláh, and is the harbinger of the New World Order that Faith must erelong establish. The destructive forces that characterize the other should be identified with a civilization that has refused to answer to the expectation of a new age, and is consequently falling into chaos and decline.

Shoghi Effendi

THE REQUIREMENTS OF A MATURE WORLD

All created things have their degree or stage of maturity. The period of maturity in the life of a tree is the time of its fruit-bearing. The animal attains a stage of full growth and completeness, and in the human kingdom man reaches his maturity when the light of his intelligence attains its greatest power and development...Similarly there are periods and stages in the collective life of humanity. At one time was passing through its stage of childhood, at another its period of youth, but now it has entered its long predicted phase of maturity, the evidences of which are everywhere apparent...That which was applicable to human needs during the early history of the race can neither meet nor satisfy the demands of this day, this period of newness and consummation. Humanity must now become imbued with new virtues and powers, new moral standards, new capacities. New bounties, perfect bestowals, are awaiting and already descending upon him. The gifts and blessings of the period of youth, although timely and sufficient during the adolescence of mankind, are now incapable of meeting the requirements of its maturity.

'Abdu'l-Bahá

54
RELIGION

THE MEANING OF RELIGION

But when we speak of religion, we mean the essential foundation or reality of religion, not the dogmas and blind imitations which have gradually encrusted it and which are the cause of the decline and effacement of a nation. These are inevitably destructive and a menace and hindrance to a nation's life...

Therefore, we learn that allegiance to the essential foundation of the divine religions is ever the cause of development and progress, whereas the abandonment and beclouding of that essential reality through blind imitations and adherence to dogmatic beliefs are the causes of a nation's debasement and degradation.

'Abdu'l-Bahá

THE PURPOSE OF RELIGION

The purpose of religion as revealed from the heaven of God's holy Will is to establish unity and concord amongst the peoples of the world; make it not the cause of dissension and strife.

Bahá'u'lláh

O ye that dwell on earth! The religion of God is for love and unity, make it not the cause of enmity or dissension. In the eyes of men of insight and the beholders of the Most Sublime Vision, whatsoever are the effective means for safeguarding and promoting the happiness and welfare of the children of men hath already been revealed by the Pen of Glory.

Bahá'u'lláh

And now concerning thy question regarding the nature of religion. Know thou that they who are truly wise have likened the world unto the human temple. As the body of man needeth a garment to clothe it, so the body of mankind must needs be adorned with the mantle of justice and wisdom. Its robe is the Revelation vouchsafed unto it by God. Whenever this robe hath fulfilled its purpose, the Almighty will assuredly renew it. For every age requireth a fresh measure of the light of God. Every Divine Revelation hath been sent down in a manner that befitted the circumstances of the age in which it hath appeared.

Bahá'u'lláh

Religion should unite all hearts and cause wars and disputes to vanish from the face of the earth, give birth to spirituality, and bring life and light to each heart. If religion becomes a cause of dislike, hatred and division, it were better to be without it, and to withdraw from such a religion would be a truly religious act. For it is clear that the purpose of a remedy is to cure; but if the remedy should only aggravate the complaint it had better be left alone. Any religion which is not a cause of love and unity is no religion. All the holy prophets were as doctors to the soul; they gave prescriptions for the healing of mankind; thus any remedy that causes disease does not come from the great and supreme Physician.

'Abdu'l-Bahá

They that are possessed of wealth and invested with authority and power must show the profoundest regard for religion. In truth, religion is a radiant light and an impregnable stronghold for the protection and welfare of the peoples of the world...

Bahá'u'lláh

THE DECLINE OF RELIGION

The face of the world hath altered. The way of God and the religion of God have ceased to be of any worth in the eyes of men. The vitality of men's belief in God is dying out in every land...The corrosion of ungodliness is eating into the vitals of human society.

Bahá'u'lláh

Religion is verily the chief instrument for the establishment of order in the world and of tranquillity amongst its peoples. The weakening of the pillars of religion hath strengthened the foolish and emboldened them and made them more arrogant. Verily I say: The greater the decline of religion, the more grievous the waywardness of the ungodly. This cannot but lead in the end to chaos and confusion. Hear Me, O men of insight, and be warned, ye who are endued with discernment!

Bahá'u'lláh

The world for the most part is sunk in materialism, and the blessings of the Holy Spirit are ignored. There is so little real spiritual feeling, and the progress of the world is for the most part merely material. Men are becoming like unto beasts that perish, for we know that they have no spiritual feeling-they do not turn to God, they have no religion! These things belong to man alone, and if he is without them he is a prisoner of nature, and no whit better than an animal.

'Abdu'l-Bahá

TRUE RELIGION SUPPORTS CIVILIZATION

A Greek philosopher living in the days of the youth of Christianity, being full of the Christian element, though not a professing Christian, wrote thus: 'It is my belief that religion is the very foundation of true civilization'. For, unless the moral character of a nation is educated, as well as its brain and its talents, civilization has no sure basis.

As religion inculcates morality, it is therefore the truest philosophy, and on it is built the only lasting civilization. As an example of this, he points out the Christians of the time whose morality was on a very high level. The belief of this philosopher conforms to the truth, for the civilization of Christianity was the best and most enlightened in the world. The Christian Teaching was illumined by the Divine Sun of Truth therefore its followers were taught to love all men as brothers to fear nothing, not even death! To love their neighbours as themselves, and to forget their own selfish interests in striving for the greater good of humanity. The grand aim of the religion of Christ was to draw the hearts of all men nearer to God's effulgent Truth.

'Abdu'l-Bahá

From this review of the history of the Jewish people we learn that the foundation of the religion of God laid by Moses was the cause of their eternal honor and national prestige, the animating impulse of their advancement and racial supremacy and the source of that excellence which will always command the respect and reverence of those who understand their peculiar destiny and outcome. The dogmas and blind imitations which gradually obscured the reality of the religion of God proved to be Israel's destructive influences, causing the expulsion of these chosen people from the Holy Land of their Covenant and promise...

...Reality does not admit multiplicity, although each of the divine religions is separable into two divisions. One concerns the world of morality and the ethical training of human nature...This is ideal and spiritual teaching, the essential quality of divine religion, and not subject to change or transformation. It is the one foundation of all the religions of God...

The second classification or division comprises social laws and regulations applicable to human conduct. This is not the essential spiritual quality of religion. It is subject to change and transformation according to the exigencies and requirements of time and place...For example, it was lawful in Abraham's cycle to eat the flesh of the camel, but during the time of Jacob this was prohibited. Such changes and transformations in the teaching of religion are applicable to the ordinary conditions of life, but they are not important or essential...

...Therefore, the fundamental basis of the revealed religion of God is immutable, unchanging throughout the centuries, not subject to the varying conditions of the human world.

'Abdu'l-Bahá

55
SUPERSTITION

SUPERSTITIOUS PRACTICES ILL BESEEMETH MEN OF KNOWLEDGE

O people of the earth! Living in seclusion or practising asceticism in not acceptable in the presence of God. It behoveth them that are endued with insight and understanding to observe that which will cause joy and radiance. Such practices as are sprung from the loins of idle fancy or are begotten of the womb of superstition ill beseem men of knowledge. In former times and more recently some people have been taking up their abodes in the caves of the mountains while others have repaired to graveyards at night. Say, give ear unto the counsels of this Wronged One. Abandon the things current amongst you and adopt that which the faithful Counsellor biddeth you. Deprive not yourselves of the bounties which have been created for your sake.

Bahá'u'lláh

EMBRACE SCIENCE AND FORSAKE SUPERSTITION

Praise be to God! The medieval ages of darkness have passed away and this century of radiance has dawned, this century wherein the reality of things is becoming evident, wherein science is penetrating the mysteries of the universe, the oneness of the world of humanity is being established, and service to mankind is the paramount motive of all existence. Shall we remain steeped in our fanaticisms and cling to our prejudices? Is it fitting that we should still be bound and restricted by ancient fables and superstitions of the past, be handicapped by superannuated beliefs and the ignorances of dark ages...?

'Abdu'l-Bahá

Such suppositions regarding lucky or unlucky numbers are purely imaginary.

'Abdu'l-Bahá

The stars in the sky do not exert any spiritual influence on this world of dust; but all the members and parts of the universe are very strongly linked together in that limitless space, and this connection produceth a reciprocity of material effects. Outside the bounty of the Holy Spirit, whatsoever thou hearest as to the effect of trances, or the mediums' trumpets, conveying the singing voices of the dead, is imagination pure and simple.

'Abdu'l-Bahá

Consider what it is that singles man out from among created beings, and makes of him a creature apart. Is it not his reasoning power, his intelligence? Shall he not make use of these in his study of religion? I say unto you: weigh carefully in the balance of reason and science everything that is presented to you as religion. If it passes this test, then accept it, for it is truth! If, however, it does not so conform, then reject it, for it is ignorance!

Look around and see how the world of today is drowned in superstition and outward form! ...

Today, men have grown into such adoring attachment to outward forms and ceremonies that they dispute over this point of ritual or that particular practice, until one hears on all sides of wearisome arguments and unrest. There are individuals who have weak intellects and their powers of reasoning have not developed, but the strength and power of religion must not be doubted because of the incapacity of these persons to understand...

God made religion and science to be the measure, as it were, of our understanding. Take heed that you neglect not such a wonderful power. Weigh all things in this balance.

'Abdu'l-Bahá

56
FREE-WILL & PREDESTINATION

GOD'S FORE-KNOWLEDGE MAN'S VOLITION

Know thou that all men have been created in the nature made by God, the Guardian, the Self-Subsisting. Unto each one hath been prescribed a pre-ordained measure, as decreed in God's mighty and guarded Tablets. All that which ye potentially possess can, however, be manifested only as a result of your own volition. Your own acts testify to this truth...God hath...through the power of His sovereign might, forbidden whatsoever He elected to forbid...Men, however, have wittingly broken His law. Is such behavior to be attributed to God, or to their proper selves? Be fair in your judgement. Every good thing is of God, and every evil thing is from yourselves. Will ye not comprehend? This same truth hath been revealed in all the Scriptures, if ye be of them that understand. Every act ye meditate is as clear to Him as is that act when already accomplished...All stands revealed before Him...This fore-knowledge of God, however, should not be regarded as having caused the actions of men, just as your own previous knowledge that a certain event is to occur, or your desire that it should happen, is not and can never be the reason for its occurrence.

Bahá'u'lláh

Thou hadst asked about fate, predestination and will. Fate and predestination consist in the necessary and indispensable relationships which exist in the realities of things. These relationships have been placed in the realities of existent beings through the power of creation and every incident is a consequence of the necessary relationship. For example, God hath created a relation between the sun and the terrestrial globe that the rays of the sun should shine and the soil should yield. These relationships constitute predestination, and the manifestation thereof in the plane of existence is fate. Will is that active force which controlleth the relationships and these incidents. Such is the epitome of the explanation of fate and predestination.

'Abdu'l-Bahá

Some things are subject to the free-will of man, such as justice, equity, tyranny, and injustice, as well as all the good and evil actions; it is evident and clear that these actions are, for the most part, left to the will of man. But there are certain things to which man is forced and compelled: such as sleep, death, sickness, decline of power, injuries, and misfortunes; these are not subject to the will of man, and he is not responsible for them, for he is compelled to endure them. But in the choice of good and bad actions he is free, and he commits them according to his own will...

In the same way, in all the action or inaction of man, he receives power from the help of God; but the choice of good or evil belongs to the man himself.

'Abdu'l-Bahá

The fore-knowledge of a things is not the cause of its realisation; for the essential knowledge of God surrounds, in the same way, the realities of things, before as well as after their existence, and it does not become the cause of their existence...

The hidden secrets of the future were revealed to the Prophets, and they thus became acquainted with the future events which they announced. This knowledge, and these prophecies, were not the cause of the occurrences. For example, to-night every one knows that after seven hours the sun will rise; but this general fore-knowledge does not cause the rising and appearance of the sun...

The mathematicians by astronomical calculations know that at a certain time an eclipse of the moon or the sun will occur. Surely this discovery does not cause the eclipse to take place. This is, of course, only an analogy, and not an exact image.

'Abdu'l-Bahá

57
NON-EXISTENCE OF EVIL

Briefly, the intellectual realities, such as all the qualities and admirable perfections of man, are purely good, and exist. Evil is simply their non-existence. So ignorance is the want of knowledge, error is the want of guidance, forgetfulness is the want of memory, stupidity is the want of good sense. All these things have no real existence.

In the same way, the sensible realities are absolutely good, and evil is due to their non-existence, that is to say, blindness is the want of sight, deafness is the want of hearing, poverty is the want of wealth, illness is the want of health, death is the want of life, and weakness is the want of strength...

Then it is proved that there is no evil in existence; all that God created, He created good. This evil is nothingness; so death is the absence of life...Darkness is the absence of light: when there is no light, there is darkness. Light is an existing thing, but darkness is non-existent. Wealth is an existing thing, but poverty is non-existing.

Then it is evident that all evils return to non-existence. Good exists, evil is non-existent.

'Abdu'l-Bahá

Evil is imperfection. Sin is the state of man in the world of the baser nature, for in nature exist defects such as injustice, tyranny, hatred, hostility, strife: these are characteristics of the lower plane of nature. These are the sins of the world, the fruits of the tree from which Adam did eat. Through education we must free ourselves from these imperfections. The prophets of God have been sent, the Holy Books have been written, so that man may be made free. Just as he is born into this world of imperfection from the womb of his earthly mother, so is he born into the world of spirit through divine education. When a man is born into the world of phenomena he finds the universe; when he is born from this world to the world of the spirit, he finds the Kingdom.

58
CONFESSION

When the sinner findeth himself wholly detached and freed from all save God, he should beg forgiveness and pardon from Him. Confession of sins and transgressions before human beings is not permissible, as it hath never been nor will ever be conducive to divine forgiveness. Moreover such confession before people results in one's humiliation and abasement, and God-exalted be His glory-wisheth not the humiliation of His servants. Verily He is the Compassionate, the Merciful. The sinner should, between himself and God, implore mercy from the Ocean of mercy, beg forgiveness from the Heaven of generosity...

Bahá'u'lláh

O Thou forgiving Lord! Thou art the shelter of all these Thy servants. Thou knowest the secrets and art aware of all things. We are all helpless, and Thou art the Mighty, the Omnipotent. We are all sinners, and Thou art the Forgiver of sins, the Merciful, the Compassionate. O Lord! Look not at our shortcomings. Deal with us according to Thy grace and bounty. Our shortcomings are many, but the ocean of Thy forgiveness is boundless. Our weakness is grievous, but the evidences of Thine aid and assistance are clear. Therefore, confirm and strengthen us. Enable us to do that which is worthy of Thy holy Threshold. Illumine our hearts, grant us discerning eyes and attentive ears. Resuscitate the dead and heal the sick. Bestow wealth upon the poor and give peace and security to the fearful. Accept us in Thy kingdom and illumine us with the light of guidance. Thou are the Powerful and the Omnipotent. Thou art the Generous. Thou art the Clement. Thou art the Kind.

'Abdu'l-Bahá

Praise be unto Thee, O Lord. Forgive us our sins, have mercy upon us and enable us to return unto Thee. Suffer us not to rely on aught else besides Thee, and vouchsafe unto us, through Thy bounty, that which Thou lovest and desirest and well beseemeth Thee. Exalt the station of them that have truly believed and forgive them with Thy gracious forgiveness. Verily Thou art the Help in Peril, the Self-Subsisting.

The Báb

O my God! O my God! Verily, I invoke Thee and supplicate before Thy threshold, asking Thee that all Thy mercies may descend upon these souls. Specialize them for Thy favor and Thy truth.

O Lord! Unite and bind together the hearts, join in accord all the souls, and exhilarate the spirits through the signs of Thy sanctity and oneness. O lord! Make these faces radiant through the light of Thy oneness. Strengthen the loins of Thy servants in the service of Thy kingdom.

O Lord, Thou possessor of infinite mercy! O Lord of forgiveness and pardon! Forgive our sins, pardon our shortcomings, and cause us to turn to the kingdom of Thy clemency, invoking the kingdom of might and power, humble at Thy shrine and submissive before the glory of Thine evidences.

O Lord God! Make us as waves of the sea, as flowers of the garden, united, agreed through the bounties of Thy love. O Lord! Dilate the breasts through the sign of Thy oneness, and make all mankind as stars shining from the same height of glory, as perfect fruits growing upon Thy tree of life.

Verily, Thou art the Almighty, the Self-Subsistent, the Giver, the Forgiving, the Pardoner, the Omniscient, the One Creator.

'Abdu'l-Bahá

59
LEADERS OF RELIGION

LEADERSHIP MUST BE TEMPERED WITH KNOWLEDGE AND GOODLY CHARACTER

Nor should it be thought for a moment that the followers of Bahá'u'lláh either seek to degrade or even belittle the rank of the world's religious leaders, whether Christian, Muslim, or of any other denomination, should their conduct conform to their professions, and be worthy of the position they occupy.

Shoghi Effendi

The divine whose conduct is upright, and the sage who is just, are as the spirit unto the body of the world. Well is it with that divine whose head is attired with the crown of justice, and whose temple is adorned with the ornament of equity.

Bahá'u'lláh

INDIVIDUAL RESPONSIBILITY CANNOT BE ABDICATED

God will ask everyone of his understanding and not of his following in the footsteps of others. How often a person, having inclined his ears to the holy verses, would bow down in humility and would embrace the Truth, while his leader would not do so. Thus every individual must bear his own responsibility, rather than someone else bearing it for him. At the time of the appearance of Him Whom God will make manifest the most distinguished among the learned and lowliest of men shall both be judged alike. How often the most insignificant of men have acknowledged the truth, while the most learned have remained wrapt in veils.

Leaders of Religion

In every nation thou beholdest unnumbered spiritual leaders who are bereft of true discernment, and among every people thou dost encounter myriads of adherents who are devoid of the same characteristic. Ponder for a while in thy heart, have pity on thyself and turn not aside thine attention from proofs and evidences...Moreover, know thou that neither being a man of learning nor being a follower is in itself a source of glory. If thou art a man of learning, thy knowledge becometh an honour, and if thou art a follower, thine adherence unto leadership becometh an honour, only when these conform to the good-pleasure of God.

The Báb

PIERCING THE VEILS OF GLORY

Notwithstanding the divinely-inspired admonitions of all the Prophets, the Saints, and Chosen ones of God, enjoining the people to see with their own eyes and hear with their own ears, they have disdainfully rejected their counsels and have blindly followed, and will continue to follow, the leader of their Faith. Should a poor and obscure person, destitute of the attire of the men of learning, address them saying: "Follow ye, O people! the Messengers of God," [Qur'án 36:20] they would, greatly surprised at such a statement, reply: "What! Meanest thou that all these divines, all these exponents of learning, with all their authority, their pomp and pageantry, have erred, and failed to distinguish truth from falsehood? Dost thou, and people like thyself, pretend to have comprehended that which they have not understood?" If numbers and excellence of apparel be regarded as the criterions of learning and truth, the people of a bygone age, whom those of today have never surpassed in numbers, magnificence and power, should certainly be accounted a superior and worthier people.

It is clear and evident that whenever the Manifestations of Holiness were revealed, the divines of their day have hindered the people from attaining unto the way of truth. To this testify the records of all the scriptures and heavenly books. Not one Prophet of God was made manifest Who did not fall a victim to the relentless hate, to the denunciation, denial, and execration of the clerics of His day! Woe unto them for the iniquities their hands have formerly wrought! Woe unto them for that which they are now doing! What veils of glory more grievous than these embodiments of error! By the righteousness of God! to pierce such veils is the mightiest of all acts, and to rend them asunder the most meritorious of all deeds! May God assist us and assist you, O concourse of the Spirit! that perchance ye may in the time of His Manifestation be graciously aided to perform such deed, and may in His days attain unto the Presence of God.

Bahá'u'lláh

THOSE WHO REJECTED THE MANIFESTATIONS OF GOD

A grievous loss hath indeed been suffered by those that have inclined their ears to the croaking of the raven, and refused to hearken unto the sweet warblings of the Bird of Heaven singing upon the twigs of the Tree of eternity.

Bahá'u'lláh

Consider those who rejected the Spirit [Jesus] when He came unto them with manifest dominion. How numerous the Pharisees who had secluded themselves in synagogues in His name, lamenting over their separation from Him, and yet when the portals of reunion were flung open and the divine Luminary shone resplendent from the Dayspring of Beauty, they disbelieved in God, the Exalted, the Mighty. They failed to attain His presence, notwithstanding that His advent had been promised them in the Book of Isaiah as well as in the Books of the Prophets and the Messengers. No one from among them turned his face towards the Dayspring of divine bounty except such as were destitute of any power amongst men. And yet, today, every man endowed with power and invested with sovereignty prideth himself on His Name. Moreover, call thou to mind the one who sentenced Jesus to death. He was the most learned of His age in His own country, whilst he who was only a fisherman believed in Him. Take good heed and be of them that observe the warning.

Bahá'u'lláh

Behold how the people, as a result of the verdict pronounced by the divines of His age, have cast Abraham, the Friend of God, into fire; how Moses, He Who held converse with the Almighty, was denounced as liar and slanderer. Reflect how Jesus, the Spirit of God, was, notwithstanding His extreme meekness and perfect tender-heartedness, treated by His enemies. So fierce was the opposition which He, the Essence of Being and Lord of the visible and invisible, had to face, that He had nowhere to lay His head. He wandered continually from place to place, deprived of a permanent abode. Ponder that which befell Muhammad, the Seal of the Prophets. How severe the afflictions which the leaders of the Jewish people and the idol-worshipers caused to rain upon Him, Who is the sovereign Lord of all, in consequence of His proclamation of the unity of God and of the truth of His Message!

Bahá'u'lláh

O concourse of divines! Because of you the people were abased, and the banner of Islám was hauled down, and its mighty throne subverted. Every time a man of discernment hath sought to hold fast unto that which would exalt Islám, ye raised a clamour, and thereby was he deterred from achieving his purpose, while the land remained fallen in clear ruin.

Bahá'u'lláh

I swear by the Day-Star that shineth above the Horizon of Utterance! A paring from the nail of one of the believing handmaidens is, in this day, more esteemed, in the sight of God, than the divines of Persia, who, after thirteen hundred years' waiting, have perpetrated what the Jews have not perpetrated during the Revelation of Him Who is the Spirit [Jesus]. Though they rejoice, at the adversities that have touched Us, the day will come whereon they shall wail and weep.

Bahá'u'lláh

LET THEM TURN TO THE WORLD ORDER OF BAHÁ'U'LLÁH

Our hope is that the world's religious leaders and rulers thereof will unitedly arise for the reformation of this age and the rehabilitation of its fortunes. Let them, after meditation of its needs, take counsel together and, through anxious and full deliberation, administer to a diseased and sorely-afflicted world the remedy it requires...It is incumbent upon them who are in authority to exercise moderation in all things.

Bahá'u'lláh

Leaders of religion, exponents of political theories, governors of human institutions, who at present are witnessing the perplexity and dismay the bankruptcy of their ideas, and the disintegration of their handiwork, would do well to turn their gaze to the Revelation of Bahá'u'lláh, and to meditate upon the World Order which, lying enshrined in His teachings, is slowly and imperceptibly rising amid the welter and chaos of present-day civilization. They need have no doubt or anxiety regarding the nature, the origin or validity of the institutions which the adherents of the Faith are building up throughout the world. For these lie embedded in the teaching themselves, unadulterated and unobscured by unwarrantable inferences, or unauthorized interpretations of His Word.

Shoghi Effendi

60
CALUMNY AND OPPOSITION

BE NOT DISTURBED

...some people may arise in opposition, heaping persecutions upon you in their bitterness, and in the newspapers there may be articles published against the Cause. Rest ye in the assurance of firmness. Be well poised and serene, remembering that this is only as the harmless twittering of sparrows and that it will soon pass away...

...Therefore, my purpose is to warn and strengthen you against accusations, criticisms, revilings and derision in newspaper articles or other publications. Be not disturbed by them. They are the very confirmation of the Cause, the very source of upbuilding to the Movement. May God confirm the day when a score of ministers of churches may arise and with bared heads cry at the top of their voices that the Bahá'ís are misguided. I would like to see that day, for that is the time when the Cause of God will spread. Bahá'u'lláh has pronounced such as these the couriers of the Cause. They will proclaim from pulpits that the Bahá'ís are fools, that they are a wicked and unrighteous people, but be ye steadfast and unwavering in the Cause of God. They will spread the message of Bahá'u'lláh.

'Abdu'l-Bahá

OPPOSITION IS THE OIL OF THE LAMP OF TRUTH

Bahá'u'lláh, speaking of these very ones who were attaching and decrying Him, said, "They are My heralds; they are the ones who are proclaiming My message and spreading My Word. Pray that they may be multiplied, pray that their number may increase and that they may cry out more loudly. The more they abuse Me by their words and the greater their agitation, the more potent and might will be the efficacy of the Cause of God, the more luminous the light of the Word and the greater the radiance of the divine Sun. And eventually the gloomy darkness of the outer world will disappear, and the light of reality will shine until the whole earth will be effulgent with its glory."

'Abdu'l-Bahá

Behold how in this Dispensation the worthless and foolish have fondly imagined that by such instruments as massacre, plunder and banishment they can extinguish the Lamp which the Hand of Divine power hath lit, or eclipse the Day Star of everlasting splendor. How utterly unaware they seem to be of the truth that such adversity is the oil that feedeth the flame of this Lamp! Such is God's transforming power. He changeth whatsoever He willeth; He verily hath power over all things...

Bahá'u'lláh

ANIMOSITY ANTICIPATED

...be aware that so soon as the full measure of the stupendous claim of the Faith of Bahá'u'lláh comes to be recognized by those time-honored and powerful strongholds of orthodoxy, whose deliberate aim is to maintain their stranglehold over the thoughts and consciences of men, this infant Faith will have to contend with enemies more powerful and more insidious than the cruellest torture-mongers and the most fanatical clerics who have afflicted it in the past. What foes may not in the course of the convulsions that shall seize a dying civilization be brought into existence, who will reinforce the indignities which have already been heaped upon it!

Shoghi Effendi

THE BAHÁ'Í RESPONSE TO HOSTILITY

Those who would have men believe that religion is their own private property once more bring their efforts to bear against the Sun of Truth: they resist the Command of God; they invent calumnies, not having arguments against it, neither proofs. They attack with masked faces, not daring to come forth into the light of day.

Our methods are different, we do not attack, neither calumniate; we do not wish to dispute with them; we bring forth proofs and arguments; we invite them to confute our statements. They cannot answer us, but instead, they write all they can think of against the Divine Messenger, Bahá'u'lláh.

Do not let your hearts be troubled by these defamatory writings! Obey the words of Bahá'u'lláh and answer them not. Rejoice, rather, that even these falsehoods will result in the spread of the truth. When these slanders appear inquiries are made, and those who inquire are led into a knowledge of the Faith...

Therefore, I say unto you, spread the Divine Truth with all your might that men's intelligence may become enlightened; this is the best answer to those who slander. I do not wish to speak of those people nor to say anything ill of them-only to tell you that slander is of no importance!

...Our part is to act in accordance with the teaching of Bahá'u'lláh in humility and firm steadfastness.

'Abdu'l-Bahá

BUSY YOURSELVES WITH THE BETTERMENT OF THE WORLD

To whatever place We may be banished, however great the tribulation We may suffer, they who are the people of God must, with fixed resolve and perfect confidence, keep their eyes directed towards the Day Spring of Glory, and be busied in whatever may be conducive to the betterment of the world and the education of its peoples. All that hath befallen Us in the past hath advanced the interests of Our Revelation and blazoned its fame; and all that may befall Us in the future will have a like result. Cling ye, with your inmost hearts, to the Cause of God, a Cause that hath been sent down by Him Who is the Ordainer, the All-Wise. We have, with the utmost kindness and mercy, summoned and directed all peoples and nations to that which shall truly profit them...

How numerous are those who, with hearts intent upon malice, have sought Our Presence, and departed from it loyal and loving friends! The portals of grace are wide open before the face of all men. In Our outward dealings with them We have treated alike the righteous and the sinner, that perchance the evil-doer may attain the limitless ocean of Divine forgiveness...

Bahá'u'lláh

BIBLIOGRAPHY

A TRAVELER'S NARRATIVE, by 'Abdu'l-Bahá Bahá'í Publishing Trust, U.S.A. 1980 edition
'Abdu'l-Bahá, by H.M. Balyuzi George Ronald, Oxford 1972 edition
'Abdu'l-Bahá in London, Addresses & Notes of Conversations Bahá'í Publishing Trust, U.K. 1987 edition
Bahá'í Institutions, A Compilation Bahá'í Publishing Trust, India 1973 edition
Bahá'u'lláh AND THE NEW ERA, by J.E. Esslemont Bahá'í Publishing Trust, U.K. 1974 edition
EPISTLE TO THE SON OF WOLF, by Bahá'u'lláh Bahá'í Publishing Trust, U.S.A. 1971 edition
GLEANINGS FROM THE WRITINGS OF Bahá'u'lláh Bahá'í Publishing Trust, U.S.A. 1971 edition
GUIDANCE FOR TODAY AND TOMORROW, from the writings of Shoghi Effendi Bahá'í Publishing Trust, U.K. 1973 edition
Huqúqu'lláh, extracts from the writings of Bahá'u'lláh, 'Abdu'l-Bahá, Shoghi Effendi Bahá'í Community of Canada, 1986
KHADIJIH BAGUM, THE WIFE OF THE BAB, by H.M. Balyuzi George Ronald, Oxford 1982 edition
KITAB-I-AQDAS, THE MOST HOLY BOOK, by Bahá'u'lláh Bahá'í World Centre, Haifa 1992 edition
PARIS TALKS, by 'Abdu'l-Bahá Bahá'í Publishing Trust, U.K. 1972 edition
PORTALS TO FREEDOM, by Howard Colby Ives George Ronald, Oxford 1983 edition
REMEMBRANCE OF GOD, A SELECTION OF BAHA'I PRAYERS Bahá'í Publishing Trust, India 1990 edition
SELECTIONS FROM THE WRITINGS OF 'Abdu'l-Bahá Bahá'í World Centre, Haifa 1978 edition
SELECTIONS FROM THE WRITINGS OF THE BAB Bahá'í World Centre, Haifa 1976 edition

Bibliography

Shoghi Effendi, Recollections, by Ugo Giachery George Ronald, Oxford 1973 edition
SOME ANSWERED QUESTIONS, by 'Abdu'l-Bahá Bahá'í Publishing Trust, U.S.A. 1970 edition
THE ADVENT OF DIVINE JUSTICE, by Shoghi Effendi Bahá'í Publishing Trust, India
THE BOOK OF CERTITUDE, by Bahá'u'lláh Bahá'í Publishing Trust, U.S.A. 1960 edition
THE CHOSEN HIGHWAY, by Lady Blomfield Bahá'í Publishing Trust, U.S.A. 1970 edition
THE DAWN-BREAKERS, NABIL'S NARRATIVE Bahá'í Publishing Trust, U.S.A. 1974 edition
THE DISPENSATION OF Bahá'u'lláh, by Shoghi Effendi Bahá'í Publishing Trust, India 1977 edition
THE DIVINE ART OF LIVING, compiled by Mabel Hyde Paine Bahá'í Publishing Trust, U.S.A. 1974 edition
THE PROMISED DAY IS COME, by Shoghi Effendi Bahá'í Publishing Trust, India 1976 edition
THE PROMULGATION OF UNIVERSAL PEACE, by 'Abdu'l-Bahá Bahá'í Publishing Trust, U.S.A. 1982 edition
THE SECRET OF DIVINE CIVILIZATION, by 'Abdu'l-Bahá Bahá'í Publishing Trust, U.S.A. 1975 edition
THE WORLD ORDER OF Bahá'u'lláh, by Shoghi Effendi Bahá'í Publishing Trust, U.S.A. 1991 edition
WOMEN, extracts from the writings of Bahá'u'lláh, 'Abdu'l-Bahá, Shoghi Effendi and the Universal House of Justice, Bahá'í Canada Publications 1986
WRITINGS OF Bahá'u'lláh, a compilation:
THE SEVEN VALLEYS
THE FOUR VALLEYS
THE HIDDEN WORDS
TABLETS OF Bahá'u'lláh
PRAYERS AND MEDITATIONS
Bahá'í Publishing Trust, India 1986 edition

INDEX

Abbas Khanum, 10, 11
'Abdul - Baha', 4, 5, 7, 20, 21, 22, 23, 26, 27, 28, 35, 36, 37, 39, 40, 42, 43, 45, 46, 51, 52, 53, 55, 59, 60, 62, 62, 63, 65, 66, 69, 70, 71, 72, 76, 77, 78, 79, 80, 81, 84, 88, 89, 93, 94, 96, 97, 98, 99, 100, 101, 103, 108, 112, 120, 123, 125, 126, 130, 132, 135, 136, 139, 142, 144, 146, 147, 152, 153, 154, 155, 156-163, 165-167, 168, 169, 170-173, 175-178, 180, 181-182, 184-186, 188-190, 191-193, 195-196, 197, 201, 202-204, 206-208, 211-213, 215-217, 218, 225, 227, 233-238, 249, 251, 255-256, 264-266, 267, 277-278, 280, 281-282, 285, 293-294, 300-301, 306-308, 309, 311, 312, 313-314, 315, 316, 317-318, 319, 320, 321, 327-329; a Christian minister's impression of, 272-73; address to an official of US, 228; appoints Shoghi Effendi as the guardian, 278-279; Blomfield's description of 273; centre of the covenant, 275, 292; defines his own station, 273-274; Effendi's clarification of the station of, 274; Hearst's account of, 273; imprisonment, 275-276; pen portrait of, 272; power of, 276; recounts Baha'u'lláh's life, 253; suffering, 257-258; the most great branch, 272-276
Abraham, 69, 246, 324
Actions, 143-145
Adhirbáyján, 3
Administrative Order, 4-6, 52, 282-83; foundation of, 285, 287; structure of, 282, 285,
Adrianople, 4, 24, 255, 256
Age of Ages, 2, 17, 239
Ákká, 1, 4, 255, 256,
'Ali Muhammad, Mirzá, 3, 43
Allenby, General, 4
Andrew, 37
Animals, treatment of, 96, 299
Annihilation, 137-138,
Áqa Ján, 251
Ásiyíh Khánum, 10, 15
Austria, 303

Báb 3, 4, 5, 7, 24, 44, 50, 61, 62, 63, 69, 74, 84, 85, 91, 110, 111, 112, 117, 118, 119, 132, 136, 206, 240-250, 251, 254, 290, 320, 322, 323; example of 244; exhorts disciples to prepare for Bahá'u'lláh's advent, 249-50; mission, 247-49; Mullá Husayn's narrative, 241-242; on his life, 246-247; on his revelation, 243, 244; on his

station, 242-243; wife's narrative, 240-241
Baghdad, 4, 254, 255, 256
Bahá'í: attitude, 28,29; attraction, 21; be active and progressive, 21; becoming a true, 19-39; betterment of the world, 34-35; detachment, 24-25; distinction, 20; gratitude, 37-38; humility, 22; kindness, 26; love, the first sign of faith, 19-20; magnanimity, 23; manking 36-37; obligation, 24-25; opposition, 35; overlooking faults, 25-26; peace, 36; promotion of the cause, 34, 35; purity, 24; relation to other faiths, 68-73; speech, 21; spiritual physician, 27-28; the cause, 33-34; virtues, 29-33; world, 37; xenophobia, 25-26
Bahá'í consultation, 215-17; and compassion, 215; serving the search after truth, 215, 216; spark of truth, 216
Bahá'í faith, 1-6, 40-58; 'Abdu'l Bahá, 4; administrative order, 4-6; Bahá'u'lláh, 3-4; basic tenets, 2-3; family of man, 52-53; fanaticism, 53-54; fundamental purpose, 40-42; guidance for the individual, 53; history and tenets, 43-46; holy life, 55; independent world religion, 1; introduction to, 1-6; imbiased investigation, 42-43; money 56; oneness of humanity, 50-51; promulgation of the, 74-83; rehabilitation of mankind, 48-51; relation to other faiths, 47-48; spirit of a new era, 40; the Báb, 3; world religion, 56, 58
Bahá'í World Commonwealth, 5
Bahá'u'lláh, 1, 2, 3-4, 5, 7, 10, 13, 19, 24, 25, 26, 27, 28, 29, 30, 31, 32, 33, 34, 35, 36, 37, 38, 39, 41, 42, 43, 44, 45, 46, 49, 50, 51, 54, 55, 56, 57, 58, 59, 61, 62, 64, 67, 68, 69, 70, 71, 72, 73, 75, 76, 78, 79, 82, 83, 86, 87, 88, 90, 93, 94, 96, 99, 101, 102, 103, 104, 106, 107, 108, 109, 111, 112, 113, 114, 118, 120, 121, 123, 124, 125, 126, 127, 128, 131, 132, 133, 136, 140, 141, 142, 143, 144, 145, 146, 147, 148-151, 159, 162-164, 167-168, 174, 179, 183, 193-194, 197, 198-200, 201-202, 205-206, 209-210, 211, 212, 215, 218-223, 225-227, 229, 232-233, 234, 247, 250, 251-263, 264, 281, 282, 283, 284, 285, 286-288, 289-290, 290-292, 295-299, 293-294, 303, 304, 305-306, 307-308, 309, 311, 313, 315, 317-318, 320, 322, 323-326, 327, 328, 329; Abdu'l's recount of, 253-256; addresses oppressors, 142; advent, 244-246; affirms truth of Báb's mission 247-49; allusion to Abdu'l Bahá's power, 276; followers of, 18; man and manifestation, 268; mission, 270-271; names Abdul' Bahá as centre of covenant, 275; pen-portrait of, 251-252; purpose, 260-261; recognition of his station, 251; revelation, 61, 261-262; station of, 267-271; stations and claims of, 46-47; suffering, 257-259; tablets, 45-46; the end of his earthly existence, 262-263; trust in God, 269-270; withdrawal to the wilderness, 259-260
Bahíyyih K͟hánum, narrative, 10-15
Balkans, 43
begging, 298
Bible, 70, 256
Blomfield, lady, 273

Index

Bombay, 44
Browne, Edward G., 8, 252, 272
Buddha, 5, 59, 69, 70, 102
Burzug, Mírzá Abbás, 10
Búshihr, 246

Calumny and opposition, 327, 329; animosity, 328; Bahá'í response to hostility, 328-329; betterment of the world, 329; oil of the lamp of truth, 327-328
Character training, 156, 161-162
Chihríq, 3
child development 156-158; age, 156; Bahá'í, 158; character training 156; from weakness to strength, 157; role of mothers, 157
Child, 5
China, 25
Christ *(See Jesus)*
Christianity, 70-71
Civilisation, 232; compassion, 233; cooperation, 233; great age to come, 238, 239; justice and moderation, 233; knowledge for positive ends, 235; liberty, 233-34; limits of material, 236-237; process of growth and adaptation, 233-235; signs of impending chaos, 232-233; spiritual, 237-238
cleanliness, 296
compassion, 233
compulsion, 77
confession, 320-321
Confucius, 45, 69, 70, 102
Constantinople, 4, 255-256
Contemplation, 112, 113
Contention, 298
Cooperation, 233
Covenant (The), 280, 288 administrative order, 282-285; firmness in, 281; guardian, 287-288; house of justice, 285-287; power of, 280; uniqueness of, 281-282
Creation 91-94; beginning 92; division of human species, 94; infinite, 93; subjected & Gods physical laws 97; worlds of God, 163
Crime, 187-190; dealing with punishment, 188-190
current age, 305-310; forces shaping humanity, 309; glorious century, 306-308; greatness of this day, 305, 306; requirements of a mature world, 309, 310; world in travail, 308, 309

deeds, 143-145
detachment, 24-25
Divine Economy, 17
Divine Purpose, 17

Economics, 181-186; absolute equality, 181, 182; alimination of extremes of wealth and poverty, 181; legislation of social order, 183-184; obligation to the poor, 182, 184; strikes, 184-186
education, 159-164; Bahá'í 159-160; children, 160; function of, 159; importance of character training, 161-162; of boys and girls obligatory, 162-163; significance, 161; speech, 162; stature of people of learning, 163-164
Effendi, Abbás, 272
Effendi, Shoghi, 1, 6, 7, 16, 17, 18, 47, 48, 52, 55, 71, 73, 115, 116, 205, 223, 228, 229-231, 239, 274, 282-288, 302-303, 305-309, 325-328; clarifies the station of Abdu'l-Bahá, 274; functions of the guardian, 277-279; recollection of, 277
egotism, 142; avoidance of, 145

Egypt, 4, 5
environment, 96
Epistles, 40, 44, 255
eternity, 79
evil: non-existence of, 319; spirit, 137

faith: gift of, 74; opened to scientists and academicians, 83; prudence, 80; teach with constancy, 78, 79; teaching by example, 74-75; teaching with wisdom, 80-81; family, 52-53, 154-155; becoming acquainted with the other's character, 155; individual choice to parental consent, 155; marriage as a spiritual lord, 154-155
fast, 293-294
faults, overlooking others', 141, 142
fear, 146
feast, 294
Formative Age, 5
France, 255
free will and predestination, 317, 318

Geachery, Dr Ugo, 277
God, 84-90, 97; above time and space, 89-90; beyond vain imaginings, 89; disbelief in God 88; foreknowledge of, 317-318; love of, 88; the Creator, 91-92; unfathomable essence, 84-88; worlds of, 93-94
Gospel, 46, 225
Government, 218, 223; advice to a king, 221-223; centralistation rejected, 227-228; future social development, 230; maturity of the world, 223; obligation of all governments, 218-219; obligation of Baháí's 218; obligation of every citizen, 219; secret of statesmanship 220; serving humanity, 220; world citizenship, 228; world civilisation, 229; World Commonwealth, 229; World unity, 231
gratitude, 37-38
Great Age, 17, 238
grief, 146

Haifa, 1, 4
Haququ'lláh, 306
health and nutrition, 191, 194, 298; greatest gift, 191; happiness, 191; importance of 192; meat-eating, 192; medical advice, 193; simple life, 191; tablet of a physician, 193-194
Hearst, Phoebe, 273
heart: pure, 75, 76; sacred, 151-152
Heroic Age, 4
Holy Spirit, 66, 313
hostility, 328-329
Husayn, Mulla, 241-242
humanity: breathing new life into, 76-77; forces shaping, 309; oneness of, 64; serving, 220-221
humbleness, 141
humility, 22
hypocrisy, avoidance of, 145

imitation: effects of 65; forsaking, 68-69; freedom from, 59
Iráq, 44, 257
Ismáil, Mirzá, 10
Israel, 66, 255
Ives, Howard Colly, 273

Japan, 25
Jesus Christ, 2, 60, 63, 66, 69, 70, 79, 102, 189, 246, 252, 262, 264, 266, 280, 302, 313, 324, 325; tribute to, 72; true greatness of, 71-72
John, 37
Joseph, Francis, 303
journalists, responsibility of, 61
justice and moderation, 233

Index

Karbilá, 246
Khadijih Bagum, 241
Kindness, 26, 96
Kirmán, 303
Kitáb-e-Aqdás (Book of Láws), 283, 285, 291-292, 301-304
Kitáb-i-Íqán, 46, 301
knowledge, 235; of God, 88
Krishna, 69, 70, 102
Kurdistan, 254

language: earth as one country 225; internal auxiliary, 225, 226; key to progress and development, 225-226; step towards world peace, 226
laws and commandments, 289, 206; anger, 298-299; apparel and appearance, 296; back biting, 293-294; begging, 298; book of, 291-292, 301-304; cleanliness, 296; contention, 298; fast, 292-293, feast, 293; happiness and protection, 289; health, 297; marriage, 293; obedience to, 289-290; reflection of the exigencies of the times, 290-91; right of God, 294-295; sacred writings, 297; slavery, 295; stature of the cause, 297; treatment of animals, 299; uncleanliness, 295-296 vices, 298-301
liberty, 234
life: after death, 133, 139; death in, 134; immortality, 134-135; reincarnation, 138; return to God, 133; review, 136; soul separation from body, 135-136
love, 19-20, 98-101; foremost teaching, 98; of God, 88; quintessential bond, 99; source of advancement, 99; spirit of, 100-101; the glorious light, 98-99; thoughts, 100

Máh-Kú, 3
man: created in the image of God, 126; dual nature of, 124-125; gift of intellect, 125-126; potential for greatness, 123; shortcomings of, 127, 128; spiritual station of, 123, 129
mankind, 36, 61, 66
manifestations: unity and purpose of, 69
marriage, 154-155, 293
Mashriqu'l-Adhkár, 285, 302
materalism, 148-153; darkness of material world, 152-153; empty show, 149; fleeting world, 150-151; preserving a lofty standard, 149-150; spiritual progress, 153; true happiness, 148
materialists, 137
meditation, 121
Mesopotamia, 41
mercy, 56, 96
Midhi, Mirzá, 13, 14
miracles, 264-266; Bahá'u'lláh's entreatment to his followers, 264; not a sound basis for belief, 265; true greatness not due to miracles, 265, 266
Moses, 60, 66, 69, 102, 246, 265
Mount Carmel, 4
Muhammad, 66, 69, 72-73, 102, 243, 246, 325
Músá, Mirzá, 11
music, 195-197; food for the spirit, 196-197; praise worthy act, 195-196

Napoleon III, 255, 303
nature, 95-97; glory of God, 95-96; man's inheritance of, 96; repository of wisdom, 96
neighbour, 143
Níavirán, 11
Nimrod, 246

Niyávarán, 257
Núr, 10

obligation, 25, 75
occupation, 179-180
opposition, 35
Ottoman, 255

parents, remembering one's, 111-112, 121
patience, 146
peace, 36, 206, 210; atomic weapons, 209; call to disarmament, 209-210; causes of war, 207-208; spiritual power and positive thoughts, 206-207; verge of war, 208; world assemby of nations, 209
Persia, 1, 7, 10, 11, 25, 43, 44, 211, 253, 254, 255, 256
Peter, 37
Pharaoh, 246
Political questions, 211; neutrality enjoined, 211-214; prohibition of seditious movements, 224; prayer, 110-116; dynamics of, 115-116; effects of, 114-115; law of, 111; selection of Baha'í, 117-118; service is also, 115
Prejudice, 170-173; breeding ground of tragedy, 170-171; freedom from, 59; human ignorance, 171; race unimportant, 171-172; rejecting, 172-173
prophets: and the leaders of religion, 109; as iconoclasts, 108; divine physicians, 106; embodiments of holy attributes, 103-104; exponents of unknowable essence, 103; luminaries of infinite splendour, 102-103; manifestation of God, 104-106; portals of God's grace, 102; unity of, 62-63; veils covering, 106-107; wisdom of unveiling, 107-108
purity, 24

Qájár dynasty, 5
Qiblih, 302
Qurán, 70, 81, 244, 249, 302

reality mirror, 169
religion, 60, 311-316; and science, 165-167; decline of, 312-313; individual responsibility, 322-323; leaders of, 322-326; meaning of, 311; piercing the veils of glory, 315-316; oneness of, 62, 67; purpose of, 311-312; test of reason, 166-167; those rejecting manifestations of God, 324-325; true, 313-314; unity of, 62; widening the basis of all, 73; world, 56-58; world order of Bahá'u'lláh, 325-326
revelation, 2, 9, 34, 40, 41, 47, 48, 55, 63, 67, 73, 82, 83 102, 104, 113, 147, 233, 241, 243-244, 247, 248, 270, 271, 274, 275, 283, 289, 298, 312, 325; continuity of, 63; necessity of, 16-17; progressive nature of, 91-64
Russia, 25; Consul, 13, 14

sacred writings, 297
science, 165, 169; religion and, 165-166, 167
self, 140-142; know thy, 140; prison of, 140-141
Shiráz, 3, 246
slavery, 295
soul, 130; after separation from body, 132; independent of the body, 131-132; nature of, 131-132
speech, 21, 81, 162
Sulaymániyyih, 254

Index

superstition, 60, 315-316; effects of, 65; forsaking, 68-69, 339-316; practices, 315
Syria, 255

Tablets, 41, 44, 45, 46, 295, 298,
Tabriz, 3, 4, 254
Tihrán, 13, 249
time and space, 89-90
Tongue of Grandeur, 48
trials, 145-146
truth: mirror the, 61; search after, 59-61
Turkey, 25, 256

Údi Khammár, 301
uncleanliness, 295-296
unity, 198-205; appearance of, 199; day of union, 202; importance among Bahá'ís, 202-203; promotion of security, 198-199; provincialism and prejudice, 263; universality, 200; well-being of manking, 200; with variety, 203-204
Universal House of Justice, 5

Vices, 299, 301
virtue, 29-33; noblest, 168-169

William I, 303
women: education, 176-178; equality of, 174-178; happiness, 175-176; lack of opportunity, 176-177; man referred collectively, 175; vital for world peace, 178
work, 179-180; contribution to quality of life, 102; status of worship, 110
world, 37; civilisation, 229; maturity of, 223-224, 309-310; peace, 178; unity, 231
World Commonwealth, 229
World Council, 5
World Order, 18, 302, 325-326
World War, 1, 4
worship, 110-116; dawning place of the remembrance of God, 120-121; function of the house of, 121-122; leading to exultation, 110-111; places of, 120-122; without fear or hope, 110

Young Turk Revolution, 4
Yusíf, Mirzá, 13, 14

zenophobia, 25-26
Zoroaster, 69, 107